CREATING
Adobe Acrobat
FORMS

JOHN DEUBERT

Creating Adobe Acrobat Forms
John Deubert
Copyright © 2002 by John Deubert

This Adobe Press book is published by Peachpit Press.
For information on Adobe Press books, contact:
Peachpit Press
1249 Eighth Street
Berkeley, CA 94710
510/524-2178 (tel) / 510/524-2221 (fax)

To report errors, please send a note to errata@peachpit.com
Peachpit Press is a division of Pearson Education
For the latest on Adobe Press books go to http://www.adobe.com/adobepress

Editor: Becky Morgan
Production Coordinators: Kate Reber, Myrna Vladic
Copyeditor: Haig MacGregor
Compositor: Phyllis Beatty
Indexer: Emily Glossbrenner
Cover Design: Hugh D'Andrade

ISBN 0-321-11221-0

9 8 7 6 5 4 3 2 1

Printed and bound in the United States of America

For Barbara, as ever

Acknowledgements

No book is really written by one person and this book is no exception. In particular, I would like to thank Becky Morgan, my editor, who was kind, patient, and helpful as the book's outline mutated before our eyes; she was excellent at whapping me upside the head when my prose became unintelligible and my illustrations uninformative. Also I owe a great debt to Kelly Ryer, whose idea this was (and who convinced everyone that it was a good idea), Peachpit/Adobe Press Publisher Nancy Ruenzel, who made it all happen, and production coordinator Myrna Vladic, who ensured that the book looked good. There are many other people at Peachpit/Adobe Press who worked on producing this book and I thank them all.

And, of course, I want to thank my wife, Barbara, for tolerating me as I turned into He Who Types for many weeks.

Table of Contents

three
Working with Forms 143

four
Appendixes

207

Introduction and Overview

one

1 Why Acrobat Forms?

Design is about control. The design of a document, as distinct from its content, is intended to evoke a certain intellectual or emotional response. If you cannot control the user's viewing experience, then you cannot predict how he or she will respond to your design.

Given this, it is significant that one of the most important communication revolutions of the last century, the expansion of the World Wide Web, is based on a file format that gives a designer only loose, indirect control of what the user sees. HTML, the language with which all Web pages are built, is a weak design tool. The pages you design in HTML are device-dependent: that is, they look different when viewed on different devices. Text fares especially poorly under these conditions, appearing in different fonts and sizes on different platforms.

At its root, HTML has always been about content, not design. The design-related features added to the language in the last decade have been squeezed into a model that was not originally meant to accommodate them.

Adobe Acrobat and PDF

Adobe Systems introduced its Adobe Acrobat software in the early 1990s as an alternative to HTML for creating electronic documents. Acrobat's file format, PDF (Portable Document Format), brought PostScript imaging abilities to electronic documentation. In particular, PDF documents are device-independent and provide excellent font support.

At this stage in its evolution, PDF files can be used among a Web site's pages just like HTML: Click on a link and your Web browser, using a free plug-in and Acrobat Reader, displays the PDF file in its own window—just like HTML. Only it's better. You will see exactly what the designer intended; fonts and artwork will be the same across all viewing platforms.

Electronic Forms

Both HTML and PDF have the ability to collect data from a user and then send that data to a server for inclusion in a database or for other processing. In a word: forms.

HTML Forms

Web commerce is based upon the use of electronic forms, usually implemented in HTML. These forms can present the user with all the familiar controls common to computer interfaces: text boxes, radio buttons, and so on.

HTML, however, has some significant disadvantages in creating forms. For one thing, it has severe design limitations. The HTML code required to create even modest forms can be surprisingly complicated. HTML forms often require tables within tables within tables. This complexity slows the display of the forms and can make it difficult for a browser to display the form correctly.

Even the simple form shown in Figure 1.1 requires a three-column table: one column for the labels, another for the radio button controls, and a column sandwiched between them for spacing, as shown in Figure 1.2.

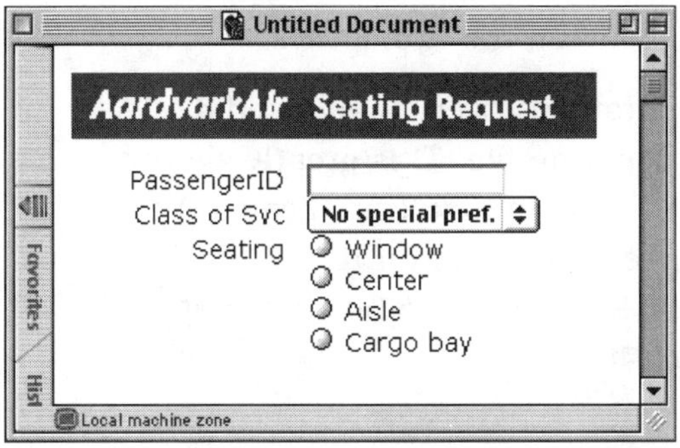

Figure 1.1 HTML forms use controls long familiar on desktop computers.

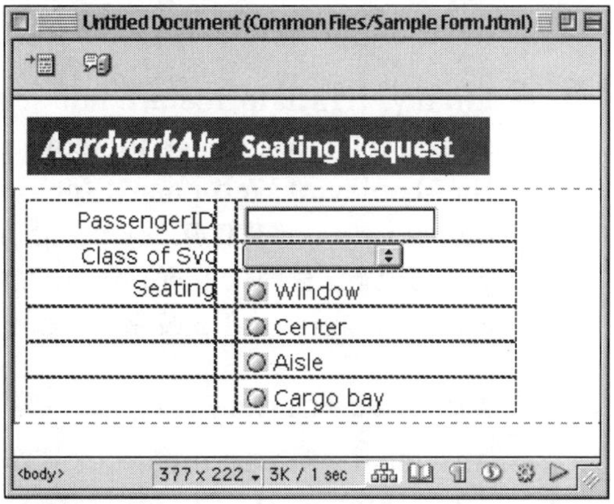

Figure 1.2 The form in Figure 1.1 actually requires a three-column table to correctly place the form fields and labels on the page.

HTML text looks different on different systems. The font and point size used to display text in an HTML form vary from one system to another. If you want your text to remain constant, you need to place it in your form as an image, rather than as actual text. Compare the appearance of the controls in Figures 1.1 and 1.3; this is the same form viewed on two different platforms. Notice how different the text size and font are in these figures. Only the title remains unchanged because it is actually an image.

Figure 1.3 Displaying the same HTML form on a different platform alters the appearance of controls and text. Only the headline (an image) remains unchanged.

Additionally, placing and sizing form fields in HTML can be trying. You generally have only indirect control over the size of the form fields in your HTML form. Precisely aligning controls with their labels is difficult at best. Furthermore, the sizes and positions of the form fields will change from one viewing platform to another. Examine Figures 1.1 and 1.3 again and notice how the size and exact placement of the various controls change between the two figures.

Finally, HTML forms are not self-contained. Every image and sound in HTML pages is kept in a separate file. This greatly slows the display of Web pages, including forms. It also complicates the distribution of HTML forms anywhere other than on the Web; if you put an HTML form on a CD-ROM, you need to be sure that *all* of the bits and pieces accompany it.

Acrobat Forms

Any form you can create in HTML you can also create in PDF. After creating the visual elements in the design software of your choice (Adobe Illustrator®, QuarkXPress™, and the like), you can add form fields to the resulting PDF file with Adobe Acrobat. The resulting form can be filled out in a Web browser exactly like an

HTML form, distributed on CD-ROM, or emailed as an attachment that end users can fill out on their computers (something that's hard to do with an HTML form).

You gain some significant benefits by using PDF for your forms.

PDF gives you freedom of design. There are few limitations to the imaging capability of PDF. You can design the visual parts of your form using Adobe Illustrator, QuarkXPress, Microsoft® Word, or any other design or page layout tool and then convert it to PDF.

Fonts are embedded in the PDF file. Therefore, text appearance and positioning will be the same regardless of the viewing system. Compare Figures 1.4 and 1.5. Here we have the same Acrobat form as displayed on two different computer systems. Note that the text is the same font and size in both illustrations.

Figure 1.4 PDF forms have all of the controls available in HTML and then some.

Another advantage is that Acrobat forms are self-contained. With a few exceptions, images, sounds, and other components in an Acrobat form are embedded in the PDF file. Thus, you have only one file that must be moved from one place to another. This makes it *much* easier to distribute Acrobat forms on CD-ROM, as email attachments, or by other means.

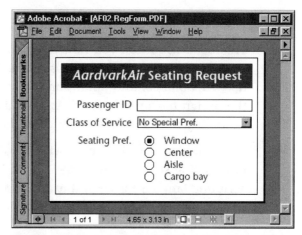

Figure 1.5 This is the same PDF form viewed on a different computer; note that the text and controls retain their fonts, sizes, and placement.

Acrobat forms support digital signatures. Among the fields you may place in a PDF form is a signature field. This field lets the user electronically sign the form, which constitutes legal proof that the user has seen, approved, or otherwise dealt with the form. HTML has no support for digital signatures.

Acrobat forms allow more efficient communication with a server. Acrobat forms can communicate with a data-consuming remote server via a format called FDF (Form Data Format). This is a much more efficient format than HTML for transmitting form data and responses.

Additionally, Acrobat forms can submit data as HTML for compatibility. Data from an Acrobat form may be sent to a server in HTML format, allowing the use of the vast array of cheap or free CGI, Perl, ASP, and other scripts for handling HTML data.

Acrobat isn't perfect, though. Among the disadvantages is the fact that there are fewer design tools for Acrobat forms than for HTML forms. Although you can use any illustration or layout software to design the visual elements of your form, you must "manually" add the form fields using Acrobat. Happily, this task is relatively easy (and is the topic of this book).

In This Book

This book will teach you how to create forms with Adobe Acrobat. We will examine the form fields available in Acrobat and see the use, capabilities, and limitations of each. We shall see how to use the design tools provided by Acrobat and look at some techniques necessary for building sophisticated forms.

We shall also see what to do with the data you collect with a PDF form, using scripts written in Perl, ASP, JavaScript, and other scripting languages. We will examine some useful scripts for common tasks associated with PDF form data.

Here, specifically, is what we shall discuss in the rest of this book:

Part I. Introduction and Overview

Chapter 1. Why Acrobat Forms? presents a high-level view of the process of creating an Acrobat form.

Chapter 2. Making Acrobat Forms: An Overview looks at the process of creating a form without talking about the mechanics. We'll look at what to do, rather than how to do it.

Part II. Controls and Actions

Here we look at the details of each of the form field types Acrobat provides us for creating forms. Additionally, in this section of the book we shall look at a variety of tools, techniques, and aids for the operation and design of a form.

Chapter 3. Basic Interaction: Links describes the appropriate use of Acrobat links within a form and introduces us to some basic concepts of interaction.

Chapter 4. The Form Tool shows you how to use the Acrobat Form tool to create form fields.

Chapter 5. Appearances and Actions looks at the properties common to all Acrobat form fields. We look at the controls that dictate the appearance of a form field and the set of actions that Acrobat should carry out when you click in that field.

Chapter 6. Buttons
Chapter 7. Text Fields
Chapter 8. Check Boxes
Chapter 9. Combo Boxes and Lists
Chapter 10. Radio Buttons
Chapter 11. Signature Fields

In these chapters, we'll look in detail at each of the control types you can create in Acrobat. We will be looking at all of the options available to each control and see how to best use these data-gathering tools.

Part III. Working with Forms

In Part III, we discuss some topics beyond the basic design of your form.

Chapter 12. Acrobat Design Tools discusses the built-in mechanisms within Acrobat that ease the creation of a form. This includes tools for copying and aligning buttons, setting tab order, and more.

Chapter 13. Form Extras presents some solutions to common problems in form design. We'll look at JavaScripts and other techniques for adding refinements to your form, such as automatic calculations and rollover help.

Chapter 14. Submitting Data describes how to save, email, submit and otherwise use data gathered from an Acrobat form and teaches you the basics of receiving Acrobat form data on a remote server.

Chapter 15. PFN, Paper, and the Web covers several short topics of interest; distributing your form on the Web, automatically filling in certain form fields using Adobe's Personal Field Names standard, and converting a collection of paper forms into PDF format.

Chapter 16. Wrapping it Up offers a number of helpful Acrobat resources from books to newsgroups.

Part V. Appendixes

Appendix A. Job Options for Forms reviews the Distiller Job Option settings that are important to an onscreen PDF file.

Appendix B. Sample JavaScripts examines four basic but useful JavaScripts for adding interactivity and efficiency to your forms.

Sample Files

This book has a set of sample files associated with it. You will find it extremely helpful to have these files on hand as we proceed through our discussions. These files are available on the Acumen Training Web site at www.acumentraining.com/AcrobatForms.html.

Acumen Training is my training consultancy. I offer programming classes in PostScript and advanced user classes in Adobe Acrobat. You may want to visit the *Resources* page on the Web site for sample files, in addition to those directly associated with this book.

A Note About Terminology

Throughout this book, we will be using terms that are nearly synonymous. In an effort to be precise and consistent in our use, let's distinguish among these terms now:

- Acrobat vs. PDF

  Acrobat is the software created by Adobe Systems to create and work with electronic documents for print and online display. PDF is the file format used for those electronic documents. Acrobat reads, displays, and otherwise manipulates PDF files. I will use PDF when referring to the file format itself or its capabilities. Otherwise, I will use the name Acrobat. We shall create Acrobat forms whose capabilities are based on the PDF format.

- Form Field vs. Control

  A form field is a data-gathering element on an Acrobat page. I use the term "control" to refer to form fields that receive mouse clicks rather than typed input. This is admittedly something of a personal preference. Still, many people make a distinction between controls (such as buttons, radio buttons, and check boxes) and more general form fields (such as text boxes). I will usually refer to buttons, combo boxes, and lists as controls, and will use the term form fields when speaking more generally or referring to text boxes and signature fields.

2 Making Acrobat Forms: An Overview

Before we dive into the details of creating a functioning form in Adobe Acrobat, let's review the process from beginning to end.

In this chapter, we shall construct a form from concept to completion. This will give you an idea as to how to proceed when creating your own forms from scratch. By the way, if you have existing paper forms that you need to convert to PDF, we'll talk about that in Chapter 15.

For now, let's presume you are creating a brand-new form.

In brief, the process is as follows:

1. Define the data you need and what type of form fields you will use to collect each piece of data.
2. Design the form: Sketch it out on paper and decide where each control will appear on the form's page.
3. Create your form's background in your favorite page layout or illustration software. This background will have all the "static" elements of your form, that is, the titles, labels, logos, decorative elements, and everything else that doesn't directly collect data from the user.
4. Convert the background file from a page layout or illustration file into a PDF file.
5. Add form fields to your PDF pages using tools within Adobe Acrobat.
6. Create the server infrastructure that will collect data from this form.

In this chapter, we shall examine each of these steps in some detail, though not exhaustively. A complete treatment occupies most of the rest of this book.

Creating the Form

Let's create an order form for a new company we are putting together: PetZoom, an online market for purchasing household pets.

The idea is that customers can fill out the form and order any kind of household pet they wish, from a giraffe to an aardvark to a kitten.

We shall create a form that will be the final page in a PDF-format catalog that we send to customers. After perusing our catalog of fauna in Acrobat Reader, customers can fill out this form, click the Submit button, and their bundle of animal joy gets sent on its way—by email, if desired.

Let's make our form.

Figure 2.1 We shall create an order form for PetZoom, a dot-com in the business of selling pets online.

Step 1. Define the data you need to collect

Before you can start making the form, you must know what data you need to collect in the form. Based on your data requirements, you can decide what types of form fields you will need.

Choose your data

In our case, this is an order form for a pet store, so we need to get shipping information and selection data on the type of pet customers wish to purchase. Specifically, we will collect the following data:

- The name and address of the customer
- What animal they would like for their pet
- How they would like their pet sent to them

Actually, in a real order form, you would need to collect a lot more information than this; you would also want to calculate a price and, perhaps, show pictures of prospective pets. For now, we'll ignore this additional data. Later in the book, we'll see how to add a calculated field.

Choose your field types

Closely related to choosing the data you need to collect is deciding what kind of Acrobat form field you will use to gather each piece of data. In Chapter 4, we will review all of the form field types available to us in Acrobat. For now, Table 2.1 shows the types of fields we shall use to collect our information.

Table 2.1 PetZoom Form Field Types

DATA	FIELD TYPE
Name, address, etc.	Text fields
Pet type	List field
Shipping method	Radio buttons

Figure 2.2 shows how they will look in the form.

Figure 2.2 Our PetZoom form will use text fields, a list and a set of radio buttons.

Step 2. Design the Form

The second step in creating a form is deciding how you will lay it out. This process includes deciding on placement for controls, labels, pictures, logos, and all the other elements on the page.

The goals here are usability and appeal. People who use your form should be able to find their way around the form easily; the layout and labels should immediately tell them what they need to do. Also, they shouldn't be repelled by the design.

You don't want to start placing elements on the page in your design software until you have decided how your form's pieces should fit together. All your form fields, labels, logos, disclaimers and other text must fit in the area you have available for the form. This will take some planning and playing with design.

Personally, I sketch my form out on paper, as in Figure 2.3, before I start implementing it with software.

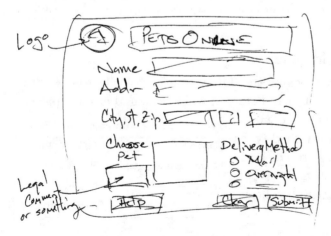

Figure 2.3 Start by sketching out your form by hand. This allows you to decide on a general layout for the form.

The sketch is rough and fast, and I will usually do several of them before I have a layout that works well. This sketch is a starting point, not a blueprint; as you lay out the form in your design software, you will find yourself adding labels or decorative doodads that weren't in the original sketch.

Step 3. Create the Static Elements

Now you're ready to create the form's "background." You will lay out all of the static parts of your form (that is, the labels, rectangles, logos, and all the other visual elements that don't actually collect information from the user) with your favorite graphic-design software.

For this task, you can use any software you wish. Pick an illustration or page-layout program with which you are comfortable and that you know well. Adobe Illustrator, QuarkXPress, Macromedia FreeHand®, Adobe InDesign®, or any reasonably capable design software will do well here. For more workaday designs, you could use Microsoft Word or Excel.

You could draw some of your static elements, such as rectangles and text labels, directly in Acrobat. (We'll do so in Chapter 9.) However, Acrobat does not give you very precise control of the size and placement of these items. For example, line widths in Acrobat can be "Thick," "Medium," or "Thin," rather than a specific line width (Figure 2.4). You are *much* better off using software that's intended for designing pages.

Width: ✓ Thin / Medium / Thick

Figure 2.4 Acrobat offers little control over static elements. Note that you cannot specify a precise line width, for example.

I tend to use Adobe Illustrator or QuarkXPress to create my forms' static elements. Figure 2.5 shows the PetZoom form as assembled in Illustrator.

Notice that this initial version of the form has all the visual elements that don't actively collect data, including labels, logos, and rectangles around the places the form fields will be placed.

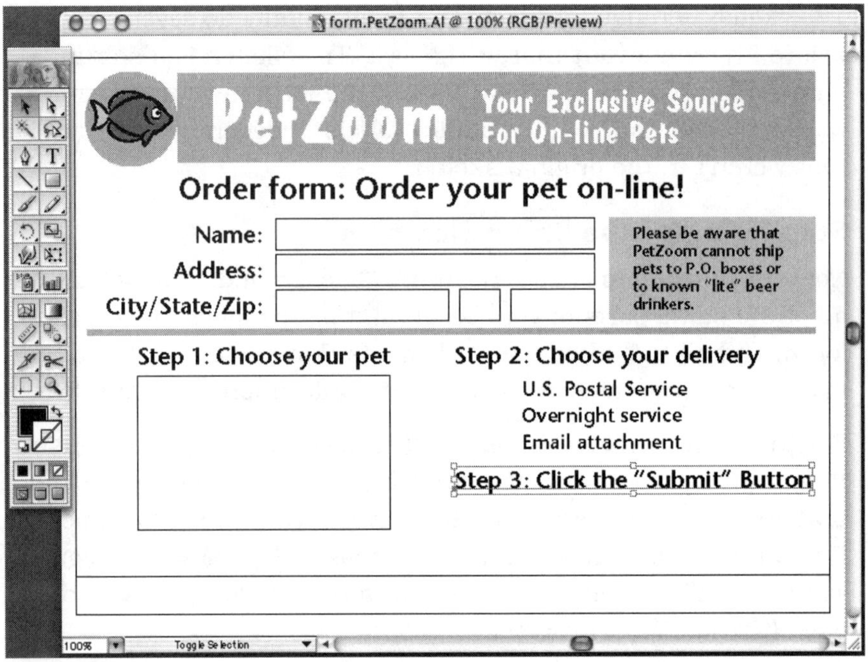

Figure 2.5 Create your form's static background in an illustration or page layout program.

Form design considerations

Form Size. In the nature of things, a PDF form is an onscreen document. You should make sure that the page size you pick works well on a typical computer screen. You may not have this luxury if you are duplicating a pre-existing paper form; in that case, you will probably need to match the page size of the original paper page.

If you are *not* reproducing a paper form, then design your form specifically for the screen. I usually design for an 800 x 600-pixel screen, using a maximum page width of 700 points, which leaves some screen space to the left and right of the form, as shown in Figure 2.6.

What if your form has a large number of fields? For example, a real version of our PetZoom order form would want to collect telephone numbers, credit card information, a name for the pet, and so on. There is no room for these additional controls in our

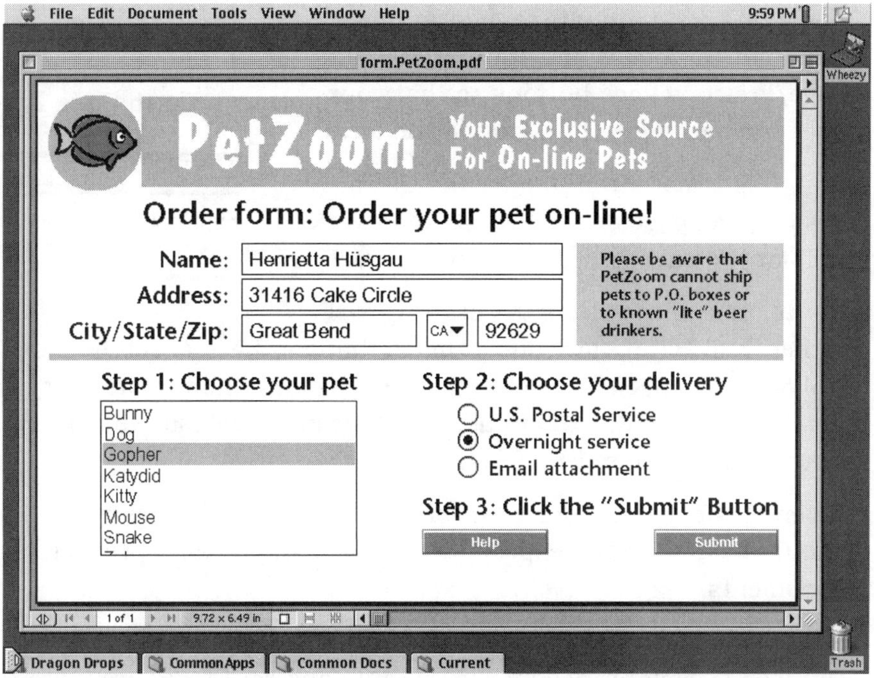

Figure 2.6 Choose a page size for your form that fits well on a computer screen. Designing for an 800 x 600 screen is safest.

current design. There are two ways you can accommodate a large, complex form.

The obvious way is to just make the form's page longer. The user will need to scroll down to get to the rest of the form, but this is not a huge imposition. (Most of us are quite used to doing this with HTML forms on the Web.)

If your form will never be printed, then the PDF page you create can be indefinitely long and may contain a very large number of form fields.

Alternatively, you can make a multi-page form whose form fields are distributed across two or more screen-size pages of the document.

I usually prefer the second method. I don't think long, scrolling, single-page forms are as easy to fill out or give as good a "user experience" as a multi-page form that uses a good onscreen layout.

If you do create a multi-page form, make sure that each page has appropriate Next Page/Previous Page buttons so that your user can easily navigate around the form.

Still, this is not a religious issue: Use a design (long page or multi-page) that works well for the particular form you are creating.

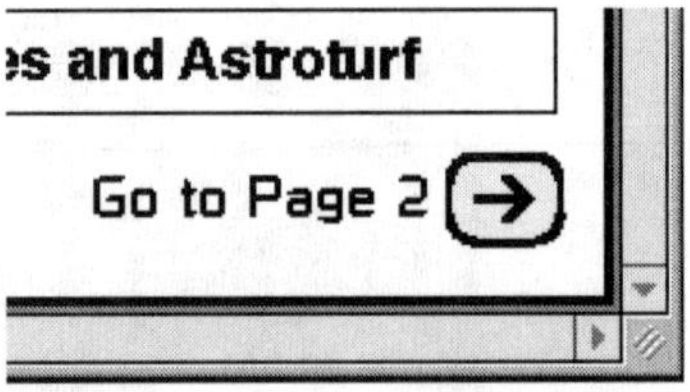

Figure 2.7 Make sure that multi-page forms have highly visible navigation controls.

Fonts. One of the strengths of using PDF, rather than HTML, for your forms is that you have absolute control over the appearance of text. By embedding the font in your Acrobat document, you are assured that users will see your form exactly as you intended.

When choosing fonts for your form, there are two things you should keep in mind, especially if you usually design printed documents.

Sans serif fonts work better onscreen than serif fonts. Serif fonts can look acceptably good for titles, but sans serif fonts are more easily read overall.

You need to use larger point sizes onscreen than you normally would for print. Twelve-point Times is very hard on the eyes when viewed onscreen, particularly in large blocks. Different fonts have different thresholds at which they become difficult to read, so you will need to experiment a bit. Pick a point size that works well with your particular set of fonts. As a rule of thumb, if you're not sure whether your text is too small, then it probably is.

Colors. One very nice thing about designing for the screen, rather than for print, is that you can depend on the presence of color on the display device. Here, too, there are a couple of things to remember.

Specify your colors in RGB (red, green, blue) rather than CMYK (cyan, magenta, yellow, black). Not surprisingly, colors specified in RGB display more consistently on RGB monitors. That is, the color displayed in the PDF file will be more like the color you specified and saw in your page layout or illustration software.

You may want to use "Web-safe" colors, depending on your circumstance. Many computer systems still use 256-color displays. If your PDF form is viewed in a Web browser running on a system that supports only 256 colors, your user will likely see colors that are very different than those you intended.

The World Wide Web defines a set of Web-safe RGB colors that are guaranteed not to change when viewed in a Web browser. Web page designers typically try to use only colors from this list. You may wish to do the same when designing your PDF form. Most high-end design applications and computer systems have a color picker like the one in Figure 2.8, which allows you to specify Web-safe colors.

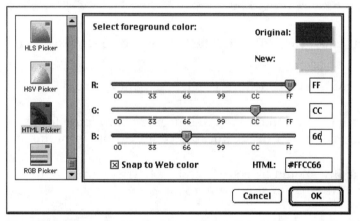

Figure 2.8 Most operating systems and high-end design applications have Web-safe color pickers.

Step 4. Convert to PDF

Now we must convert our form document from the design software's format into PDF. There are a couple of ways of doing this. You can export directly to PDF from within most professional design applications (Figure 2.9), or you can print your document to a PostScript file and then use Acrobat Distiller to convert the PostScript to PDF.

This book presumes you have some experience in making PDF files. If you would like a reminder, Appendix A presents a reminder of what Job Option settings are important to creating a PDF form.

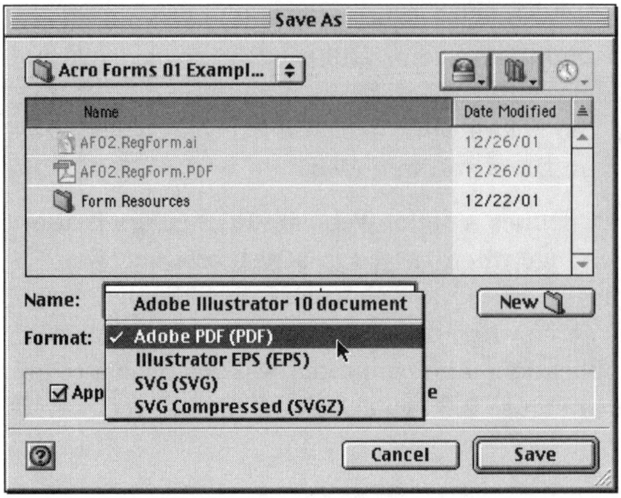

Figure 2.9 Most high-end design applications can export directly to PDF. Some of these use Acrobat Distiller in the background.

However you make your PDF file, the following characteristics are important:

- Fonts must be embedded in the PDF file. They should also be subset.
- Images should be compressed to a degree appropriate for onscreen PDF files. I use Automatic compression at minimum quality.
- Compatibility should be set to Acrobat 4. There are a *lot* of people out there who still use Acrobat 4.

Step 5. Add Form Fields

Now, at last, you are ready to add form fields to your PDF file and truly turn it into a form.

You do this by opening the PDF file in Acrobat and using the Form tool to draw form fields onto the document's pages. When you draw each control on the page, you will use the Field Properties dialog box, shown in Figure 2.10, to specify the type of control it should be, and what properties and behavior it should exhibit. We shall see how to do this in detail beginning with Chapter 4.

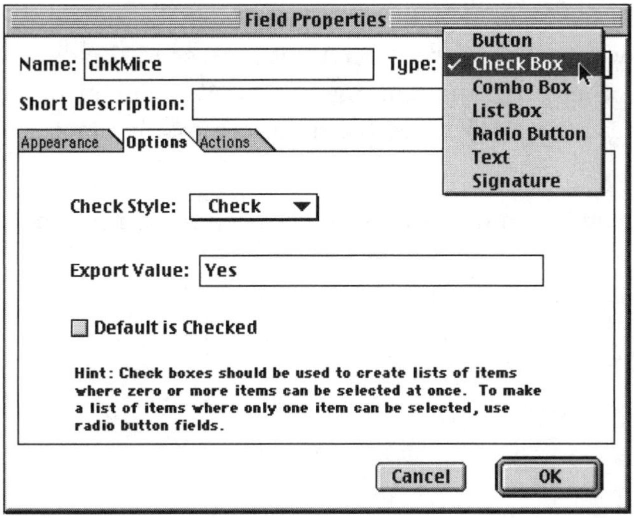

Figure 2.10 When you create a form field in Acrobat, you must specify what type of field it is, its properties, and its behavior.

Once you have drawn all the controls on the page and specified their properties, you have a functioning Acrobat form. You may place this on a Web site for people to fill out in a Web browser, or you can distribute it on CD-ROM or other media for users to fill out on their own computers.

Step 6. Create the Server Infrastructure

Once people fill out your form in Acrobat, you will need to do something with the form data. You will most often provide a button that sends the form's data to you in some way. Most commonly, you will have your form submit its data in one of two ways: as an email attachment or submitted to a CGI (Common Gateway Interface), ASP (Active Server Page), or other data-handling program on a remote host.

If the data is submitted to an email address, the data will be attached to the email message as an *FDF file,* an Acrobat-specific file format that encapsulates the data collected in a form. When you receive this emailed data, you can import the FDF file into your copy of the same form. Acrobat will populate your form fields with the user's responses, at which point you can do anything you wish with the information.

Working with a remote host implements a completely automated data-processing system. Your form tells Acrobat to send the data to a CGI, ASP, or other program running on your Web site or other server. That program then processes the data, commonly placing it in a database.

We shall explore how to handle data once it's been submitted in Chapter 14.

Controls and Actions
two

3   Basic Interaction: Links

We are going to begin our discussion of active elements in Acrobat forms with something that is not, properly speaking, a form field at all: the link.

Links are ubiquitous; they are more commonly used than any other interactive feature in Web pages, online help systems, and Acrobat. Links are also remarkably easy to create in Acrobat.

Anything you can do with a link you can do with a button. Nonetheless, links have their place in form design. Linking to other locations in an Acrobat file is much more conveniently accomplished with Acrobat links than with buttons; the latter don't have the same explicit "Go Somewhere" ability. Links are very compact and add much less to the size of a PDF file than a button. Links are very easily created in Acrobat; the process involves fewer steps than creating form fields.

These characteristics make links very useful for jumping to Help pages and other locations within an Acrobat form. Furthermore, since links are so easy to create, they serve as a good starting point for our discussion of form components.

Creating Links

Consider the form pictured in Figure 3.1. We shall discuss its menus and other form fields in the next chapter. For now, consider the word "disclaimer" in the lower-left corner. This colored, underlined text should take us to a disclaimer page that absolves our fictional company from

Figure 3.1 Let's add a link to a disclaimer page to this form.

blame if anything goes wrong with delivery, food quality, and so on.

Like all the form's static elements, the word "disclaimer" was placed on the page, then colored blue and underlined in the original illustration application. We need to add a link to the PDF page, laying the link on top of the blue, underlined text. Later, when the customer moves the cursor over the link, the cursor will turn into a pointing finger. When he or she clicks on this text, Acrobat will go to the Meals by Mail disclaimer page (Figure 3.2). After reading this text, the customer can click on the button that returns to the original order form. Let's see how we create this link in our Acrobat form.

Figure 3.2 Here's the disclaimer page. This will be the destination for our link.

The Controls Layer

As we create our link, it will be useful to know that links and form fields effectively occupy a separate "layer" in a PDF file. The link is a separate entity from whatever text or artwork it may overlay. Speaking precisely, you do not place a link in the text; rather, you lay the link on top of the text, as in Figure 3.3. Each Acrobat page, in effect, has two layers: a Content Layer that contains the text and artwork for that page, and a Controls Layer that contains the page's links and form fields.

Figure 3.3 Links and form fields occupy a separate layer of the page from the text and artwork.

Using the Link Tool

The Link tool is what we use in Acrobat to create links. When you click on this tool and then move the cursor onto the Acrobat page, the cursor turns into a crosshair that you will use to create the link.

To make a link that moves you to another page in the PDF file:

1. Click on the Link tool.

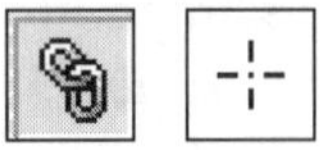

   The cursor will turn into a crosshair when you move it onto the page.

2. Click and drag a rectangle where you want the "hot" part of the link to be.

   In our case, we'll drag a rectangle around the text "disclaimer," as in Figure 3.4. When you release the mouse button, Acrobat will present you with the Link Properties dialog box (Figure 3.5). In Acrobat 4, this dialog box is entitled "Create Link."

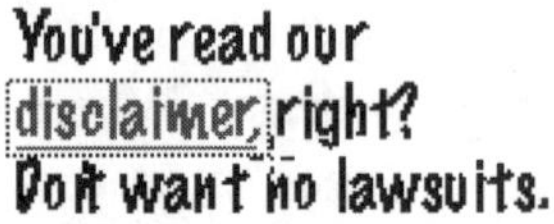

   This dialog box lets you specify the link's appearance and behavior. We shall talk about the controls in this dialog box later in the chapter.

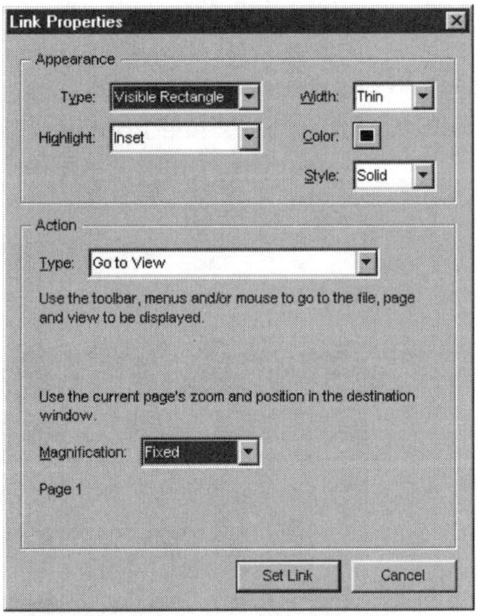

3. Using the standard Acrobat navigation buttons, move the view of your document in the Acrobat window to the page you want for the link's target destination.

   It seems surprising at first that, even though the Link Properties dialog box is the frontmost window on your screen, your PDF file is still active in the background (Figure 3.6). That is, all the Acrobat tools and menus, including the Next Page button and other navigation tools, are still active and apply to your open PDF file. So while the Link Properties dialog box is in the foreground, you have complete freedom to move to the target page of your link. You may find it useful to move the dialog box off to one side so you can see what you are doing.

You've read our disclaimer, right? Don't want no lawsuits.

Figure 3.4 To create a link, click on the Link tool and drag out a rectangle where you want the link to go.

Figure 3.5 The Link Properties dialog box allows you to specify the appearance and behavior of a link.

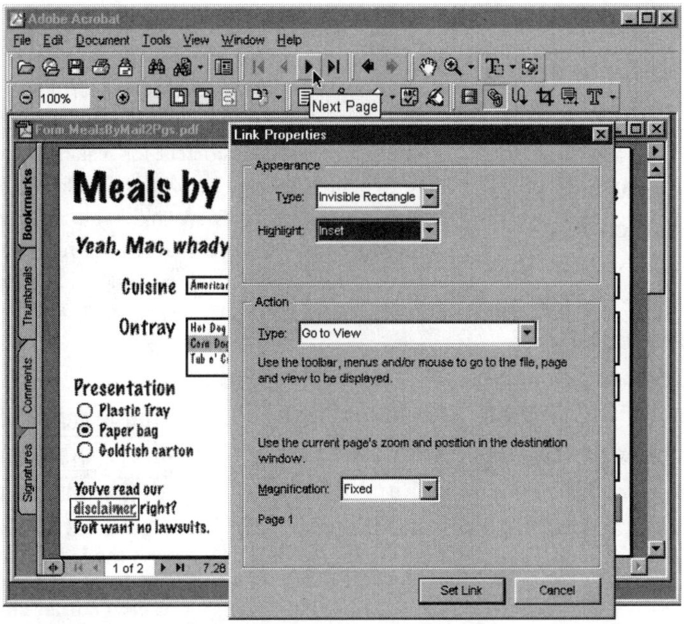

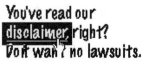

Figure 3.6 While the Link Properties dialog box is up, all of the Acrobat navigation controls are active in the background. Move to the link's destination page and click Set Link.

4. Click the Set Link button. Acrobat will return you to the page on which your link appears.

You have now created a link in your Acrobat document.

This new link will appear on the page as a rectangle until you click on the Acrobat Hand tool (or any tool other than the Link tool). At that point, the link will adopt the look specified in the Link Properties dialog box. By default, links have a visible rectangle around the clickable area, which is fairly unattractive. We'll see how to change it in a moment.

Once you have returned to the Hand tool, you can click on the new link. It will highlight briefly and then take you to the destination page (Figure 3.7).

We now have made a functioning link!

You've read our disclaimer, right? Don't want no lawsuits.

Figure 3.7 Click on the link and it will highlight briefly and take you to its target destination.

Editing Links

Changing position and size

After creating a link, you can easily change its position and size on the page. When the Link tool is selected in Acrobat, all links within the document become visible as rectangles. Click on one of these rectangles, and Acrobat adds "handles" at the corners and sides of the link (Figure 3.8). You can reposition a link by simply dragging it to its new position; you can resize a link by dragging its handles (Figure 3.9).

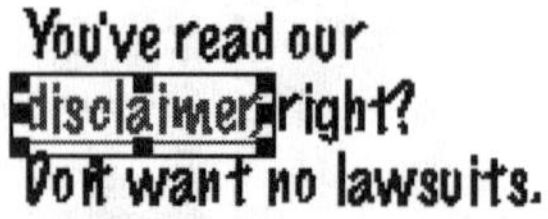

Changing properties

You can change the target, appearance, and other properties of a link by returning to the Link Properties dialog box. With the Link tool selected, you can regain access to this dialog box in any of three ways:

- Double-click on the link.
- Right-click (Control-click on the Mac) the link and select Properties from the resulting menu (Figure 3.10).
- Click once on the link to select it, and then select Properties from the Acrobat Edit Menu.

Whichever of these three things you do, you'll see a variant of the Link Properties dialog box. It differs from the version you saw when you first made the link in that there is an Edit Destination button in the lower half, rather than a Magnification menu (Figure 3.11).

You've read our disclaimer, right? Don't want no lawsuits.

Figure 3.8 Click on a link with the Link tool selected and Acrobat places handles at each corner and side of the link's bounding box.

Figure 3.9 Drag the handles to resize the link.

Figure 3.10 You can edit the properties of a link by right- or Control-clicking on the link and selecting Properties from the resulting menu.

You can now change any of the properties associated with this link. When you click the Set Link button, the link will exhibit its new properties. For example, if you click on the Edit Destination button, Acrobat will instruct you to navigate to a new target destination for the link, exactly as you did when you first created the link. We will talk about the controls in this dialog box in the next section.

Tip

Recent versions of Microsoft Word allow you to specify links within a Word document. Just go to Insert > Hyperlink in Microsoft Word, and you will be prompted for destination information for where you want to link. If you export your Word as a Web page, Word will turn the hyperlinks into HTML links.

Word ships with a macro named PDFMaker that creates a PDF file from the currently open Word document. PDFMaker will convert any hyperlinks in the Word document to Acrobat links. This can be very convenient if you are creating a PDF form from a Word document.

Link Properties

Links are pretty simple creatures, possessing relatively few properties. Here we shall discuss what those properties are.

Looking at Figure 3.11, we can see that there are seven controls in the Link Properties dialog box. Some of these may be hidden at times.

The controls at the top of the dialog box specify the appearance of the link on the page. The two controls in the bottom half determine what the link should do when you click on it.

Let's look at each of these sets of controls in turn.

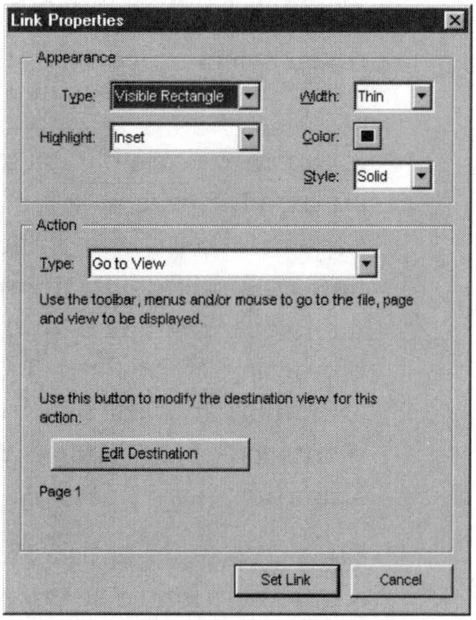

Figure 3.11 Double-clicking on a link with the Link tool active returns you to the Link Properties dialog box, where you may change the characteristics of your link.

Setting Link Appearance

The five controls at the top of the Link Properties dialog box determine the appearance of the link on the page.

Type

The Type pop-up menu specifies whether the link is visible on the page or is an invisible overlay. You have two choices here: Invisible Rectangle or Visible Rectangle.

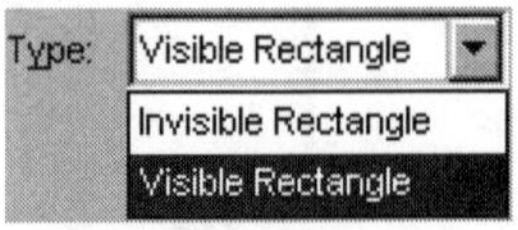

Figure 3.12 The Type menu specifies the appearance of the link on the page.

If you choose Invisible Rectangle, the link will not be visible on the page, although its underlying text will be visible. The link's presence will be directly indicated only by the cursor's changing to a pointing finger when it moves over the link.

This is the most common choice, since you will have likely placed an indication of the link's presence in the original design of the form (for example, making underlying text blue and underlined).

If you select this option, the controls that specify the color and width of the outline will disappear from the dialog box.

If you choose Visible Rectangle, the link is visible on the PDF page as a rectangle. Use this if you have no other way of indicating the presence of a link. It is pretty ugly, however. I strongly recommend building a clue to the link's presence into the design of the form: Text should be colored and underlined, or make underlying graphic elements look like buttons. You'll be happier in the long run.

Figure 3.13 If you select Visible Rectangle in the Type menu, your link will be surrounded by a, well, visible rectangle.

Still, if no other option is available (perhaps you're adding links to a page someone else created), the Visible Rectangle selection does indicate to the user that a link is present.

Highlight

This control specifies what visible feedback the link should deliver to indicate it has been clicked. Your choices are:

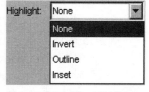

Figure 3.14 The Highlight menu specifies what visual feedback the link should supply when you click on it.

- **None.** The link will not provide any visual indication that it has been clicked. I recommend against this: Good interface design principles dictate that something should happen when the user clicks an active element. It "feels wrong" to click on a link that doesn't highlight, push in, or otherwise look like it's been clicked.

- **Invert.** The link will reverse its color when you click on it, as in Figure 3.7. I think this is the best choice for links that are poised over text.

- **Outline.** The link will draw a rectangle around itself when you click on it. This looks a little odd, I think.

- **Inset.** The link mimics the appearance of a button that has been pushed in, as in Figure 3.15. This is the best choice if the link overlays a graphic element, rather than text. It makes links look very much like buttons.

Figure 3.15 An inset link looks like a real button when it's clicked.

Width

This control specifies the width of the outline surrounding the link if you chose Visible Rectangle in the Type control. You are given the rather imprecise-sounding choices of Thin, Medium, or Thick, which correspond to one, two, or three pixels thick, respectively.

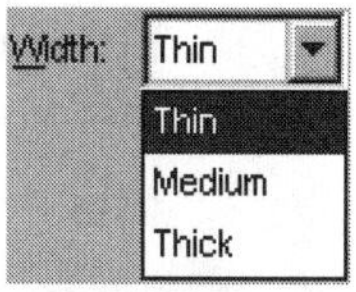

Figure 3.16 The Width menu specifies the width of the link's visible rectangle.

This thickness is independent of the zoom percentage you are using for the PDF file. That is, when you zoom to 500%, the link outlines remain the same number of pixels thick.

Color

This little square control lets you specify the color of the border for visible links. What exactly happens when you click on this control depends on your computer system. On Windows systems, you get a little drop-down palette of colors from which to choose (Figure 3.17). On the Macintosh, you are immediately presented with the default Macintosh Color Picker.

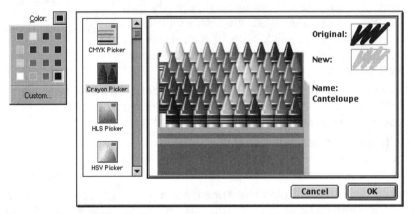

Figure 3.17 The Color control lets you pick the color of the link's border. In Windows, it gives you a little drop-down palette; on the Mac, it takes you to the standard Macintosh Color Picker.

Style

This specifies what kind of line should be used to draw a link's visible rectangle. You may choose between a solid and a dashed line.

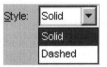

Figure 3.18 The Style menu lets you specify what kind of line you want drawn around your link.

Setting the Link Action

A link is expected to carry out some activity when you click on it, usually to move you to another place in the PDF document. However, links can actually carry out any one of a number of actions defined by Acrobat or its plug-ins. The default action for a link is Go to View, which sends you to another view of the document.

However, Acrobat defines several kinds of actions that a link can carry out, such as running a movie, going to a Web page, sending an email, or opening a spreadsheet. The range of possible activities associated with a link is surprisingly broad. As we'll see later, these actions are also available to buttons and other form fields.

The controls in the lower half of the Link Properties dialog box allow you to specify the action the link should take when clicked upon.

Action type

This pop-up menu specifies the type of action that should be associated with this link. In this chapter, we shall discuss the one action that is unique to Links: Go to View. Chapter 5 will describe the other actions in detail.

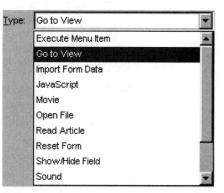

Action details

The control at the bottom of the Actions section changes its label and nature depending upon the Action you have selected. I refer to it as the "Details" control because it lets you

Figure 3.19 The Action Type menu lets you specify what you want the link to do when you click it. We will discuss these actions in detail in Chapter 5.

specify the details of the action you select. If you are executing a menu item, it lets you specify which menu item; if you are playing a sound, it lets you select the sound. Whatever action you select, it presents you the options appropriate to that action.

Go to View

The Go to View action is unique to links; it is not available to form fields. This action sends you to another view of the current document; it also can send you to a view of another PDF file entirely. This is the default action for a link and is, indeed, the most common use of links.

This is the action we described when we first made a link earlier in this chapter: With the Link Properties dialog box in the foreground, you navigate to the destination you want for the link and then click the Set Link button.

The process is pretty straightforward, and I have only a couple of additional points to add to what you already know.

Acrobat Views

A link doesn't just take you to a new page in your document—it takes you to a new *view*. The word "view" has a specific meaning in Acrobat. Think of it as the combination of four things:

- A PDF document
- A page within that document
- A location on that page
- A magnification

There are some implications to this. A link can take the user to an entirely different Acrobat document. A link can also take the user to a zoomed view of the destination.

Let's discuss these points in a little more detail.

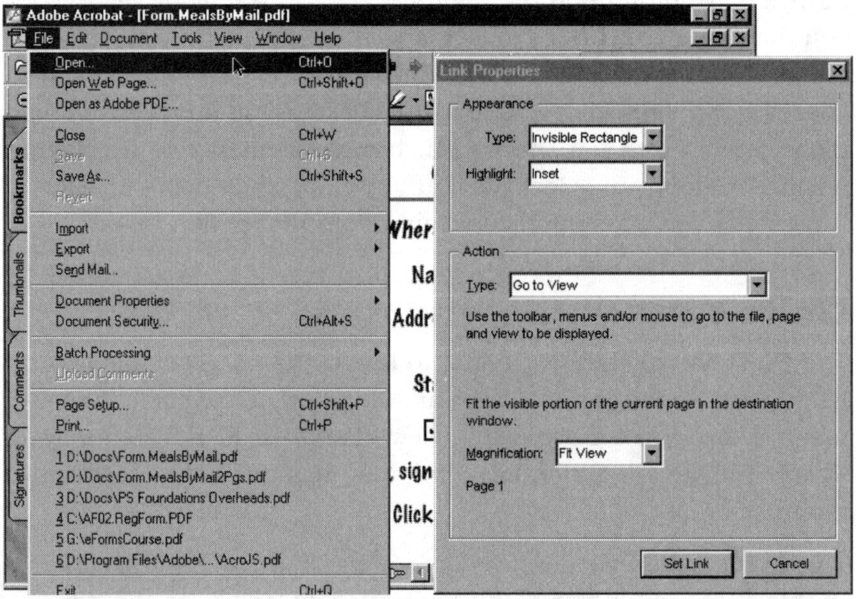

Figure 3.20 The destination page for a link can be in a different PDF file. Just select Open from the Acrobat File menu, select the target PDF file, and navigate to the link's destination in that file.

Links to other PDF files

A link can take you to another document. The File menu is among the navigation tools available to you when the Link Properties dialog box is visible. You can open another PDF file and move to a place in that file (Figure 3.20). When you click Set Link, that position in the other file will be the destination of your link.

To link to a location in another PDF file:

1. Click and drag a new link, as usual.

   Acrobat will present you with the Link Properties dialog box.

2. In the Acrobat File menu, select File > Open.

   You will see a standard Open dialog box.

3. Open the destination PDF file.

   The new PDF file will be visible behind the Link Properties dialog box.

4. Navigate to the page and zoom that you want for your link's target.

5. Click the Set Link button.

When you click on the link, Acrobat will go to the other file (opening it if necessary) and will move to the page (and the position and magnification) that was current when you made the link.

It is perfectly possible to seamlessly link together a number of PDF files. The frosting on the cake is that when you click on a link to another document, the Previous View button in the Acrobat toolbar will take you back to the original document. Very slick, indeed.

Linking to a zoomed view

Your link's destination includes position on the page and magnification. Acrobat's Zoom tool is available while the Link Properties dialog box is up. You can not only move to another page in the document, but also zoom in on a place on the page (an illustration, perhaps). When the user clicks on that link, Acrobat will zoom to that place on the destination page. This allows you to focus the reader's attention on what you want them to see. The Previous View button will return the user to the earlier page and zoom level.

Note that the zoom can be overridden by the Magnification control, discussed next.

Magnification

When you select Go to View for your link's action, the details control becomes a Magnification menu. This allows you to specify a magnification associated with the destination.

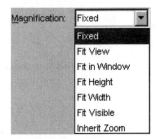

If you examine the entries in this menu, you will see that most of them adjust the magnification of the destination view to match the size of the window *at the time the user clicks on the link.* Fit to Width, for example, adjusts the zoom so that the destination page fits the width of the user's Acrobat window.

Figure 3.21 The Magnification menu specifies the type of zoom applied when the link takes you to its target.

The options in this menu are:

- **Fixed.** Adopt the magnification that was current when you clicked the Set Link button. This is generally the most useful choice for forms; it gives you the most control over what the user sees.
- **Fit View.** Scale the destination page so that its contents fit within the user's window at viewing time.
- **Fit in Window.** Scale the destination page so that the entire page fits within the user's window at viewing time.
- **Fit Height.** Scale the destination page so that the height of the page fits the height of the user's window at viewing time.
- **Fit Width.** Scale the destination page so that the width of the page fits the width of the user's window at viewing time.
- **Fit Visible.** Scale the destination page so that the contents of the page fit across the width of the user's window at viewing time.
- **Inherit Zoom.** Use whatever magnification the user was using when the link was clicked.

For a form, you will almost always want to use Fixed for your magnification. This gives you the most control over what the user will see when filling out your form.

The Form Tool 4

The Form tool is the tool you will use to draw form fields onto your Acrobat document. This tool is very easy to use: You simply drag out a rectangular area for each of the form fields you want to make. Acrobat then allows you to specify the characteristics of each form field.

In this chapter, we shall discuss how to use the Form tool to create form fields, as well as the types of form fields available to you in Acrobat and the proper use of each. In later chapters, we shall discuss each type of form field in detail.

Using the Form Tool

As we discussed earlier, before you can start creating your form fields, you must have already created a PDF file that contains all the inactive parts of the form. These inactive components include the form title, explanatory text, and all the form field labels, as in Figure 4.1.

Now you can use the Form Tool to add the active elements—text boxes, radio buttons, signature fields, and so on—to turn your PDF file into a usable form, as in Figure 4.2.

Meals by Mail   Good grub with postage due

Yeah, Mac, whadya want?   **Where we sendin' it?**

   Cuisine   Name

   On tray   Address

Presentation   State   Zip
   Plastic Tray
   Paper bag   ☐ This is a gift (you gotta be kiddin')
   Goldfish carton
                    Awright, sign here:

                       Click here:

Figure 4.1 Create all the static elements of your form in an illustration or page layout program.

To create a form field with the Form tool:

Start with your "raw" form—without active elements—open in Acrobat.

1. Click on the Form tool in the Acrobat toolbar.

   This will be at the top of the document window in Acrobat 5; it is on the left side of the window in Acrobat 4.

   The pointer will turn into a crosshair.

2. Click and drag out the region on the PDF page where the form field should appear. Precision is not necessary at this point; you can easily reposition and resize your field later.

   Acrobat will now display the Field Properties dialog box. This dialog box gives you detailed control over the nature and behavior of your form fields. In the chapters that follow, we shall discuss these controls in great detail; you're going to become an expert at using this dialog box. (Figure 4.3)

3. In the Type pop-up menu, select what kind of control this should be.

Figure 4.2 You add the active form fields using the Form tool in Adobe Acrobat.

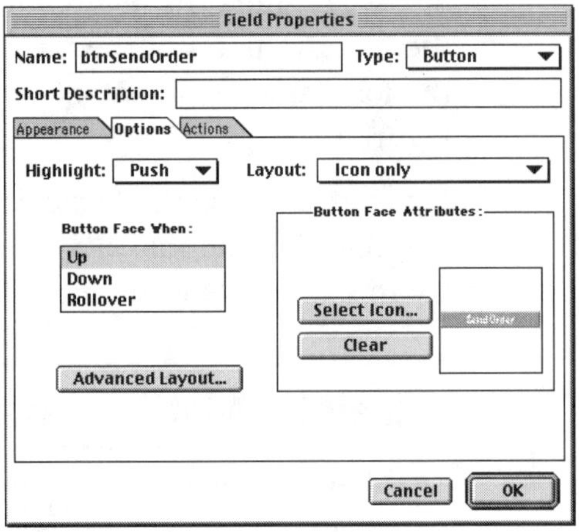

Figure 4.3 The Field Properties dialog box allows you to specify the properties and behavior of form fields.

The set of options available in the dialog box will change according to the type of control you are making. Text fields, not unreasonably, have different features than radio buttons. We'll discuss all the controls in great detail in Chapters 6 through 11.

4. Specify a name for the control in the Name text box.

   This name is internal to the form; the user of your form does not see it. In particular, it does not become the visible label for a button, check box, or radio button. See the next section for more information on naming controls.

5. Supply a short description of the control, if you wish.

   This text will become tool tip text for your control.

6. Click OK.

   Acrobat will return you to your form page. The newly created form field will appear as a colored rectangle with handles at each corner, as in Figure 4.5.

   At this point, you can drag the control to its final position and resize it as needed. (Note that you can "nudge" a control's position using the arrow keys and its size using Shift–arrow keys; we'll talk more about Acrobat's design aids later.)

Figure 4.5 While you are editing, form fields appear as colored rectangles with handles at each corner.

That's all there is to it. The control will continue to look like a colored rectangle until you click on an Acrobat tool other than the Form tool, at which point it will take on the look it presents to the user (Figure 4.6).

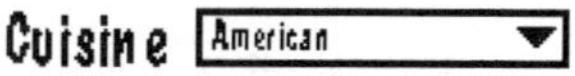

Figure 4.6 When you click on any tool other than the Form tool, the new form field will take on its final appearance.

Field Names

You must supply a name for every field you place in your form. This name is internal to the form and is never seen by the end user. This is the name by which this field will be addressed by JavaScripts and other controls to carry out a variety of interesting activities: calculate values, change appearance, show or hide the field, and so on.

The name you give to your control can be anything you wish. Several points are good to keep in mind when naming a form field. First, you may find it useful to make the first three letters of the field name reflect the field type. For example, the text fields in the Meals By Mail form are named txtName, txtAddress, and so on. This makes it much easier to remember the field names when you are writing JavaScripts.

There are no standards for these prefixes, but Table 4.1 presents the prefixes I use.

TABLE 4.1 Suggested Field Name Prefixes

FIELD TYPE	PREFIX	EXAMPLE
Button	btn	btnSendOrder
Check Box	chk	chkGift
Combo Box	cbo	cboCuisine
List Box	lst	lstOntray
Radio Button	rdo	rdoPresentation
Text Box	txt	txtName
Signature	sig	sigSignHere

Second, make your field names descriptive. Field names may contain embedded spaces and can be reasonably long, so there's no reason to be terse. A name like "txtClassFee" is preferable to "txtCF."

Third, field names don't need to be unique within the document. If two fields have the same name, they are really instances of the same field. When the user makes a change to one of the fields (typing text into a text field, for example), the change will be seen in all instances of that field.

This can be useful in some circumstances. For example, you could have a multi-page form with a "Your Name" text box at the top of each page, all of which share the same internal name. When the user types his or her name into any of these text boxes, the name will immediately appear at the top of all the pages in the form. If two fields require different values or behaviors within the form, they should be given different names.

Lastly, if you will be performing calculations with the contents of several fields (for example, summing a series of text boxes containing individual item costs), you should use Acrobat's hierarchical naming convention for those fields.

This convention is pretty easy to use and has some of the flavor of Web address names. The procedure is to assign names to related fields using the following pattern:

```
Name.subname.subname
```

Thus, a series of form fields that contain expense item amounts might be named

```
txtExpense.Amt1
```

```
txtExpense.Amt2
```

```
txtExpense.Amt3
```

The benefit of adopting this naming scheme is that JavaScripts and other form fields can refer to the entire set of fields by the higher-level name or subname. For example, you can derive the total of the expense items by calculating the sum of "txtExpense," rather than "txtExpense.Amt1 + txtExpense.Amt2 + txtExpense.Amt3."

We shall return to this discussion of the Acrobat naming convention in Chapter 7, where we'll talk about calculated fields.

Fields Palette

The Fields palette is an occasionally useful tool for working with form fields in your Acrobat document. You can make it visible by selecting Windows > Fields in Acrobat. You will then be looking at the palette, shown in Figure 4.7.

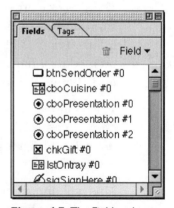

This palette shows the type and name of every form field in the current Acrobat document. Double-clicking on one of these entries in the palette is the equivalent of clicking on the actual field on the page. This will have one of two results.

Figure 4.7 The Fields palette shows all of the form fields in the current Acrobat document.

If the Form tool is active and you are editing form fields, double-clicking an entry in the Fields palette will select that tool, showing its corner handles and allowing you to make changes to the field.

This is very useful if you have two or more form fields in the same place on the page, with one covering the others. It's easy to select buried fields using the palette, but otherwise it's very difficult.

If you are not editing fields (that is, the Form tool is not selected), then double-clicking an entry in the Fields palette will give that form field the focus, ready for you to enter data: Select an item in the combo box, type text into the text box, and so on. I've never found a reason to do this. Entering a form field by double-clicking the palette strikes me as less convenient than clicking on the same field on the page.

The "Fly-out" menu attached to the Fields palette duplicates the Forms submenu in the Acrobat Tools menu (Figure 4.8). We shall discuss these menu items in more detail later in the book.

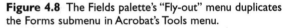

Figure 4.8 The Fields palette's "Fly-out" menu duplicates the Forms submenu in Acrobat's Tools menu.

The Fields palette can be dangerous

There is one other, highly objectionable thing you can do with the Fields palette: You can change the internal names of your controls. If you click once on a control name within the palette, you can edit and change the name.

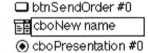

Figure 4.9 The Fields palette lets the user change the internal names of your form fields. This is very bad.

This is dangerous because the palette lets you change controls' names *even when the Form tool is not selected*. That is, your user could inadvertently change the internal names of your form fields when filling out the form.

This will almost certainly break something: JavaScripts will stop working, data submission will fail, rollover help may cease to function. Small nations may have their entire legislatures resign. These are all bad scenarios. Happily, almost no one uses the Fields palette, since it doesn't have much use, so this will probably not be a problem for you.

Editing Form Fields

You can change the position and properties of a form field any time the Form tool is selected and your field is in its rectangle-with-handles state.

Changing position and size

You can change the position of a form field by clicking on it and dragging it around the page with your mouse. You can change the size of the form field by clicking and dragging any of the handles at its sides or corners.

Having clicked on a field to select it, you can nudge its position and size using your keyboard's arrow keys. Each press of an arrow key will move the field one pixel in the appropriate direction. If you hold the Shift key down, the arrow keys will change the size of the form field by one pixel.

Changing properties

When the Form tool is selected, you can regain access to the Field Properties dialog box in any of three ways:

- Double-click on the control with the Form tool selected.
- With the Form tool selected, click once on the control to select it and then choose Edit > Properties.
- Right-click (Control-click on the Mac) the field in the Fields palette and select Properties in the resulting menu.

Any way you do it, you will again be looking at the Field Properties dialog box. You can make whatever changes you wish to the field's behavior.

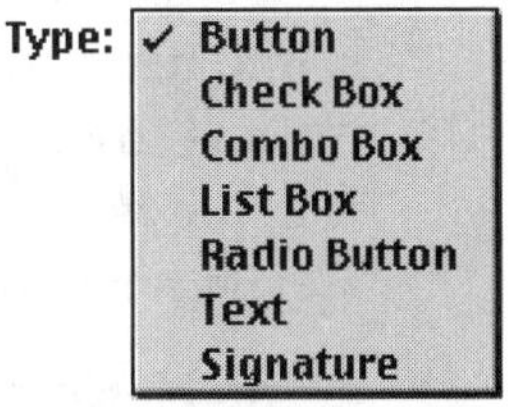

Form Field Types

Acrobat provides you with seven field types for building your forms. Most of these are the equivalent of standard controls in the Macintosh and Windows user interfaces. Over the next several chapters, we will get to know these field types

Type: ✓ Button
Check Box
Combo Box
List Box
Radio Button
Text
Signature

Figure 4.10 There are seven types of form fields available in Acrobat.

very well. For now, let us briefly examine each control type and see how they are used.

Button

This is a standard pushbutton control that initiates an action. When the user clicks on a button, your form should do something: submit data, perform a calculation, or some other action appropriate to your form's purpose.

Figure 4.11 A button initiates an action.

Acrobat buttons can be labeled with either text, a picture, or both.

Check box

A check box collects Boolean (for example, true or false, yes or no) information from the user. Typical labels for check boxes would be:

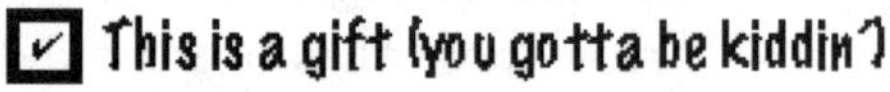

☑ **This is a gift (you gotta be kiddin')**

Figure 4.12 A check box collects true-or-false (Boolean) information.

- I am a carbon-based life form.
- I will need an aardvark.
- This is an obligatory gift for my sister-in-law, whom I have never particularly liked. But it's OK because she doesn't like me either.

Note that these are all statements that are either true or false.

Combo box

A combo box is a useful combination of text box and pop-up menu.

Figure 4.13 A combo box combines a text box with a pop-up menu.

Use this when you want to let the user select one item from a list of items, as in picking a class from a list of classes offered by a school. If you wish, a combo box can allow a user to type a response not included on the list.

The Macintosh has no native support for combo boxes. Acrobat draws a control that has the same functionality: a text field with a pop-up menu that appears when you click on the control.

Figure 4.14 The Macintosh has no native support for combo boxes, so Acrobat must simulate it.

List box

A list box shows the user a list of selections from which he or she may choose. It differs from a combo box in the following ways:

- Selections are presented to the user as a scrolling list rather than a pop-up menu.

Figure 4.15 A list box presents a list of choices from which the user must choose.

- Users may pick only items on the list; there is no mechanism by which they can enter other responses.

- Users can select multiple items by using the Shift and Ctrl/Command keys.

- List boxes take up more room on the page, since some or all of the choices are always visible.

Figure 4.16 List box choices may be accessed by a scroll bar.

List boxes change their appearance when the user clicks in them; scroll bars appear if they are needed, and the font changes to something that the computer system can manipulate more easily. This may be a different font, a different point size, or both. Both effects are temporary. When the user clicks on something else, the scroll bars disappear, and the font reverts to whatever you specified for the list.

Radio button

Here the user can choose from among two or more mutually exclusive responses. All the responses are visible all the time, as in Figure 4.17. (Contrast this with combo boxes or list boxes, whose unused responses are often hidden.)

Presentation
- ○ Plastic Tray
- ⦿ Paper bag
- ○ Goldfish carton

Figure 4.17 Radio buttons allow the user to select among mutually exclusive choices, all of which are visible.

Text field

This is the workhorse of most forms. At its simplest, the text field is just a text box into which the user may type information. However, this field type has several options that make it very broadly useful:

- A text field can apply a variety of automatic formats to whatever the user types in: number, telephone, ZIP code, and so on. Text entered by the user is automatically reformatted to your specification.

- Text fields can perform calculations and display the results.
- "Read-only" text fields can be used for labels and rollover help.
- You can specify rules that define what constitutes valid input for a text box. If users enter invalid text, Acrobat will not let them leave the field. This is useful for such things as passwords and numeric values that must be within a certain range.
- Text fields can display a series of bullets, rather than the text the user actually typed, allowing them to be used for passwords.

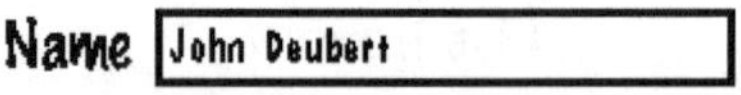

Name John Deubert

Figure 4.18 Text boxes are useful for a wide variety of tasks: validated input, calculated values, passwords, and, of course, just collecting text input.

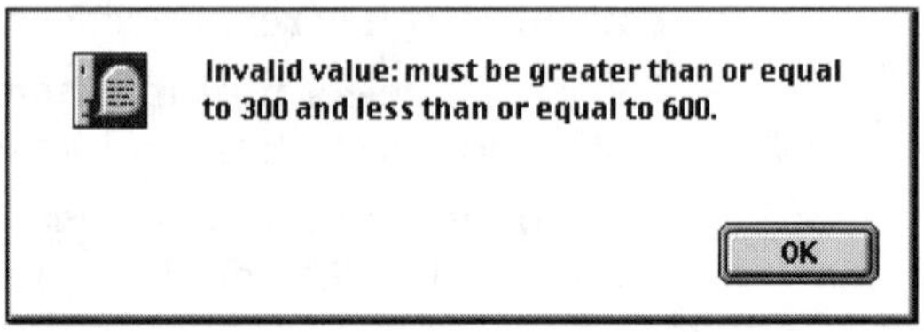

Invalid value: must be greater than or equal to 300 and less than or equal to 600.

OK

You will use a *lot* of text fields.

Figure 4.19 Text fields may restrict user input to values you consider valid.

Signature field

This field type is unique to Acrobat. A signature field can hold an electronic signature of the person who fills out the form.

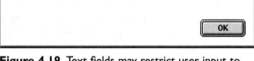
Awright, sign here: ✔ John Deubert

Figure 4.20 Signature fields allow a user to place a legally valid signature on the PDF page.

An electronic signature in Acrobat is an electronic mark placed in a PDF file that constitutes proof that a particular person has made that mark. Many organizations accept such electronic signatures as legally binding commitments.

We will discuss Acrobat signatures in detail in Chapter 11.

Appearance and Actions   5

As we saw in the previous chapter, when you click and drag out a form field using the Form tool, Acrobat immediately presents you with the Field Properties dialog box. You must supply the type of field, the name that field will have within the form, and perhaps some descriptive text for the tool tip. Then you need to specify the properties of that form field.

The Field Properties dialog box is a multi-tab dialog box. Each tab is attached to a panel full of controls that specify some set of properties for that field. The exact set of panels available to you depends on what type of control you are making. Buttons, text fields, and combo boxes are all going to have different properties that you can set.

However, there are two tabs in the Field Properties dialog box that are always available to you: the **Appearance tab** and the **Actions tab.** The controls in these panels are identical for all form field types. The Appearance tab affects what the form field should look like on the page. Here you specify the color, the type of border, the font, and several other visual properties of the field. The Actions tab specifies what should happen when you click on the field, when the cursor rolls over the field, and so on. The actions you specify here carry out your purpose for the field.

In this chapter, we shall look at the controls available in these two panels, and then we shall look in detail at the actions that a form field can carry out in collecting, displaying, and submitting data.

The Appearance Tab

The Appearance tab (Figure 5.1) allows you to specify how a button or other form field should look on the page.

The Appearance panel lets you specify the border, background, font, and other visual properties of a form field.

Border controls

At the top of the Appearance panel is a set of six controls that specify the color and style of the border drawn around the form field. The controls are these:

The **Border Color** and **Background Color** check boxes determine whether the form field will have an outline and whether it will be filled with a color. If these are both unselected, the button will be invisible, existing as an overlay on top of the visible page. This can be very useful for text fields whose visual representation was created in the original artwork for the PDF file.

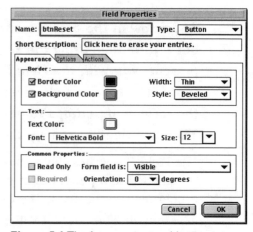

Figure 5.1 The Appearance panel lets you set the appearance of field borders and text, and a handful of properties.

The **Color Well** controls are small, square buttons with a color swatch in the middle. These allow you to specify the colors of the field's border and background. Click on one of these, and Acrobat for Windows drops down a palette of colors from which to choose; the Macintosh version sends you to the standard System color picker. (You may recall the Link Properties Color Well control worked the same way.)

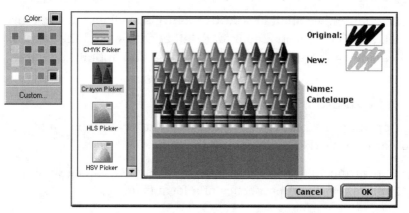

Figure 5.2 Clicking on one of the Color Well controls yields a drop-down palette of colors in Windows (left). On the Macintosh (right), you are presented with the standard System color picker.

The **Width** pop-up window allows you to specify the thickness of the border. You may choose Thin, Medium, or Thick lines, corresponding to line thicknesses of 1, 2, or 3 pixels, respectively. These widths do not change with zoom level; a Thin line will always remain one pixel wide on the screen as you zoom in and out.

Figure 5.3 The border widths you can select for your button correspond to thicknesses of 1, 2, or 3 pixels. This border width does not change as you zoom in and out on the Acrobat page.

The **Style** pop-up menu lets you specify what kind of border should be applied to the field. Your choices, more easily demonstrated than described, are illustrated in Figure 5.4. The most common style for form fields is Solid, although Beveled looks best for buttons labeled with text.

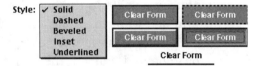

Figure 5.4 These are the border styles available for form fields. Solid is the most common choice, except for text-labeled buttons, which look best with beveled borders.

The Underlined style can be useful for text fields, giving you a blank line to be filled in, as in Figure 5.4. As is often the case, however, this doesn't give me enough control for true happiness; in particular, you can't directly specify how close the text is placed to the underlining stroke. I still prefer drawing the underline in my graphics program and placing a text field with no border on the Acrobat page.

Text controls

The Text controls in the center of the Appearances panel are pretty self-explanatory. You can pick the font, size, and color of the text in the form field.

There are some limitations to your font choice. In Acrobat 5, you may pick any font installed on your system; in Acrobat 4, you may only choose among the 14 standard Acrobat fonts (including Times, Helvetica, Courier, Symbol, and Zapf Dingbats). If you intend your form to be accessible to people using Acrobat 4, I strongly recommend you restrict yourself to the standard 14 fonts.

Common properties

These four controls define miscellaneous characteristics of the form field.

Read-only tells Acrobat that the user is not allowed to change this control. Relatively few of your form fields will be read-only. The one exception may be text fields, which, if made read-only, can be used as labels.

Required prevents the user from submitting the form without placing a value in the field. This is most useful for text fields; you wouldn't want to submit the form without the user's name and contact information, for example. This property doesn't apply to buttons and, indeed, the Required check box is grayed out if the current form field is a button.

The **Visibility** pop-up menu allows you to specify whether the field is visible or not, and whether it should print. An invisible button does not respond to mouse clicks; it is as though it wasn't there. The button can be made visible later by a Show/Hide or JavaScript action executed by another control. (For example, you may not want a "Donations amount" field to appear unless the user has selected the "I donated" check box.)

The Acrobat 4 version of this pop-up menu is a marvel of precise, yet somehow annoying, labeling (Figure 5.5).

The **Orientation** menu lets you choose a rotation for your form field in multiples of 90 degrees (Figure 5.6). This is of limited use in forms.

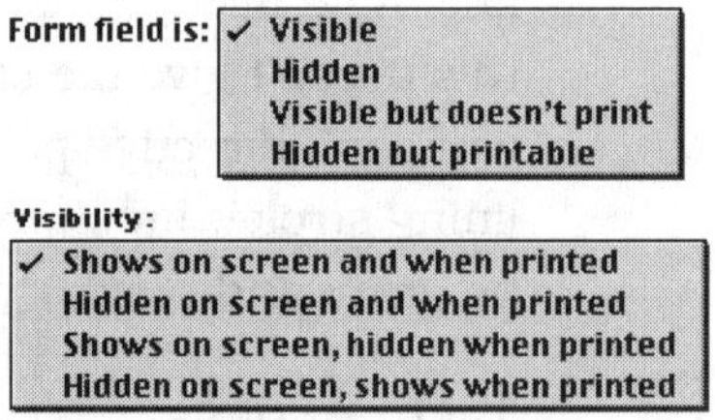

Figure 5.5 The Visibility menu lets you specify when your form field should appear. The wording is much more concise in Acrobat 5 (upper) than in Acrobat 4.

The Actions Tab

Form fields are active beasts. When you click on them, Acrobat should do something: move to another page, play a movie, submit form data to a server, display a menu, or collect data. Perhaps some help text should appear when the cursor moves over a check box. Maybe when you select a product from a combo box, Acrobat should calculate the total price and place it in a text field.

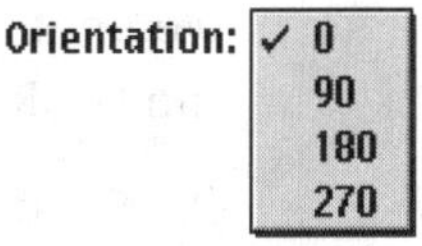

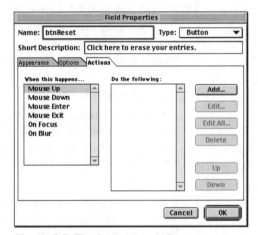

Orientation:
✓ 0
90
180
270

Figure 5.6 Button text may be oriented in any multiple of 90 degrees.

The Actions tab allows you to associate one or more actions with each of six events that may occur in a form field. These are the same actions we mentioned with regard to links, except that form fields don't have the Go to View action available to them.

Form field events

A form field action is triggered by an event, such as a mouse click, that occurs in that form field. The "When this happens" box (Figure 5.7) lists the six events that may have actions attached to them:

Figure 5.7 The Actions panel allows you to associate a list of actions with each of six events. This panel is identical for all form field types.

- **Mouse Up.** The mouse button was released in the form field. This is what you use to respond to mouse clicks on a button.

- **Mouse Down.** The mouse button was pressed down in the form field. This is the best event to use for "feedback" sounds, such as clicks.

- **Mouse Enter.** The cursor has entered the form field. This event, together with Mouse Exit, lets you implement such things as rollover help.

- **Mouse Exit.** The cursor has left the form field.

- **On Focus.** The form field is receiving input from the user, either because the user clicked on the control or tabbed into it. You can use this to provide feedback to the user; perhaps the field could change color when it's the current field.

- **On Blur.** The user has clicked on some object other than the form field or has tabbed out of the form field. You can use this to perform calculations based on the new values of the form field. (The On Blur event, of course, is the opposite of the On Focus event.)

We shall see all of these events used in our examples later in the book.

On Focus and On Blur were added in Acrobat 5. Do not use them if you want people to be able to use your form in Acrobat 4. This is a pity because these are very useful events.

Attaching an action

The remaining controls in the Actions tab let you attach and manipulate a list of actions associated with each of these events.

To attach an action to an event:

1. With your desired form field selected, click on the event to which you want to attach an action.

2. Click the Add button.

   Acrobat will present you with the Add an Action dialog box. This dialog box allows you to select an action and specify its details.

3. Select from the Type pop-up menu the action you want to associate with the event.

4. Click the button in the lower half of the dialog box (labeled "Edit Menu Item" in Figure 5.9) and specify the details of this action. This button will change its label to match the action type you have selected.

5. Click Set Action in the Add an Action dialog box.

You will now be looking at the Field Properties dialog box again, but now there will be an action listed in the Do the Following box.

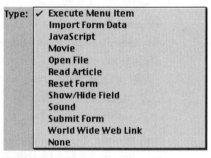

Figure 5.8 You select from the Type menu an action you want to associate with your form field.

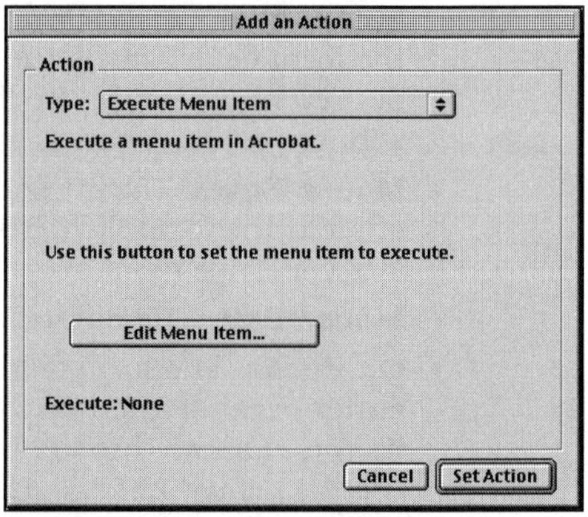

Figure 5.9 The Add an Action dialog box allows you to select an action to associate with your form field. The button will change its label depending on the action you choose.

You can add as many actions as you wish to each of the events. For example, when the user clicks on our job application's Clear Form button, you may want to play a "beep" sound and then clear the form. This would require two actions: Sound and Reset Form (Figure 5.10).

The other buttons on the right of the Actions tab, beneath the Add button, allow you to edit and delete the actions in the list, and move them up and down the list, changing the order in which they are carried out.

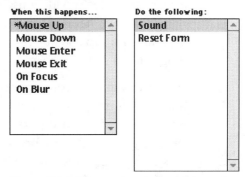

Figure 5.10 You can associate several actions with each event. Here, when the mouse button is released, the button will play a sound (a beep, maybe) and then clear the form.

Page actions

You can also associate an action with the opening or closing of a page in your Acrobat document. Select Document > Page Actions, and Acrobat will present you with the Page Actions dialog box (Figure 5.11). This is similar to the Actions panel in the Field Properties dialog box: It allows you to associate a list of actions with the opening and closing of the current page in the Acrobat file.

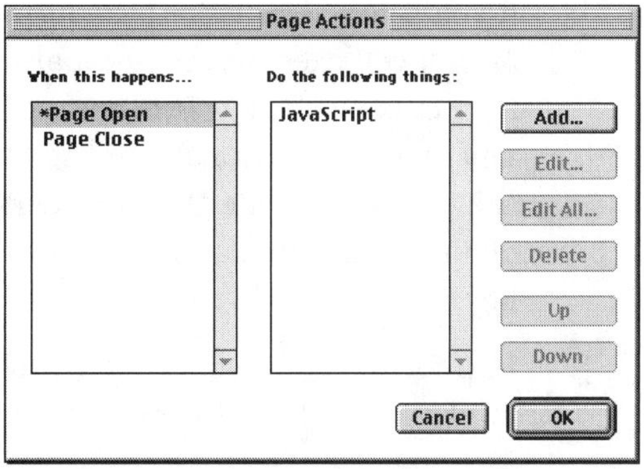

Figure 5.11 You can associate an action with the opening or closing of a page. Clicking the Add button takes you to the same Add an Action dialog box used by form fields.

This can be very useful. For example, if your form used Acrobat 5 features (perhaps associating an action with the On Focus event), you can enable a Page Open action that checks the current Acrobat version and informs the user of problems that will occur with Acrobat 4 or earlier. We do this with a JavaScript action; the version-checking JavaScript code is presented in the discussion of JavaScript, below.

Action Types

Acrobat provides a wide variety of actions that may be associated with your form fields. Here we are going to look in detail at the behavior and purpose of each of the actions that are useful in designing an Acrobat form.

We shall examine these actions in the order in which they occur in the Action Type pop-up menu. However, we shall skip the actions that have no relevance to forms. If you are curious about these actions, you can find information about them in the Acrobat Help file (choose Help > Acrobat Help) or in any number of books on Adobe Acrobat. You can also get detailed information about some of these actions from the Acumen Journal (www. acumentraining. com/AJournal.html).

Execute Menu Item

If you select this action, the form field or link will execute the Acrobat menu item of your choice. This can be literally any menu item available in Acrobat at the time you create the form field. The dialog box for this action is pictured in Figure 5.8.

Figure 5.12 The Execute Menu Item action is often used to implement navigation controls, such as Next Page and Previous Page buttons.

In a form, the Execute Menu Item action (Figure 5.12) is used to implement a broad range of controls, including:

- Navigation buttons that take the user to the next or previous page. These use items in the Document menu, such as Next Page, Previous Page, Previous View, and Go to Page
- Print Form buttons, executing File > Print
- Save Form buttons that use File > Save

We shall see Execute Menu Item in use several times as we go through the exercises in this book.

Sample File on the Web site

There is a file on the Acrobat Forms Web page that has samples of each of the actions. Go to http://www.acumentraining.com/AcrobatForms and download the file Chapter05.zip.

The Edit Menu Item button

When you select the Execute Menu Item action, the Add an Action dialog box acquires a button labeled Edit Menu Item (see Figure 5.8). When you click this button, Acrobat lets you choose which menu item should be executed when the action is carried out.

What exactly happens when you click Edit Menu Item depends on what version of Acrobat you have. Acrobat 5 for the Macintosh makes the Acrobat menu bar active and asks you to choose the menu item you want associated with this action (Figure 5.13). Acrobat 5 for Windows and all versions of Acrobat 4 present you with a dialog box that reproduces Acrobat's menus and asks you to pick from among those menus' items, as in Figure 5.14.

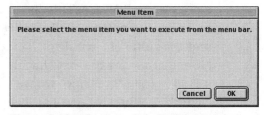

Figure 5.13 When you click the Edit Menu Item button, Acrobat 5 for the Mac asks you to pick an item from among Acrobat's menus.

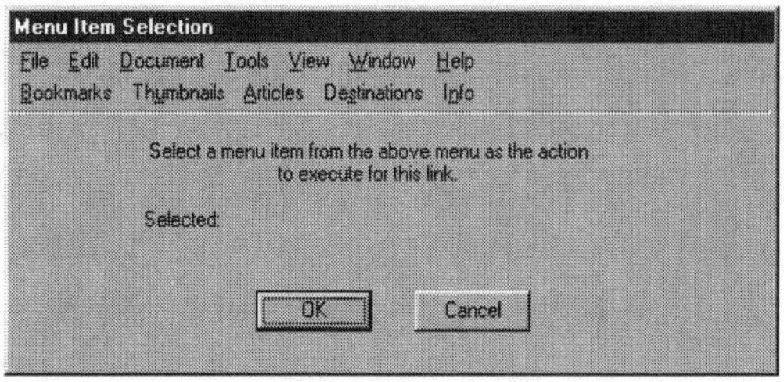

Figure 5.14 Acrobat 5 for Windows presents you with a window that reproduces the Acrobat menus and asks you to select an item. Acrobat 4 does this also in both the Mac and Windows versions.

Be sure that the menu item you choose for this action will exist on users' computers. When you create this action, you can pick from all of Acrobat's menu items available to you at that time (Figure 5.15). This includes menu items inserted by Acrobat plug-ins, such as Enfocus' PitStop or Quite a Box of Tricks.

If you pick a plug-in's menu item for this action, the action will not work unless the user also has that plug-in. If the plug-in and its menu item are not available, the action does nothing at all. The user will click your button a few times and then give up with a shrug. This constitutes bad form design.

Import Form Data

This action tells Acrobat to import values for this form from a Form Data Format (FDF) file on your hard disk.

Data gathered by an Acrobat form can be stored in an FDF file. This file is a compact record of the names of all the fields in a form and the value of each field. (Thus, the FDF file might record the fact that the form has a field named "txtName" whose value is "Asterix.") When an Acrobat form imports data from an FDF file, it populates its form fields with the values taken from the FDF file. The field names in the form must match the field names in the FDF file, of course.

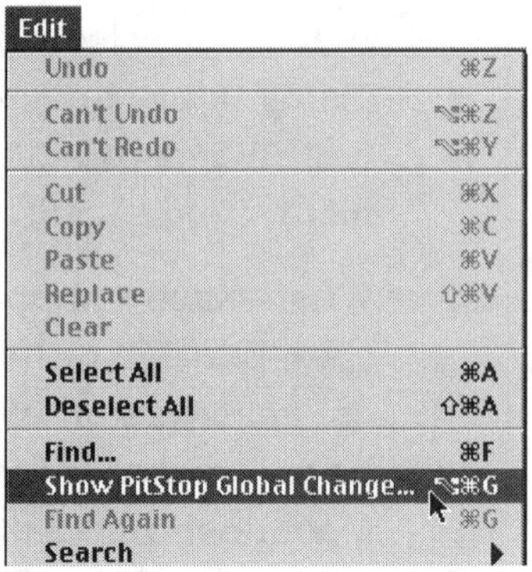

Figure 5.15 Do not execute added menu items unless you are sure your customers will also have your plug-in.

The Import Form Data action imports form data from a specific FDF file. Among other things, this would allow you to set up different default form field values for your user, perhaps selectable by a pop-up menu. For example, an expense account form might let the user select his or her job title from a pop-up menu and then fill in default values for daily allowance from an appropriate FDF file; each selection in the pop-up menu would import data from a different FDF file. We shall talk in much more detail about exporting and importing form data in Chapter 14.

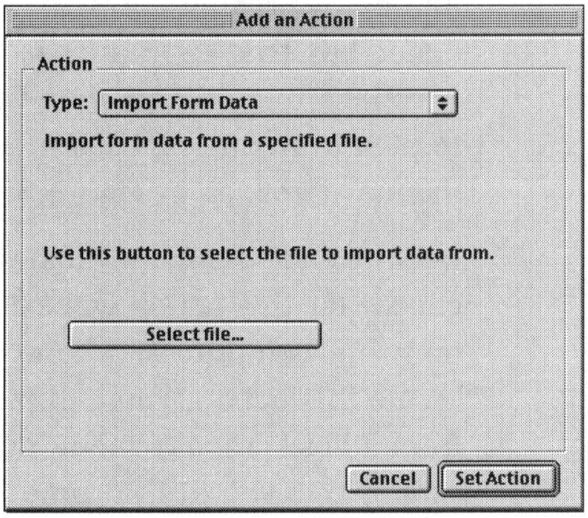

Figure 5.16 The Import Form Data action imports data from a preselected FDF file. Acrobat will fill in your form fields with values taken from this file.

The Select File button

The Select File button allows you to specify the FDF file from which data should be imported. When you click on this button, Acrobat presents you with a standard Open dialog box. Simply select the FDF file from which data should be imported.

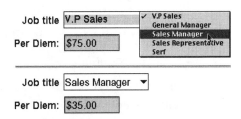

Figure 5.17 By associating an Import Form Data action with the "Job Title" combo box, you can have all the form field values automatically change to defaults appropriate to the user's job.

Data will always be imported from a file with this name in this location; the user will *not* have the opportunity to pick a different file upon invoking this action. This makes this action most appropriate for situations where form data has been created ahead of time, as in our per diem example in Figure 5.17.

JavaScript

The JavaScript action executes a JavaScript (which seems reasonable, somehow). This is an extremely powerful action, allowing a JavaScript programmer to do some remarkably complicated activities. If you cannot do what you want with the predefined actions, you very possibly can do it with a JavaScript.

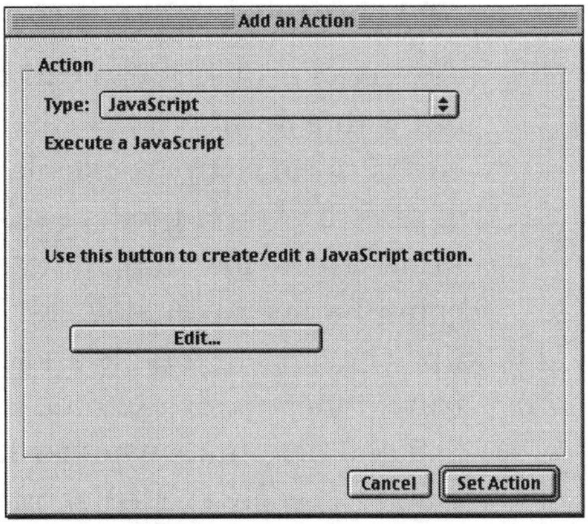

JavaScript is a relatively simple programming language, more similar to C++ than anything else. It is a simple enough language that

Figure 5.18 The JavaScript action will execute a JavaScript. This is a very powerful action for people with some programming skills.

many programs contain interpreters for it and use it as their internal scripting language. Acrobat is among them.

A course in JavaScript is far beyond the bounds of this book, but if you have ever had an inclination to learn programming,

JavaScript is an excellent place to start. From the standpoint of a novice, JavaScript's main virtue is that you can do very useful things with only a small snippet of JavaScript. For example,

```
this.pageNum += 5
```

will cause Acrobat to move your view of the document ahead five pages. Here's another example: You could use the following JavaScript as a Page Open Action to warn users off if their version of Acrobat is too old for your form.

```
var v = app.viewerVersion;

if (v < 5)
    app.alert("This form requires Acrobat 5 or later; you
are using Acrobat " + v);
```

This JavaScript will put up the alert shown in Figure 5.19 if the form page is opened with any version of Acrobat earlier than 5.0.

The set of activities you can carry out with a JavaScript is vast: You can perform complex calculations of price based on product selected, number of items, and add a discount for special customers; look up schedules in a table and present the user with a customized travel itinerary; or examine the serial number entered in a text box and determine whether it is valid. Endless possibilities. I get embarrassingly excited about it.

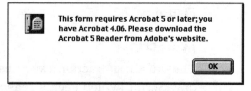

Figure 5.19 A Page Open JavaScript Action could check the version number of the user's copy of Acrobat and report if it is too old. This is strongly recommended if your form uses Acrobat 5 features, such as the On Focus/On Blur events.

The Edit button

If you click on the Edit button in the Add an Action dialog box, Acrobat will present you with a very simple text-editing window named JavaScript Edit (Figure 5.20). Here is where you type in your JavaScript code.

Using an external editor

I find the text editor in the JavaScript Edit window to be annoyingly basic. It is fine for very simple JavaScripts, but if I am doing something more than a few lines long, I yearn for a more sophisticated text editor.

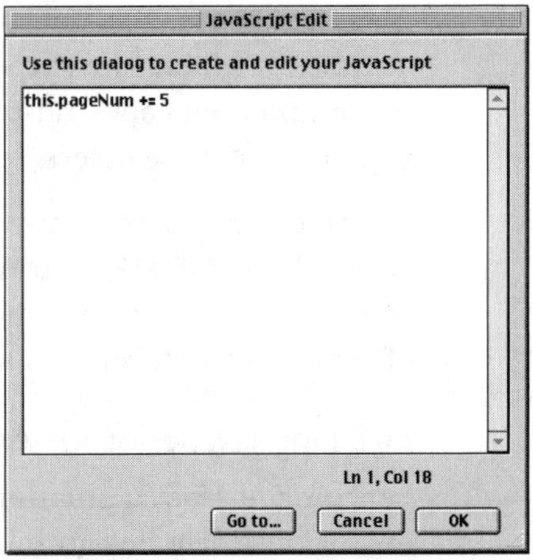

Acrobat 5 for Windows lets you specify an external editor for defining a JavaScript action. If you go to Edit > Preferences and go to the JavaScript preferences, you can specify the text editor that you want to use for writing your JavaScripts (Figure 5.21). Later, when you click on the Edit button

Figure 5.20 When you click the Edit button, Acrobat presents you with a very simple text-editing window. Type your JavaScript into this window.

for the JavaScript action, Acrobat will launch your specific text editor, rather than bringing up its own simple text-editing window.

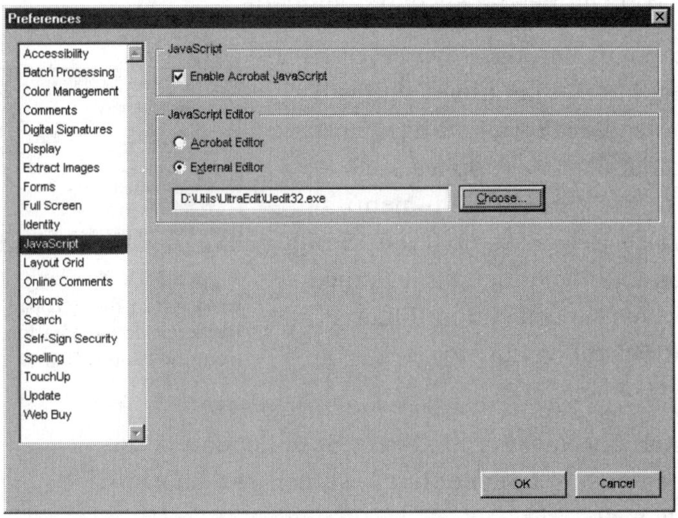

Figure 5.21 Acrobat 5 for Windows lets you specify an external text editor for working with JavaScripts. When you go to edit your Java-Script, Acrobat will automatically launch this text editor.

Alas, Acrobat for the Macintosh does not let you specify an external JavaScript editor. I just type my JavaScript code into my favorite text editor and then copy-and-paste it into the Acrobat JavaScript Edit window. Not as seamless as in Windows, but it gets the job done.

If you're curious, my favorite free or shareware text editors are UltraEdit and TextPad in Windows and BBEdit on the Mac. BBEdit Lite is an excellent text editor, considering it's free. You can find all of these on whatever Web site you go to for shareware software.

Learning JavaScript for Acrobat

Learning at least a smattering of JavaScript is well recommended for serious form design in Acrobat. There are so many useful things you can do with JavaScript that are not otherwise possible.

If you want to learn JavaScript, you will need two references. First, you'll require a book on the JavaScript language. There are many very good books that will teach you the language, including *JavaScript for the World Wide Web: Visual QuickStart Guide*, published by Peachpit Press. Most such books teach you JavaScript in the context of the World Wide Web, rather than for use with Acrobat. This is why you will need a second document.

Your second resource is an Acrobat Java Reference. Having learned the JavaScript language, you will need to learn how to use JavaScript within Acrobat. Actually, an Acrobat installation supplies such a document. If you go to the Acrobat Help menu (Figure 5.22) and choose Help > Acrobat JavaScript Guide, Acrobat will open a PDF document named Acrobat JavaScript Object Specification (Figure 5.23). This document describes how to use JavaScript in Acrobat.

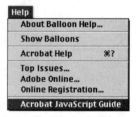

Figure 5.22 You can easily get to the Acrobat JavaScript documentation from the Help menu.

Be warned that the Acrobat JavaScript Object Specification is not a tutorial. It is a quite dense reference that assumes you know JavaScript reasonably well.

If you are just learning to use JavaScript, you may want to go to the Planet PDF Web site (www.planetpdf.com). Among its developer resources are a large number of articles and tutorials on using JavaScript in Acrobat.

I also distribute a free monthly newsletter, the Acumen Journal, which has a series of articles on JavaScript. You can get back issues at www.acumentraining.com/AJournal.html.

Reset Form

This action sets form field values to their defaults.

When you create a form field, you must specify its initial value. Users will enter their own values into the fields as they fill out the form. This action is what you would use in a Clear Form button to remove user data from the form fields, presumably because they made a mistake and want to start over.

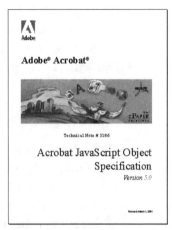

Figure 5.23 The Acrobat JavaScript Object Specification shows you how to use JavaScript in Acrobat. This is a reference, not a tutorial: It presumes you know JavaScript.

The Select Fields button

You may not want your Clear Form button to clear all the fields in the form. For example, perhaps you want to leave user name and address fields untouched and reset only the list of products ordered.

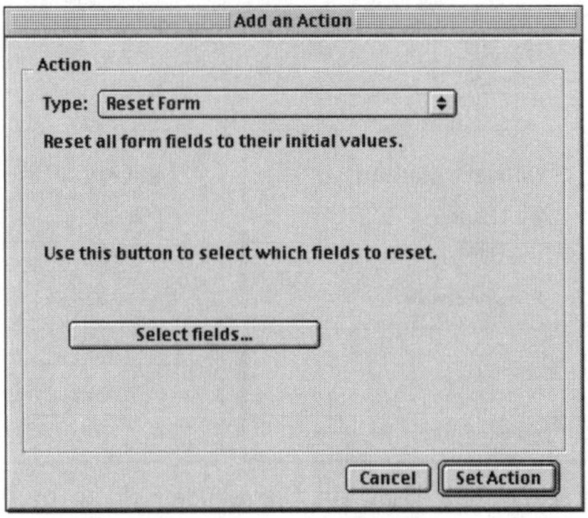

Figure 5.24 The Reset Form action will set the values of your form fields to their defaults.

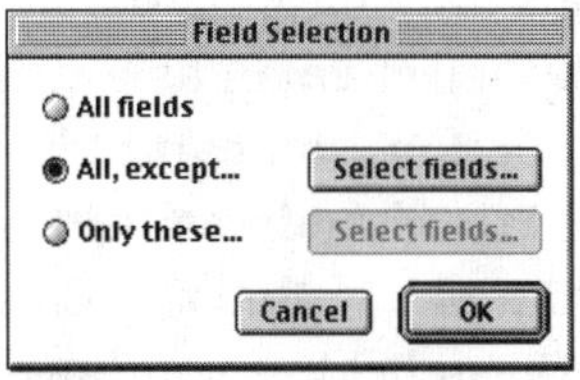

Figure 5.25 The Select Fields button lets you choose which form fields should be reset. You can choose to reset all fields, only certain fields, or all fields with exceptions.

When you click the Select Fields button in the Add an Action dialog box, Acrobat presents you with a dialog box that lets you choose which fields you want to reset to their original values (Figure 5.25).

The radio buttons here are self-explanatory: You can have Acrobat reset all the fields in the form, only certain fields, or all except certain fields. If you click a Select Fields button in this dialog box, Acrobat presents you with a two-pane window that lets you select among the fields in your document (Figure 5.26).

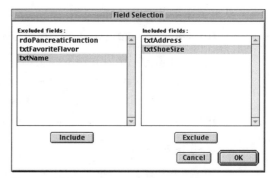

Figure 5.26 Acrobat presents you with a two-pane dialog box when selecting form fields.

Show/Hide Field

This action makes a selected field visible or invisible on the Acrobat page (Figure 5.27).

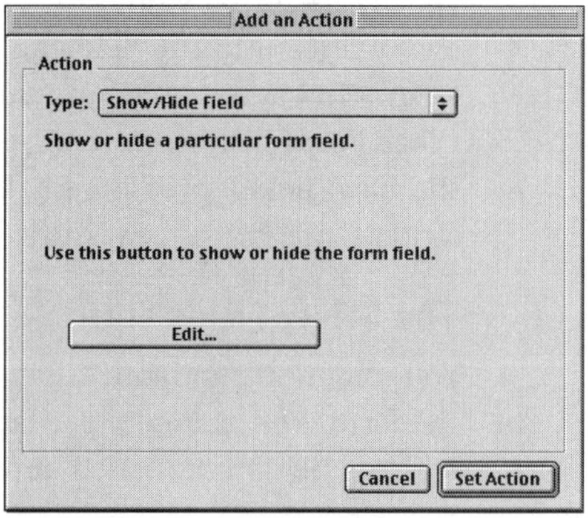

This action is very useful for creating dynamic forms that vary the form fields presented to users according to other selections they have made. If they select email as a delivery option, you can hide the Postal Address field and make visible the Email Address field. If you have a very large number of form fields you want to swap in and out in this manner, you would be better off

Figure 5.27 The Show/Hide Field action will make form field visible or invisible.

Figure 5.28 Using the Show/Hide Field action, different form fields may be presented to the user, depending on circumstance.

using a template. Show/Hide field is most useful for manipulating the visibility of a small
number of fields. We will use the Show/Hide
Field action in our sample forms in Chapter 9.
We discuss templates in Chapter 13.

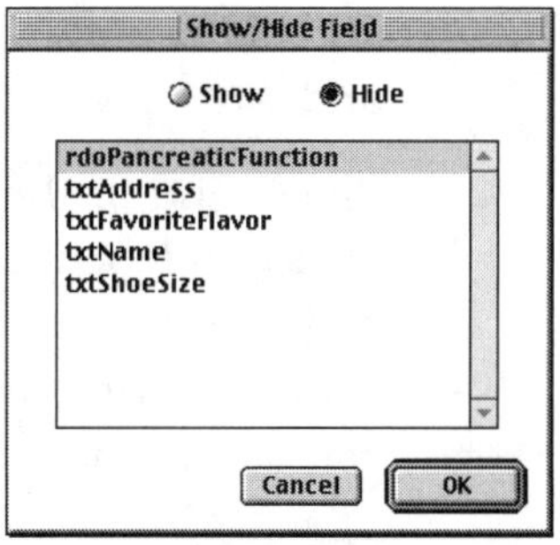

The Edit button

Clicking on the Edit button lets you select
which form field you want to affect. The resulting dialog box presents you with a list of form
fields in the document and a pair of radio
buttons that let you select show or hide.

Figure 5.29 When you click
the Edit button, Acrobat lets you
select a form field in the current
document and asks you whether
you want to show or hide it.

Sound

The sound is embedded in the
Acrobat document in Acrobat's
own PDF sound format. When the
action is triggered, the sound plays
to the end; there is no way to halt
the playback, short of closing the
PDF file. This makes the Sound
action inappropriate for long
sounds, such as mp3 files; if you
want to make a page with buttons
for all your favorite mp3 songs,
you would do better to embed the
mp3s as sound-only movies. The
Sound action is intended for short,
small feedback sounds, such as
the "tick" that indicates you have
clicked on a button.

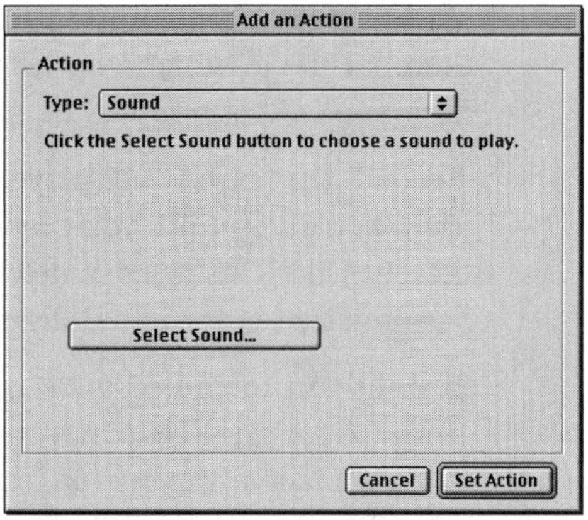

Figure 5.30 The Sound action plays a sound.
Be careful with this one: Once you start the
sound, it can be hard to stop.

The Select Sound button

This button takes you to your system's standard Open dialog box.
Select the sound file that contains the sound you want embedded
in your Acrobat file. You may select any sound file compatible with
QuickTime. On the Mac, this includes AIFF, Sound Mover, WAV,

and old System 7 Sound files. On Windows, you may select AIF and WAV files.

The sound in the file you select will be converted to the PDF device-independent sound format so that the sound will play correctly on any computer platform. QuickTime must be installed on your computer when you embed the sound and also on the user's computer when the sound is played back.

Small, short sounds

I hate to beat this to death, but it's important to remember that the Sound action is intended for very short sounds of the "audible feedback" variety. There are two reasons this is so:

First, the sounds are embedded in the PDF file. Each sound you embed adds significantly to the size of your Acrobat file. The Acrobat file in which you have embedded your entire mp3 collection as PDF sounds will be gigabytes in volume.

Second, the sounds are played asynchronously—that is, once started they won't stop until you reach the end of the sound or you close the Acrobat file. This is extremely annoying to a user, who will naturally assume that going to a different page will shut down the sound.

If you want to embed a sound that goes on for some time— perhaps an audio explanation of how to fill out your form—you should place it in your page as a QuickTime movie. Among other benefits, the sound will stop playing when you move to another page. By the way, if you select an AIFF or other sound file with the Acrobat Movie tool, Acrobat will automatically convert it to a sound-only QuickTime movie.

Submit Form

This action submits the data in your form to a program on a remote server for processing.

We shall defer a complete discussion of data submission until Chapter 14. For now, let's discuss the basics.

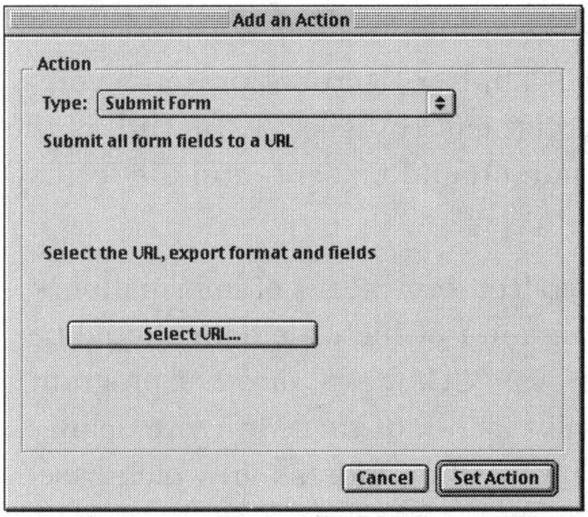

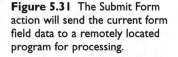

Figure 5.31 The Submit Form action will send the current form field data to a remotely located program for processing.

Submitting form data, in Acrobat parlance, means sending form data to some program that resides on a remote server for processing. A typical program would be a utility written in ASP or Java that collects the incoming data and places it in a customer database for later action by a human.

When assigning the Submit Data action to a control, you must provide the URL for the remote program; such a URL would look something like this:

```
http://www.at.com/registration.asp
```

Acrobat can send its form data in a variety of formats, depending on what is expected by the remote program. The most common formats currently used with Acrobat form data are FDF and HTML. Acrobat can also send the data as XML or send the entire PDF file, complete with filled-out form fields (Figure 5.32).

If you wish, Acrobat can instead send the data as an email attachment to a specified email address. Simply supply a mailto for the URL:

```
mailto:registration@acumentraining.com
```

The recipient will receive the FDF or HTML file as an attachment to the email.

The Select URL button

When you click on the Select URL button, Acrobat presents you with a dialog box (Figure 5.32) that lets you specify the URL of the remote program to which the data should be sent, and the format that should be used for that data.

The controls in this dialog box collect four pieces of information. First, the URL of the remote program to which the data should be sent. This will be the URL of an ASP, CGI, Java, or other program that will receive the data. We will talk about these in more detail later in the book. It can also be a "mailto" address, in which case the data will be emailed to the specified address as an attachment.

Second, the controls collect the fields whose data you want sent to the remote processor. By default, Acrobat will submit data from all the form fields in the document. You can elect to send only certain fields' values or to omit certain fields.

The third piece of information that gets collected is the format that should be used for dates. By default, dates are submitted exactly as the user types them in. Hence, a variety of bits of text can be sent to represent a date: "Sunday, January 24," "1/24/02," "24 January 2002," etc. If you select the Convert Dates check box, Acrobat will convert all date fields to a standard "D:YYYYMMDD" format, as in "D:20020124," for January 24, 2002. Your selection

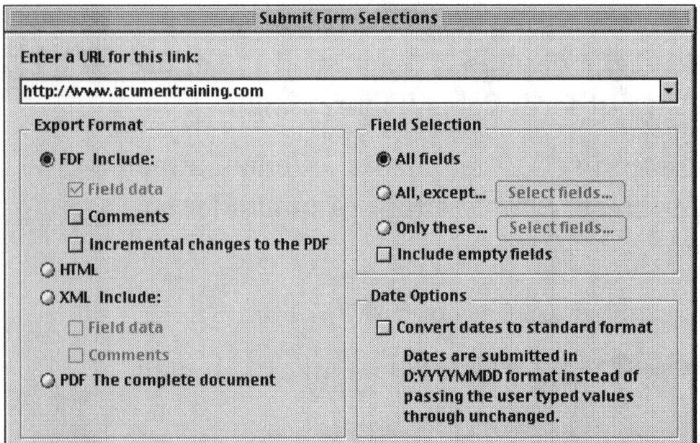

Figure 5.32 The Submit Form Data action needs the URL of the processing program, the format in which to send the form data, the fields whose data you want to send, and the format you want to use for dates.

of the date format is decided by what the processing program expects for its dates. Dates are more easily processed if they are expressed in a known format. Keep in mind that it is you who will be setting up the processing program, so you should be able to decide what date format is appropriate. (We will discuss form data processing programs in Chapter 14.)

Finally, the Select URL dialog box lets you specify the format in which the form data should be sent. You are given your choice of sending the data in FDF, HTML, or XML format. You can also have Acrobat send the entire PDF file.

Your choice here is dictated by what the processing program is expecting. If the program is written to process HTML form data, then you must send the data in HTML format. If you are sending the data as an email attachment using mailto, you may want to send the entire PDF file; the recipient can then open the file and see how you have filled out the form.

We shall compare the advantages and disadvantages of each of these data formats in Chapter 14.

Note that for FDF and XML, you can include user comments with the form data. These comments are placed on the form page using the Acrobat annotation tools. Perhaps your user has pasted an electronic "sticky note" onto the form's page with a question.

John Deubert

This is perhaps the oddest excuse for student notes I have seen in a long time. Do you really make a living at this?

Figure 5.33 Form data sent in FDF or XML format can include comments attached to the Acrobat document.

Finally, FDF files can contain the incremental data for past versions of the form. When you change an Acrobat file and save it, Acrobat actually adds the new changes to the end of the previous Acrobat file; the old contents are still in the file. If you select the Incremental Changes check box, the FDF file that Acrobat submits will contain all the old, superceded data, as well as the current PDF form field values. For form fields, I recommend against this: it increases the size of the FDF file to no purpose.

World Wide Web Link

This action links to a Web page or email address. You can use this action to create buttons that send users to your Web page for more information, or that launch their email client, presenting them with a blank email form so they can email you a question or comment.

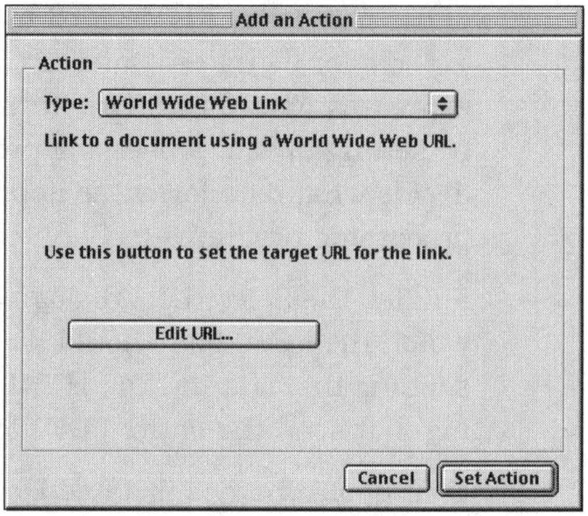

If the action links to a Web address, Acrobat will open the Web page in one of two ways. Acrobat may launch your Web browser and tell it to go to the

Figure 5.34 The World Wide Web Link action connects your form field to a Web page or email address.

specified page, or Acrobat may convert the Web page to PDF and open it in an Acrobat window. The latter method often looks a bit odd, since the handling of text is very different in PDF and HTML.

You can tell Acrobat which method to use in opening Web pages by choosing Edit > Preferences > Web Capture; the resulting dialog box allows you to choose between opening Web pages in a browser or in an Acrobat window. Unless you have strong objections, I suggest you have Acrobat open Web links in your Web browser.

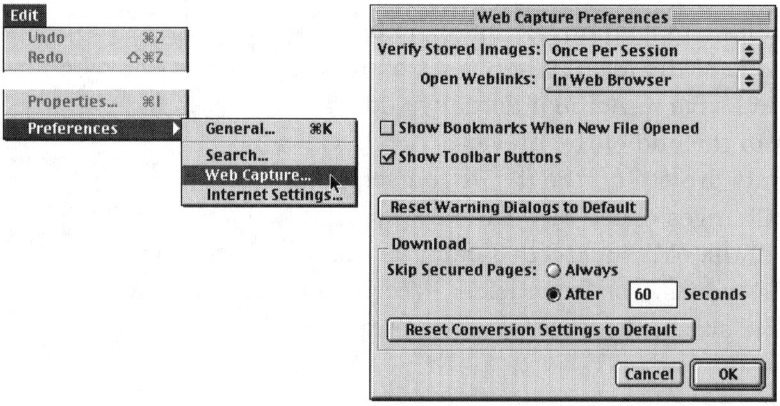

Figure 5.35 Acrobat's Web Capture preferences let you specify whether Web pages should be opened in your Web browser or converted to PDF and opened in an Acrobat window. I prefer "Web browser," myself.

It looks much better. Unfortunately, it is your readers' preference settings, not yours, that will determine this. Also unfortunately, Acrobat 5 defaults to opening Web links in an Acrobat window. Acrobat 4 opens Web pages only by launching your Web browser; it does not automatically convert them to PDF.

The Edit URL button

When you click on the Edit URL button, Acrobat presents you with a dialog box that lets you type in the URL that should be associated with the action. Your URL should start with one of two sets of characters: http:// or mailto. The former is the start of a Web page address. Acrobat will open the specified page in either your Web browser or in an Acrobat window, depending on your Web Link preferences. Thus, `http://www.adobe.com` would take you to Adobe's Web site.

Again, in Acrobat 4, there is no choice: The Web page will always be opened in your Web browser.

Mailto identifies an email address. Acrobat will launch your mail client and present you with a blank email form addressed to the specified address. Thus, `mailto:acroforms@acumentraining.com` would present you with a blank email form addressed to the Acrobat Forms comment box.

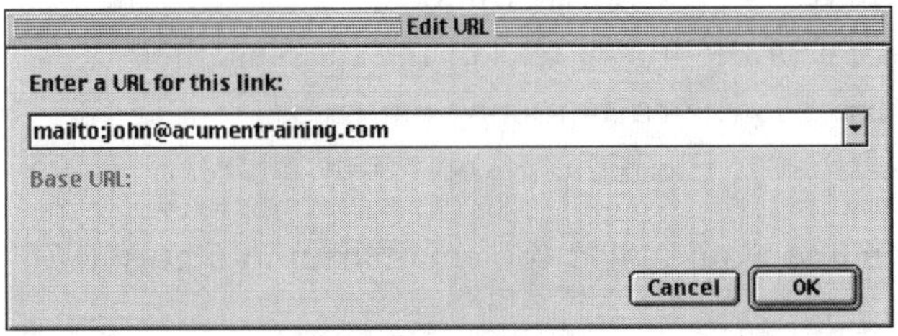

Figure 5.36 The Edit URL dialog box lets you specify the Web address or email address associated with the action.

Mailto options

The mailto: URL can accept a series of options that let you specify the initial values of several characteristics of your blank email form, including subject and body text. Each of these "commands" is separated from those preceding with a question mark (Figure 5.37). This is more easily demonstrated than described:

```
mailto:john@acumentraining.com?subject=Today's rainfall
```

The above entry in the URL dialog box would present the user with a blank email form addressed to john@acumentraining.com, and with the subject line set to "Today's rainfall."

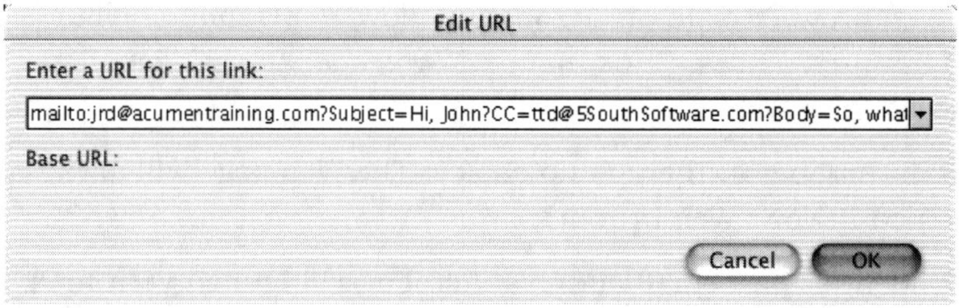

Figure 5.37 A mailto can have options that present the user with a blank email form with several of the fields already filled in. This mailto will present the user with the email form in Figure 5.38.

The options available to mailto are:

- **?subject=Any text** sets the subject line.
- **?body=Any text** sets the initial text in the message body.
- **?CC=emailAddress** is the carbon copy address.
- **?BCC=emailAddress** is the blind carbon copy address.

The following mailto line would yield the email form in Figure 5.38.

```
mailto:jrd@acumentraining.com?Subject=Hi,
John?CC=ttd@5SouthSoftware.com?Body=So, what's new?
```

Figure 5.38 The mailto options let you fill in the subject, CC, BCC, and initial text of the email form presented to the user.

Other Action Types

There are several other types of actions available to your form fields. Since these have no application to Acrobat forms, I shall just list them here:

- **Movie** plays, pauses, stops, or resumes playing a QuickTime movie on the current page.
- **Open File** opens another file on your computer system. This file can be of any type: an Excel spreadsheet, an Illustrator drawing, a Photoshop image, or anything else. The file will be opened with whatever application your system associates with that file type.
- **Read Article** takes you to an Acrobat article in the current document. Articles are an extremely useful means of making a document originally formatted for print work as an onscreen document; they have no real use in Acrobat forms.
- **None** does nothing. This makes the link a placeholder for a future, active link.

You can get more information on these actions by choosing Help > Acrobat Help.

6 Buttons

In this chapter, we shall look at the properties and abilities of buttons in an Acrobat form. Buttons are unique among the Acrobat form fields. They do not collect data; rather, they initiate commands. When you click on a button, Acrobat should do something: go to the next page, submit data for processing, or clear the form.

This Chapter's Exercise: a Job Application

Over the course of the next several chapters, we are going to construct a useful form: a corporate job application (Figure 6.1). This is a PDF form that may be emailed to a candidate or posted on a corporate Web site for filling out online or on the applicant's hard disk.

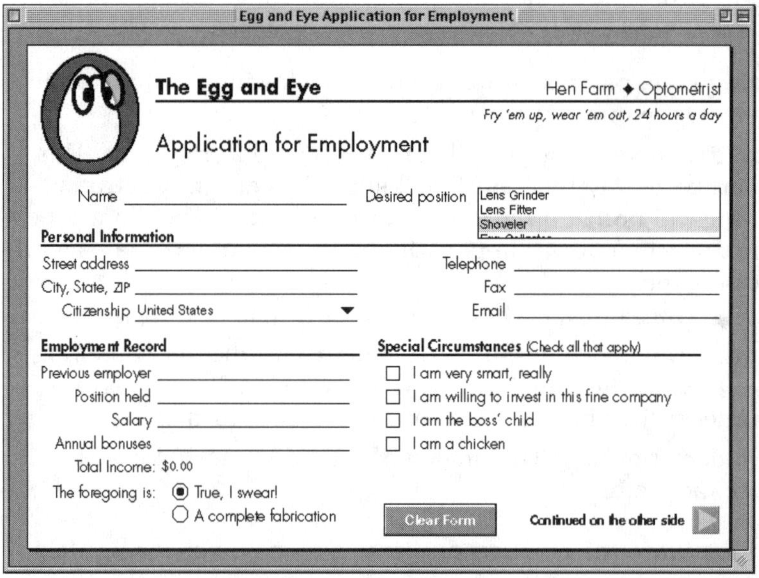

Figure 6.1 This is the first page of a Job Application form we shall assemble over the next five chapters.

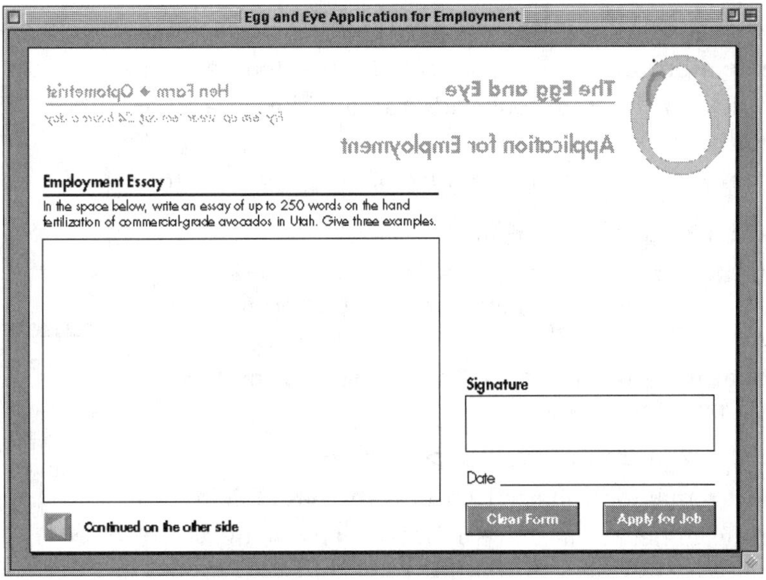

Figure 6.2 This is the second page of our project.

This two-page form contains examples of every type of form field Acrobat supports and will give you an opportunity to create these form fields as we go.

The Files

If you want to construct the Job Application form yourself, you will need some files from the Acumen Training Web site.

If you haven't done so already, go to *www.acumentraining.com/AcrobatForms* and grab the .zip file for Chapter 6. After unzipping, you will find several files that we will use for our discussion of buttons:

- Form.Employment.pdf is the final, finished form, as pictured in Figures 6.1 and 6.2.
- Form.Chapter 6 Start.pdf is the form file with no controls. This is your starting point for Chapter 6.
- Form.Chapter 6 End.pdf is the form file as it should be at the end of this chapter. This is your starting point for Chapter 7.
- Button Art is a folder of PDF files that contain artwork for our Next Page and Previous Page buttons, which we shall use later in this chapter.

Periodically through the chapter, we will perform exercises that let you add buttons to your form.

Creating and Editing Buttons

You create a button using the Acrobat Form tool, as usual. Simply click on the Fom tool and drag out the area to be occupied by the button, as we described in Chapter 4. As a reminder, here are the mechanics of creating a button.

To create a button in Acrobat:

1. With the Acrobat Form tool selected, click and drag out a rectangle where you want the button to go on the page (Figure 6.3).

   Acrobat will present you with the Field Properties dialog box (Figure 6.4).

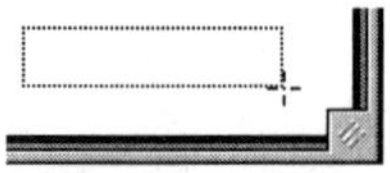

2. Select Button in the Type pop-up menu.

3. Type a name for your button into the name field.

   Every form field must have an internal name by which the field is referenced by scripts and other fields in the Acrobat file. See Chapter 3 for more information on naming form fields.

4. If you wish, you may enter a phrase into the Short Description field (Figure 6.5).

   This will become tool tip text for this button.

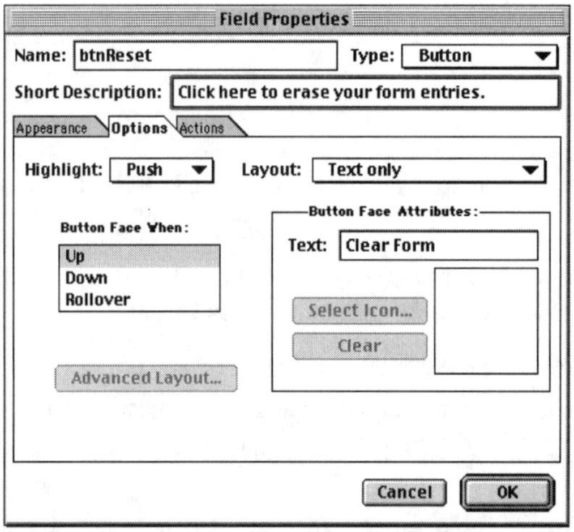

Figure 6.3 Start a button by dragging a rectangle on the page using the Form tool.

Figure 6.4 The Field Properties dialog box lets you specify the appearance and behavior of a form field. All fields need a name and a type (Button," in our case).

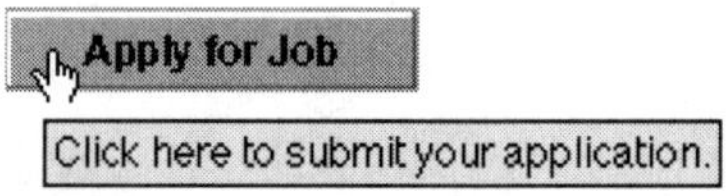

Figure 6.5 The Short Description field in the Field Properties dialog box will become tool tip text in the final button.

5. Set whatever properties you wish among the three tabs in the Field Properties dialog box.

   We will talk about all of these controls in detail in this chapter.

6. Click OK.

   You will return to the Acrobat page. The newly minted button will be represented by a rectangle with handles at each side and corner. You can drag the button to a new position and size when it is in this state.

7. Click on the Hand tool when you are finished with making buttons.

   All your controls will take on their final appearance when you leave the Form tool.

Button Properties

The Field Properties dialog box, when conjured for a button field, is a three-tabbed dialog box that dictates the appearance and behavior of the button. Two of these tabs, Appearance and Actions, are identical for all field types.

The **Appearance Tab** specifies what the button should look like on the page. Here you specify the color, the type of border, the font, and all the other visual properties of the button, except for its label.

The **Options Tab** specifies properties specific to buttons and not shared by other field types. Here you can specify the button's label and what visual feedback the button should provide when the user clicks on it.

The **Actions Tab** specifies the actions the button should carry out. This can be any combination of the actions we described in the previous chapter.

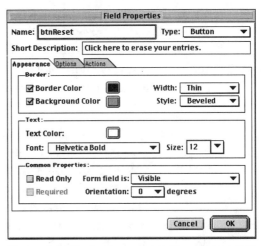

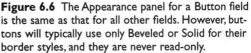

Figure 6.6 The Appearance panel for a Button field is the same as that for all other fields. However, buttons will typically use only Beveled or Solid for their border styles, and they are never read-only.

Tip

Although the Appearance panel is the same for buttons as for any other form field type, you will find that the Border Style that you pick for buttons will invariably be either Beveled, for buttons with text labels, or Solid, for buttons that use icons as labels. We shall talk about this in more detail later in this chapter. Also notice that the Read Only attribute is pretty useless when applied to buttons.

We talked about the Appearance and Actions tabs in the previous chapter. Here, we'll talk in detail about the controls on the Options tab.

The Options Tab

When you click on the Options tab in the Field Properties dialog box, you are faced with a set of controls that are unique to buttons. These controls specify the labeling of your button.

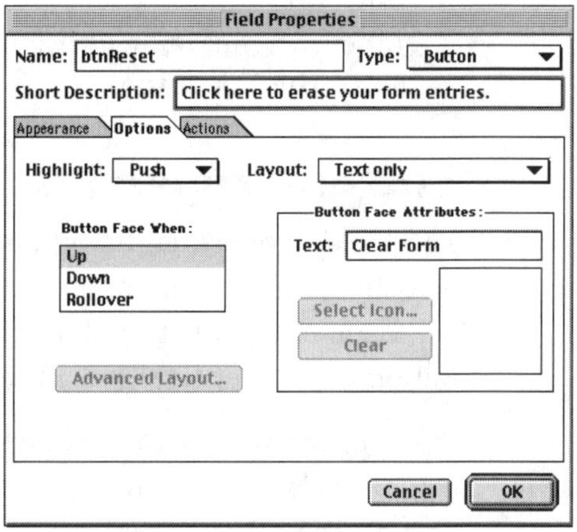

The **Highlight** pop-up menu specifies how the button should visually respond when the user clicks on it. The options are reasonably self-explanatory, except for Push, which causes the button to be offset in such a way that it looks as though it has been pushed in. Push is the most common choice—it looks best.

Figure 6.7 The Options panel lets you specify how your button should be labeled. These controls are unique to button fields.

The **Layout** pop-up menu lets you choose whether the button should be labeled with text, a picture (an icon, in Acrobat terminology), or both. If both text and an icon are used, you may specify how they will be arranged. The icon used to label a button is PDF artwork taken from a specified Acrobat file and embedded in the button definition. Let's defer talking about button icons until later in the chapter.

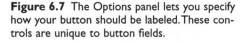

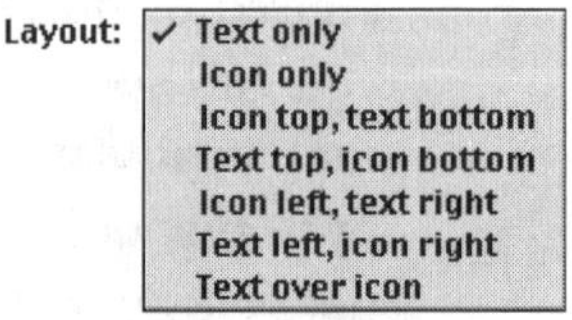

Figure 6.8 The Layout menu lets you specify whether the button is labeled with text, an icon, or both, and how they should be arranged.

The **Button Face Attributes** controls let you specify the label for your button. You may enter a text label into the text box or click on the Select Icon button and choose the PDF file that contains your button art.

The **Button Face When** control allows you to associate a picture with any of the three states a button may occupy. The **Advanced Layout** button allows you to precisely control how pictures are placed in your button. Again, we'll put off talking about these controls until later in the chapter, when we discuss using pictures as button labels.

Exercise: Text Buttons

In our first exercise, we will create the text buttons that appear on our Job Application form. There are three of these: two Clear Form buttons, one for each page of the form, and an Apply for Job button that submits the form data to the company's human resources department (Figure 6.9).

Figure 6.9 There are three text buttons in our sample form: two that clear the form, and a third that submits the application to the company.

There are two other buttons in this form: the Next Page/Previous Page buttons labeled with arrowheads. We shall look at these in a later exercise, since they use pictures for their labels.

Start by opening the file Form.Chapter 6 Start.pdf among the files for this chapter. You will see the Job Application with no form fields in it at all, as in Figure 6.10.

Create the Clear Form Button

Let's begin by creating the Clear Form (or Reset Form) button on the first page of the form. I will be very detailed on the steps here. Follow closely, since I'll be brief on this procedure in later exercises.

1. Click on the Form tool.
2. Click and drag out the rectangle where the Clear Form button should be located on the page, just to the left of the "Continued..." label. (Refer to Figure 6.1 to see where this is.)
   You will now see the Field Properties dialog box.

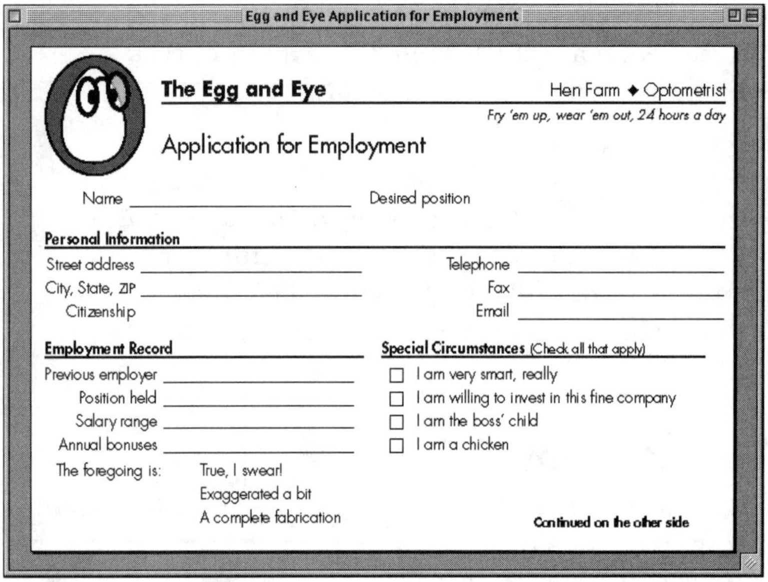

Egg and Eye Application for Employment

The Egg and Eye
Hen Farm ✦ Optometrist
Fry 'em up, wear 'em out, 24 hours a day

Application for Employment

Name ______ Desired position

Personal Information
Street address ______ Telephone ______
City, State, ZIP ______ Fax ______
Citizenship Email ______

Employment Record
Previous employer ______
Position held ______
Salary range ______
Annual bonuses ______
The foregoing is: True, I swear! / Exaggerated a bit / A complete fabrication

Special Circumstances (Check all that apply)
☐ I am very smart, really
☐ I am willing to invest in this fine company
☐ I am the boss' child
☐ I am a chicken

Continued on the other side

Figure 6.10 Your starting point for this exercise is the file form.Chapter 6 Start.pdf. This contains the static artwork with no form fields in place. We'll add the form fields later.

3. In the Type menu, select Button.
4. Type the name "btnReset" (or whatever you prefer) into the Name text box.
5. If you wish, type a descriptive phrase into the Short Description box.
6. Click on the Appearance tab and set the properties as they're shown in Figure 6.11.

   I picked a medium blue for the button's background color and white for the text color. Of course, you may use whatever colors strike your fancy.
7. Click on the Options tab and set the properties as they appear in Figure 6.12.
8. Click on the Actions tab.
9. Select the Mouse Up event and click the Add button

   You'll now see the Add an Action dialog box (Figure 6.14).
10. In the Type menu, select Reset Form.

    The Select Fields button will appear in the dialog box.
11. Click on the Select Fields button and make sure the All Fields button is selected (Figure 6.15).

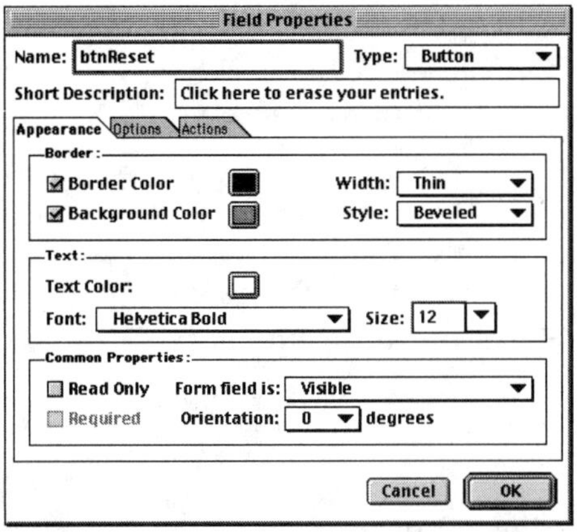

Figure 6.11 Set the controls in the Appearance panel to match these settings for your Clear Form button. Note that beveled is usually the best-looking style for text-labeled buttons.

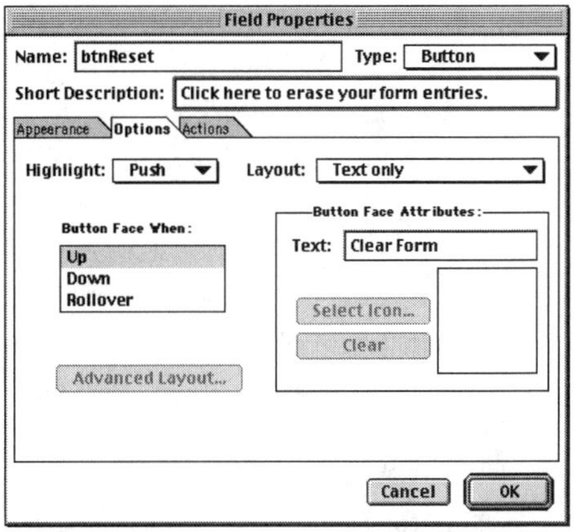

Figure 6.12 Set the controls in the Options panel to match these settings for your Clear Form button.

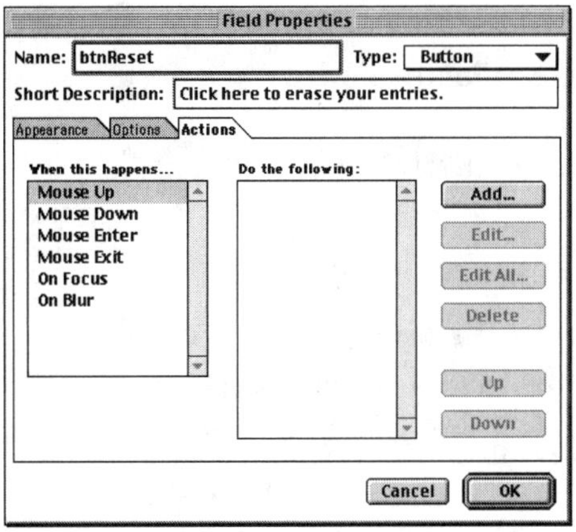

Figure 6.13 We shall add an action, Reset Form, to the Mouse Up action.

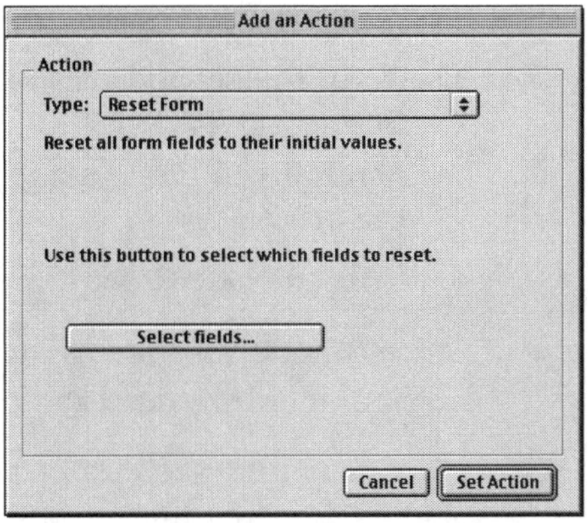

Figure 6.14 In the Add an Action dialog box, select Reset Form in the Type menu.

12. Click the OK and Set Action buttons, returning to the Field Properties dialog box.

13. Click OK again, returning to your form's page.

Excellent! We have now created the Reset Form button. Of course, at the moment it looks like a red rectangle with handles. Click on the Hand tool and you will see your button sitting on the page.

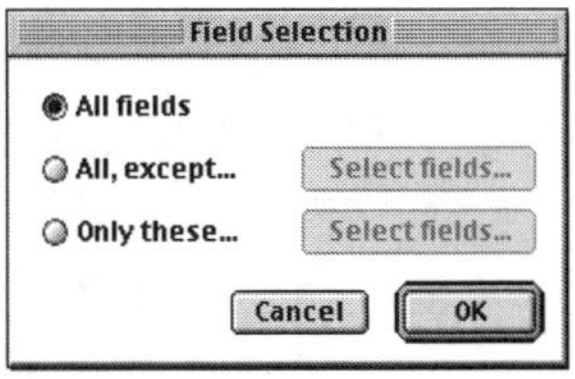

Figure 6.15 Our Clear Form button should reset all the fields in the form.

If the size and position look off, click on the Form tool again, and reposition and resize as you wish. Remember that you can nudge the position and size with your arrow keys. (Hold down the Shift key to nudge the size with your arrows.)

Look good?

Then do the other Reset Form button on your own. Go to the second page of the form and make a Reset Form button in the position you see it in Figure 6.2.

Copy and paste

Now that you've made your second Reset Form button, I should point out a shortcut: You can copy and paste form fields. The easy way to make your second Reset Form button is to do the following:

1. With the Form tool active, click on the first Reset Form button.
2. Select the menu item Edit > Copy or press Command-C/Ctrl-C.
3. Go to the second page and select Edit > Paste or press Command-V/Ctrl-V.

    Acrobat will paste a copy of your Reset button in the middle of the screen.
4. Drag the new Reset Form button to its proper place on the page.

Since this button has the same purpose as the original, there is nothing more we need to do to create this second Reset button.

I use copy and paste *a lot* when making a form. It's a convenient way of ensuring my buttons are the same size and color. After pasting a new button on the page, I can edit it and make whatever changes I want to its name, actions, and other properties.

Create the Apply for Job Button

The final text button in this form is the Apply for Job button on the form's second page. (Again, see Figure 6.2 to see what this button looks like.)

The procedure for making this button is similar to that for making the Reset Form button. It should have a different name and label, of course. (I used "btnSubmit" and "Apply for Job," but pick your own names, if you wish.) The most important difference is that this button should execute a Submit Form action, rather than a Reset Form action.

1. Carry out steps 1 through 10 from "Create the Clear Form Button," changing name and label as needed.

2. In the Add an Action dialog box, in the Type menu, select Submit Form. A Select URL button will appear.

3. Click on the Select URL button and set up the resulting dialog box as in Figure 6.16. Click OK when you're done.

   By the way, the URL listed here will just discard the data you send it.

4. Keep exiting dialog boxes until you are back at the Form page.

Drag the new button around and nudge its size until it looks right, then click on the Hand tool to see how it looks.

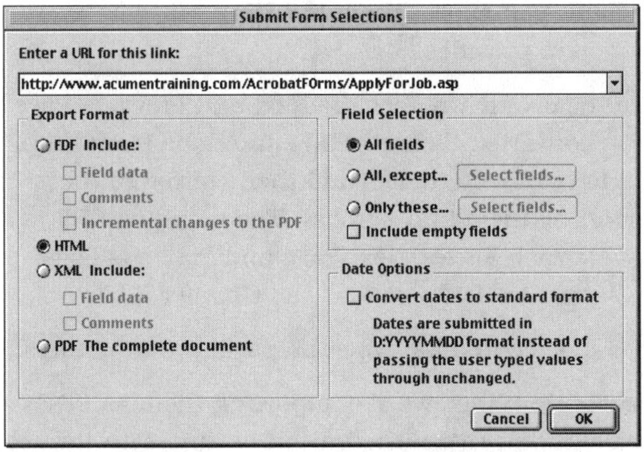

Figure 6.16 Here are the URL settings for the Submit Form action. The program at this URL will do nothing with the data you send it.

Using Pictures as Labels

The Next Page/Previous Page buttons in the lower corners of the application (see Figures 6.1 and 6.2) are graphic buttons. When the cursor moves over them, the arrow in the center brightens; when you click on these buttons, the button pushes in and the arrow glows (Figure 6.17).

Figure 6.17 The Next Page and Previous Page buttons change their appearances.

This type of button uses pictures as its label. Actually, the labels for these buttons are each made up of three separate pictures: one for when the button is idle, a second for when the cursor moves over the button, and a third for when you click on the button. Acrobat displays whichever of the three label pictures is appropriate at any given moment.

Preparing the Pictures

Acrobat wants button label pictures to be supplied as pages in a PDF file. This means that you will create them in whatever combination of drawing or image-editing software you wish. When you have them looking right, you export them to PDF using whatever mechanism your software provides.

For example, I made the six pictures for the Next and Previous Page buttons in Illustrator, converted them to TIFFs in Adobe Photoshop, applied a glow effect to the Down image, and then converted the TIFFs to PDF by importing them into Acrobat. The resulting PDF files (one three-page file each for the Next Page and Previous Page buttons) are in the Button Art folder among the Chapter 6 files.

Here are some things to keep in mind when preparing your pictures:

The pictures are scalable. Since we are importing them as PDFs, the pictures can scale as you resize the button outline with the Form tool. You specify the details of how or whether the art resizes itself in the Advanced Layout button, which we'll discuss later.

Design at the final size, if possible. Even though the button pictures can scale, you should design your button art at the size it will finally appear on the page. The small pictures used for buttons can change their appearance dramatically as they scale. You will have much better control of the appearance of your button if you design its icons at the final, displayed size. One hundred percent is always the best scale.

The button art file's page size does not need to match the button size. Your button's PDF file can have a quarter-inch button picture sitting in the middle of a letter-size page. Acrobat will grab only the artwork out of the page.

You can have more than one piece of button art in a PDF file. Each page within a PDF file becomes a candidate for button art. When you attach the art to a button, Acrobat lets you scroll through the pages in the PDF file.

Button pictures can be line art. If you come to Acrobat from the HTML world, there is a tendency to use only images for your button art. This is fine but not necessary; button art can be line art from Illustrator, FreeHand, or any other source that can generate a PDF file.

Button pictures are stored in the form file. This means that the button artwork files do not need to travel with the form file. It also means you shouldn't use 6 MB image files for your button pictures; this would yield very big PDF files. Incidentally, if you copy and paste or otherwise duplicate a button, all the copies make reference to the same artwork within the PDF file; Acrobat does not store a separate copy of the button pictures for each instance of the button.

Assigning Pictures to a Button

The Field Properties Options tab is where you specify how a button should be labeled (Figure 6.18). The Layout pop-up menu lets you label a button with some combination of text and artwork. If you select any layout other than Text only, you will have access to the controls that let you select an icon.

To the left of the Select Icon button is a list of the three states a button can have: up, down, and rollover (meaning the cursor is over the button, but the mouse button has not been clicked). You may assign a picture to the button in each of these three states. You must supply an Up picture; the others are optional.

To assign a picture to a button:

1. In the Options panel, select a Layout that includes an icon as a label.

2. Click on the button state (Up, Down, Rollover) to which you want to assign a picture.

3. Click on the Select Icon button.

   Acrobat presents you with the Select Appearance dialog box (Figure 6.19). Its Sample box will display the icons in the most recently selected PDF file, if any. (If this is the first set of icons you have looked for, the Sample box will be blank.)

4. If there are no icons displayed, or if the picture you want is not in the Sample box, click on the Browse button, and from the resulting Open dialog box select the PDF file that contains your button art. Each page in the PDF file will become a picture that is available in the Sample box and accessible using the scroll bar.

5. If necessary, scroll through the list of pictures in the Select Appearance dialog box until the picture you want is displayed.

6. Click the OK button.

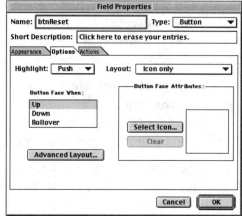

Figure 6.18 The Options panel lets you associate an icon with each of three states the button can occupy.

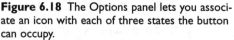

Figure 6.19 The Select Appearance dialog box lets you choose an icon for your button.

That's all there is to it. The Options panel will now display the picture associated with the state you have selected. Repeat these steps for each of the states you want to associate with a picture.

Highlight, appearance, and button pictures

There are a couple of other controls in the Field Properties dialog box that need to be set correctly for your button pictures to look good.

- In the Options panel, the Highlight pop-up menu should be set to Push.
- In the Appearance panel, both the Border and Background Color check boxes should be unchecked if you are using only icons.
- Also in the Appearance tab, you may want to set the Style pop-up menu to Solid. Do some experimentation here; some button pictures need beveling, depending on the picture's content.

The Appearance tab should look like the one in Figure 6.23 if you are using button pictures without text. If you are using both text and pictures to label your buttons, you will need to experiment with borders, backgrounds, and style to see what works best with your particular button art.

Button Picture Layout Controls

If you click on the Advanced Layout button in the Options tab, Acrobat presents you with the Icon Placement dialog box (Figure 6.20). This dialog box lets you specify how your button picture is placed within the control's border.

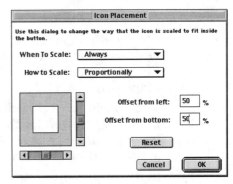

Figure 6.20 The Icon Placement dialog box lets you specify how icons should be positioned within a button.

Looking at the controls in this dialog box, you can specify whether and when the picture should be scaled to match the size of the border; whether the scaling should maintain the original proportions of the artwork; and exactly where the icon should be located within the button's border.

Figure 6.21 The two menus in the Icon Placement dialog box determine when and how icons should scale as you resize the button.

Exercise: Button Pictures

Let's finish up the buttons for our Job
Application form. There are two buttons
we still need to place on our Job Application:
Next Page and Previous Page. Let's start by making the Next Page
button, the right arrow button at the bottom of the first page.

Start with the form as we left it at the end of the previous
exercise. Alternatively, you can just start with Form.Chapter 6
Start.pdf among your Chapter 6 files; this contains the form
with no form fields placed on the pages.

The icons for this button are in the file Right
Arrow.pdf in the Button Art folder. This three-
page file has a button icon on each page for the
Up, Over, and Down states, as in Figure 6.22.

Figure 6.22 There are
three pictures in Right
Arrow.pdf: One each for
the button in its Up,
Rollover, and Down states.

Create the Next Page Button

Start with the Job Application turned to Page 1 and the
Form tool selected.

1. Click and drag out a small rectangle for the button form
   field, as before. The button should be just to the right of
   the "Continued on the other side" text at the bottom right
   of the page, as in Figure 6.1.

2. In the Field Properties dialog
   box, select Button for the control type and type in a name
   and a short description.

3. In the Appearance tab, set the
   controls as they are shown in
   Figure 6.23.

4. In the Options tab, set the
   Highlight pop-up menu to
   Push and the Layout menu to
   Icon only, as displayed in
   Figure 6.24.

5. Select Up in the list of button
   states and click on the Select
   Icon button.

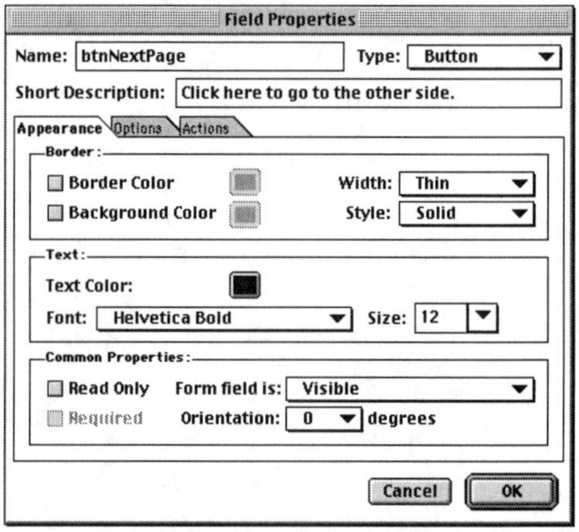

Figure 6.23 Set the controls in the Appearance
panel to match these settings for your Next Page
button.

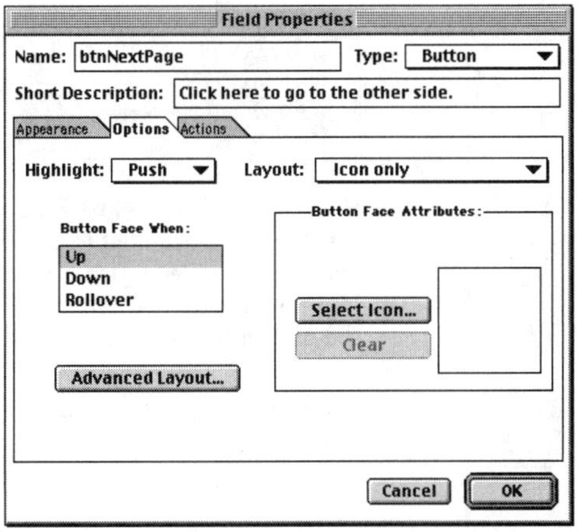

Field Properties

Name: btnNextPage   Type: Button ▼

Short Description: Click here to go to the other side.

[Appearance] [Options] [Actions]

Highlight: Push ▼   Layout: Icon only ▼

Button Face When:
- Up
- Down
- Rollover

Button Face Attributes:

[Select Icon...] [Clear]

[Advanced Layout...]

[Cancel] [OK]

Figure 6.24 In the Options panel, set the Highlight menu to Push and the Layout menu to Icon only. Then assign a picture to the Up state.

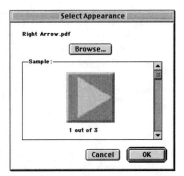

Select Appearance

Right Arrow.pdf

[Browse...]

Sample:

1 out of 3

[Cancel] [OK]

Figure 6.25 Having browsed to Right Arrow.pdf, you can look at the pictures it contains by clicking on the scroll bar in the Sample box.

Acrobat will present you with the Select Appearance dialog box.

6. Click the Browse button and, in the resulting Open dialog box, select the file named Right Arrow.pdf.

The Sample box will now display the graphic on the first page of the button art PDF file. You can look at the other button pictures in the file using the scroll bar in the Sample box (Figure 6.25).

7. Make sure that the Up button picture is showing in the Sample box (it is the first picture in the set) and click the OK button.

You will be back in the Options tab, this time with the Up picture displayed to the right of the Select Icon button, as in Figure 6.26.

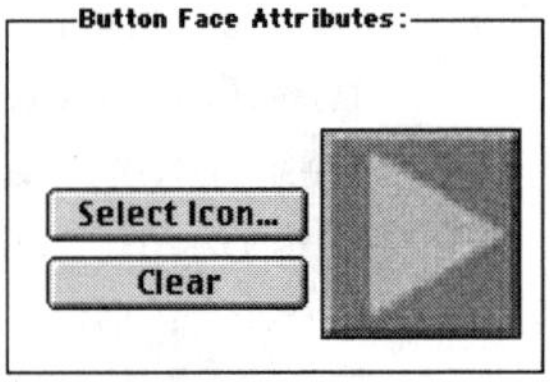

8. Repeat steps 5 through 7 for each of the other two button states.

9. Go to the Actions panel and set the action for the Mouse Up event to Execute Menu Item, as shown in Figure 6.27.

The menu item, in this case, is Document > Next Page. See the discussion of the Execute Menu Item action in the previous chapter if you need a refresher.

10. Click OK in the Field Properties dialog box.

Button Face Attributes:

[Select Icon...] [Clear]

Figure 6.26 Once you have chosen an icon, it will appear in the Button Face box of the Options panel.

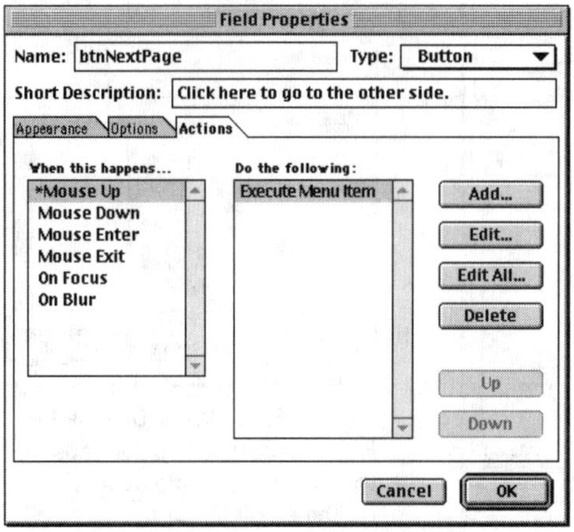

Figure 6.27 Finally, you must assign a Mouse Up action to the button. You want to use an Execute Menu Item action, selecting Document > Next Page for the item.

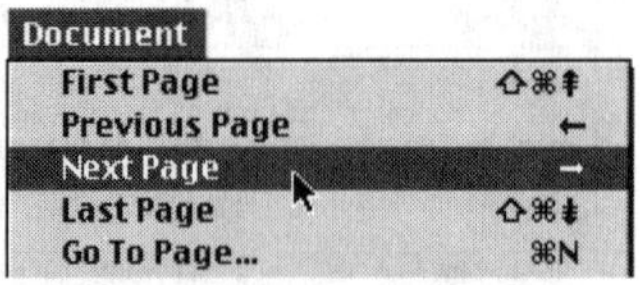

Figure 6.28 Select Next Page in the Acrobat Document menu for your Execute Menu Item action. Use the Previous Page item for the button on page 2 of the form.

You should now have returned to your Acrobat page, and your new button should be a red rectangle in the lower right corner. Click on the Hand tool to see your button in action. Put it through its paces: pass the mouse over it and click on it, so you can see the different button pictures in play.

Now create the Previous Page button (with the left arrow) on page two. Check out Figure 6.2 to see where it should go. The file with this button's artwork is Left Arrow.pdf. The Mouse Up action for this button will be Execute Menu Item, executing Document > Previous Page.

(Hint: the easy way to make this second button is to copy and paste the button we just made. You'll need to change the pasted button's name, description, button art, and action.)

Done!

So now we have all the buttons in place on our form. Perhaps we should collect some data?

In the next chapter, we'll add text fields to the form so we can get our applicants' names, addresses, and other vital statistics.

Text Fields 7

Most of the fields you create for your Acrobat forms will be text fields. They are the best field type for collecting a wide range of data, everything from names and addresses to salaries and dates to requests for clarification.

Acrobat provides a remarkable set of options for its text fields. The text in your form fields can be automatically formatted as a numeric value, checked for validity, and calculated from other form fields.

In this chapter, we shall see how to create text fields and examine the properties associated with them.

This Chapter's Exercises

In the preceding chapter, we placed the buttons on our Job Application form. As we proceed through this chapter, we shall add all of the text fields. The form's two pages contain a total of 12 text fields.

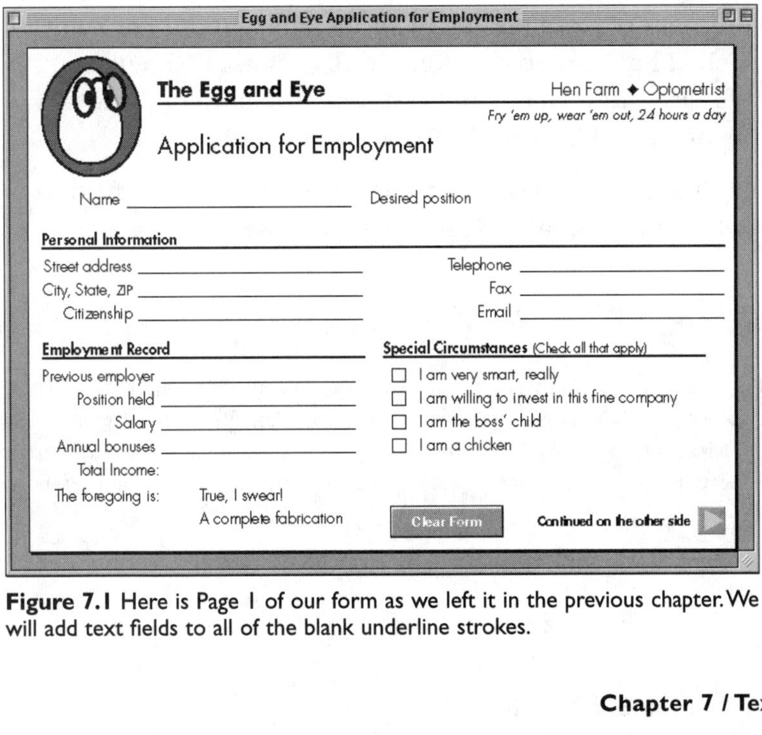

Figure 7.1 Here is Page 1 of our form as we left it in the previous chapter. We will add text fields to all of the blank underline strokes.

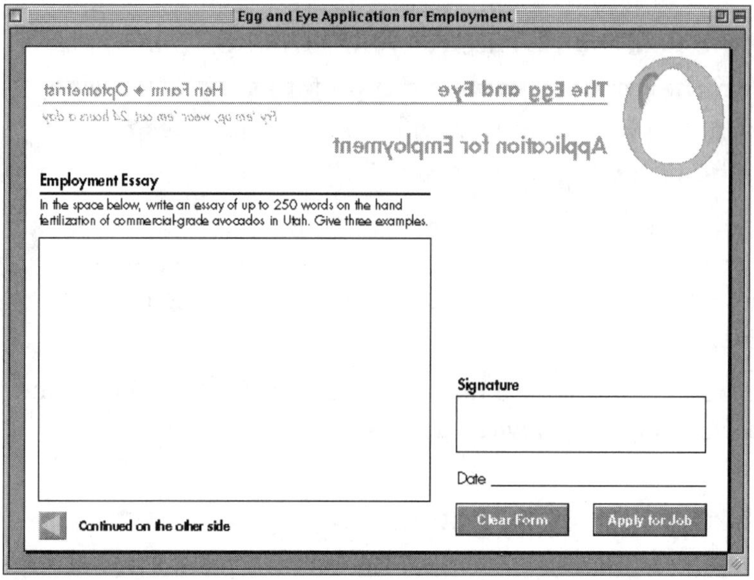

Figure 7.2 On Page 2 of our form, we shall place a text field in the Essay box and another to the right of the Date label.

Looking at Figure 7.1, we shall be laying a text field on top of each of the blank "fill-in" lines on Page 1 of the application. For some of these, we shall have Acrobat automatically reformat the user's input. We'll also put a calculated text field (the sum of the salary and bonus amounts) next to the Total Income: label.

On Page 2 (Figure 7.2), we'll place a large, multi-line text field in the Essay box and a small text field for the date.

This chapter's files

If you worked on the exercises in the previous chapter, you can use your form with buttons as the starting point for this chapter's exercises. Alternatively, you can start with the file Form.Chapter 07 Start.pdf among the Chapter 7 files on the Acrobat Forms web page (www.acumentraining.com/AcrobatForms). This has the Job Application with only buttons in place, exactly as it should be after finishing the exercises in Chapter 6.

You create a text field in the same manner as any other form field: Select the Form tool and then drag out a rectangle roughly where you want the control to go on the page. In the resulting Field Properties dialog box (Figure 7.3), select Text in the Type pop-up menu, give your field a name and (if you wish) a short description, and then sit back and contemplate the field properties.

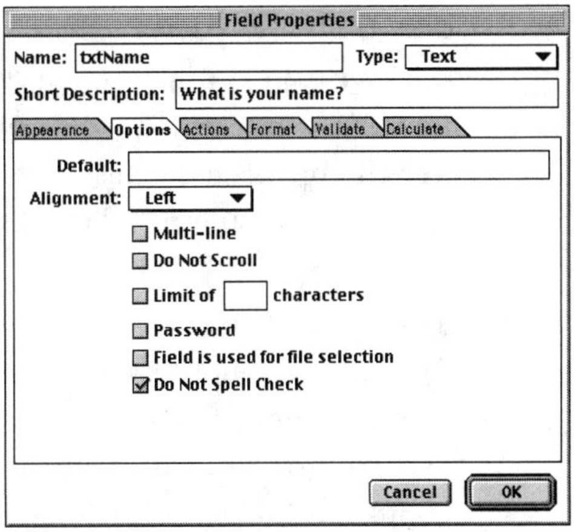

Figure 7.3 Text fields have a large number of properties spread across six tabs in the Field Properties dialog box.

Text Field Properties

Text fields have *a lot* of properties, spread across six panels in the Field Properties dialog box. These six panels are:

- The **Appearance** panel, as described in Chapter 5.
- The **Options** panel, containing controls that dictate the default field contents, text alignment, and other text-specific properties.
- The **Actions** panel, which, as always, lets you assign actions to this field. Text field actions are used in a variety of special-purpose activities, including rollover help.
- The **Format** panel, which lets you decide whether and how the text field should reformat the text the user types in, displaying it as a monetary value, a phone number, a ZIP code, and so on.
- The **Validate** panel, wherein you supply a function that establishes whether the text supplied by the user is valid. Acrobat will not let users place invalid text in the field.
- The **Calculate** panel provides information by which Acrobat can calculate the value that should go in this text field. Perhaps this is a Total field, that calculates by adding the numeric values of several other text fields.

The Appearance and Actions panels are the same as in all other field types. Look at Chapter 5 if you need a review of the contents of these panels. We shall now look at the other, text-specific panels.

The Options Panel

The text field Options panel (Figure 7.3) lets you set a number of properties that will apply to all kinds of text fields. That is, whatever the purpose of these fields in your form (number, telephone number, and so on), you will need to make decisions on these properties.

Default holds the default contents of the field. Type in whatever text the user should see when he or she opens the form. For example, the default text for a field that collects information on your country of birth might be "United States" (or whatever would be appropriate for your form).

Alignment lets you left- or right-justify or center the text in the field.

Multi-line tells Acrobat that the form field can have multiple lines of text. Text will be wrapped within the field and, when the user hits the return key, the field will start a new line of text within the field. This lets you use text fields for such things as user comments and questions. See the section on multi-line fields, below, for more information.

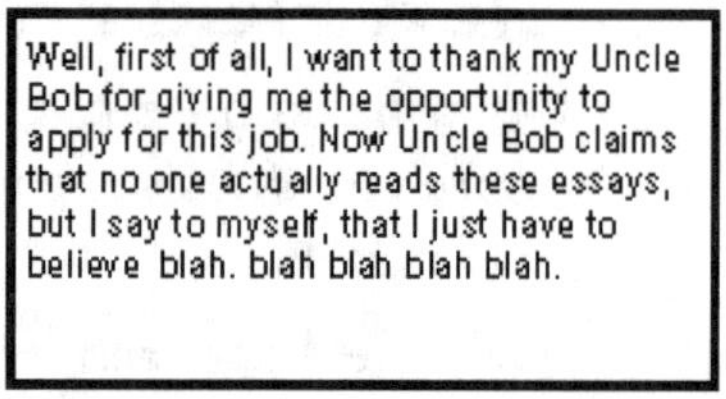

> Well, first of all, I want to thank my Uncle Bob for giving me the opportunity to apply for this job. Now Uncle Bob claims that no one actually reads these essays, but I say to myself, that I just have to believe blah. blah blah blah blah.

Figure 7.4 A multi-line text field can have multiple lines of text in it. This makes it appropriate for such things as comment boxes.

Do Not Scroll limits the text the user can enter to the boundaries of the visible form field. When the user tries typing below the bottom of the field, Acrobat will beep. If this check box is off, then users can type as much text as they wish; the text will scroll as needed to accommodate the additional text.

Limit of ___ characters lets you specify the maximum number of characters that may be typed into the field. This is common in text fields that collect such information as passwords, zip codes, and other text of a known length.

Password causes Acrobat to display asterisks when the user enters text into this field. This is standard in password fields, preventing bystanders from reading the text being entered into the field.

Password [*********]

Figure 7.5 A password field displays an asterisk every time the user presses a key. This prevents passersby from reading the password.

Field is used for file selection indicates that this field contains the name of a file. If the form is submitted to a remote processor in FDF format, the file named here will be embedded in the FDF file. For example, an expense report form could include scanned receipts as a TIFF file embedded in the submitted FDF file. See the section below on File Selection Fields.

Do Not Spell Check tells Acrobat to ignore this field when it performs a spell check. (You can tell Acrobat to check the spelling in your PDF form fields by selecting Tools > Spelling > Check form fields and comments.)

Multi-line text fields

If you click on the Multi-line check box in the text field options, users may type large amounts of text into a text field. The exact way the text field will behaves when its text box capacity is exceeded is determined by the text size you have chosen, and whether the text field is allowed to scroll.

If you have chosen Auto in the Appearance panel's text size menu, then, once your text hits the bottom of the text box, Acrobat will decrease the point size of the text box every time it needs to, in order to add a new line of text. The text will always fit in the box, though it will quickly get *very* hard to read as the point size becomes increasingly microscopic.

Well, first of all, I want to thank my Uncle Bob for giving me the opportunity to apply for this job. Now Uncle Bob claims that no one actually reads these essays, but I say to myself, that I just have to believe blah. blah blah blah blah.	Well, first of all, I want to thank my Uncle Bob for giving me the opportunity to apply for this job. Now Uncle Bob claims that no one actually reads these essays, but I say to myself, that I just have to believe blah. blah blah blah blah. Furthermore, I personally have always assumed that as long as the first line or each paragraph looks like a real essay, the rest of the paragraph can blah blah blah blah blah blah blah blah blah blah blah blah blah blah blah blah blah blah blah

Figure 7.6 When the text size is set to Auto, Acrobat will always choose a point size that allows all the text to fit in the multi-line text box. This can be hard on the eyes if the user types in 15 or 20 paragraphs of text.

If you use a fixed text size for your text box, then Acrobat looks at the Do Not Scroll check box to determine how your text box should behave when your text hits the bottom.

If Do Not Scroll is selected, then the user is simply not allowed to type beyond the bottom of the text box; Acrobat will beep and refuse to accept further keystrokes. If Do Not Scroll is unchecked, then Acrobat will just scroll the text box contents as needed to let you type more text.

> Well, first of all, I want to thank my Uncle Bob for giving me the opportunity to apply for this job. Now Uncle Bob claims that no one actually reads these essays, but I say to myself, that I just have to believe blah. blah blah blah blah.
>
> Furthermore, I personally have always

Figure 7.7 If the text size is a fixed number and the Do Not Scroll property is unchecked, the text field will scroll up and down as needed to display your text.

File selection fields

If you select the "Field is used for file selection" check box, the contents of the text field are assumed to be the path and filename of a file that the user wants to have submitted with the rest of the form field values. Note that the entire contents of the file are embedded in the FDF file, not just the name. The typical use would be to send supporting documentation with a form: The classic case is embedding a file of scanned receipts in an expense report form.

Although you can just let the user type a pathname, such as C:\MyComputer\docs\receipts\mytrip.xl, into the text field, this is tedious at best. It would be much kinder to give your users some way of browsing to the file they want to attach to the form. You do this with a JavaScript action. This action could be attached to the text field's On Focus event; in that case, they users would get a Open dialog box when they click in the text field.

Personally, I think having the text field automatically produce the dialog box is bad user-interface design: it doesn't give users any clue what they are supposed to do. I think it is better to give them a Browse button, as in Figure 7.8.

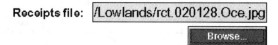

Receipts file: /Lowlands/rct.020128.Oce.jpg

Browse...

Figure 7.8 A filename text field names a file that Acrobat should embed in the FDF file when the form is submitted. The Browse button uses a JavaScript to let users pick a file.

The JavaScript that should be attached to the button's Mouse Up action is:

```
var fld = this.getField("txtFilename");

fld.browseForFileToSubmit();
```

The above assumes that the name of the text field is txtFilename.

The Format Panel

Acrobat can automatically reformat the text that the user enters into a text field, converting it to some standard format, such as a number, an American telephone number, a ZIP code, and so on. The Format panel lets you specify how the text should be formatted.

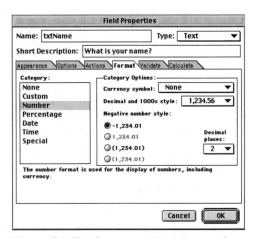

Most of the options in the Format panel are pretty clear. Click on a data type (number, date, time, and so on), and you get a set of controls that specify the details of how the text should be reformatted. The Special format type lets

Figure 7.9 The Format panel lets you specify whether and how Acrobat should reformat text that the user enters into a text field.

you choose among telephone numbers, social security numbers, and two flavors of ZIP code.

If none of the predesigned formats work for you, you can do your own formatting by selecting Custom. The Category Options turn into a set of controls that let you enter two kinds of JavaScript.

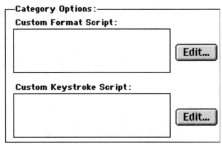

The first type of JavaScript is called when users leave a text box. This JavaScript should reformat all the text entered by a user.

Figure 7.10 Custom Formatting lets you write a JavaScript to reformat the text. This gives you vast reformatting capabilities, if you know JavaScript.

The second type of JavaScript is called upon each keystroke, and checks the characters that users type into a text box. You can program in a beep if users hit an illegal key.

When you click on one of the two Edit buttons, Acrobat presents you with the standard JavaScript Edit window, letting you type in your JavaScript.

For example, here is a Custom Format JavaScript that turns the user's text entry to uppercase when he or she leaves a text field.

```
var s = new String(event.value);

event.value = s.toUpperCase();
```

To enter the above code, you would click on the Edit button next to the Custom Format Script box and then type the JavaScript snippet into the JavaScript Edit window, as in Figure 7.11.

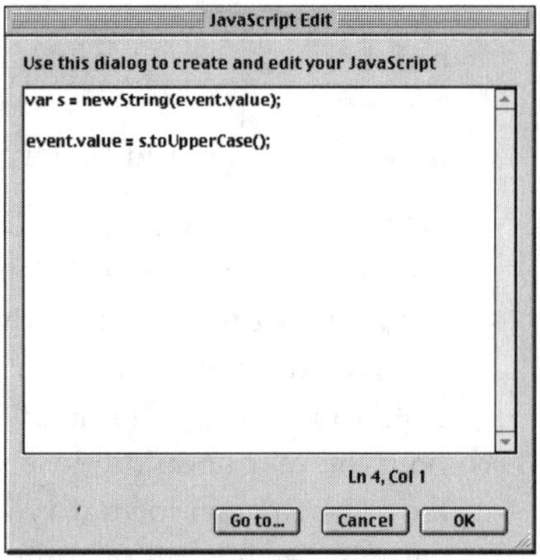

In a similar vein, the following is a keystroke JavaScript that inspects each character typed by the user and beeps if he or she types anything other than a capital letter. Only capital letters are actually entered into the text box.

Figure 7.11 The JavaScript Edit dialog box is where you type your JavaScript code. In Windows, you can specify your own text-editing program.

```
event.rc = (event.change >= 'A' && event.change <= 'Z');

if (!event.rc)
        app.beep();
```

Keystroke JavaScripts allow you to prevent the user from entering illegal characters into the text field.

For more information on the Event object in JavaScript, see the Acrobat JavaScript Guide, available in the Acrobat Help menu.

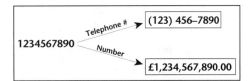

Figure 7.12 Reformatting a text field has no effect on the underlying data. The value of the field is always the exact text typed by the user.

The Validate Panel

The fifth panel in the text field properties lets you specify rules by which Acrobat can determine whether the user's input is valid for the purpose of that text field. For example, if the text field is collecting a tax percentage, you might want to limit the text typed by the user to numeric values between 0 and 100.

If you specify a validation condition, Acrobat will not let the user submit the form data if the text fails the validation test.

The top radio button in the Validate panel turns off validation, which frees users to type in any text they wish.

The second radio button and its corresponding text boxes appear only if you have selected Number in the Format panel. These allow you to supply a numeric range within which the user's input must lie, as in Figure 7.13.

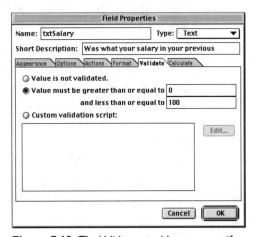

Figure 7.13 The Validate panel lets you specify a JavaScript program or a range of numeric values that determine whether the user's text input is valid. The text field will not accept invalid text.

Finally, you can supply a Java-Script that tests the user's text in any way you wish. You can check that the text conforms to your company's serial number format, that the text consists of only numbers, or that the text is a valid name and password combination (Figure 7.14).

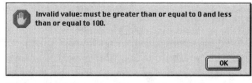

Figure 7.14 If you specify a valid numeric range, the user must enter a number within that range. Otherwise, Acrobat will complain when they try to leave the field.

The possibilities are extremely broad; they also require a bit more JavaScript skill than we can detail here. The Acrobat Forms page on the Acumen Training Web site has some sample forms with validation JavaScripts that you may wish to examine.

The Calculate Panel

This final panel among the text field properties lets you calculate a value for the text field, rather than allowing the user to enter text.

Generally, you supply a JavaScript that calculates the value of the text field. If your text field is a numeric field (that is, you have chosen Number in the Format panel), you may select one of a set of common numeric calculations supplied by Acrobat (Figure 7.16). The Pick button allows you to select the text fields that should be used in the calculation; alternatively, you can just type the field names into the text box.

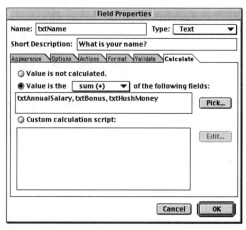

Figure 7.15 The Calculate panel tells Acrobat to calculate the value that should be placed in the text field.

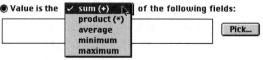

Figure 7.16 For convenience, Acrobat can calculate the value of the text field by performing a mathematical operation on a set of form fields that you specify.

Consider the three text fields in Figure 7.17. These three fields—named "txtAmount.Price," "txtAmount.Tax," and "txtAmount.Total"—are each formatted as a number with a preceding dollar sign and two decimal places. The only value that the user actually types in is the price; tax and total are both calculated from this value.

Price:	$100.00
Tax:	$8.00
Total:	$108.00

Figure 7.17 Of these three text fields, only Price needs to be entered by the user. The Tax and Total field values can be calculated.

The tax needs to be a JavaScript, since calculating it requires multiplication by a number, which is not one of the short-cut calculations provided by Acrobat. The calculation JavaScript for our txtAmount.Tax field is the following:

```
var priceField = this.getField
("txtAmount.Price");

event.value = priceField.value
* 0.08;
```

Figure 7.18 The Select a Field dialog box lets you select the form fields whose values should be the basis for the final calculated value.

The Total field is just a simple sum of the price and the tax, so we'll use the Acrobat shortcut for the calculation of txtAmount.Total.

If we click the second radio button in the Calculate panel, we can then select sum (+) in the pop-up menu. Clicking on the Pick button yields a dialog box (Figure 7.18) that lets us pick the fields we want to add together: in this case txtAmount.Price and txtAmount.Tax (Figure 7.19).

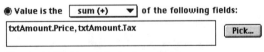

Figure 7.19 You pick the form fields you want Acrobat to add together or otherwise work with.

Because of the way we named our Price and Tax text fields, we can take advantage of a shortcut available in Acrobat. The names txtAmount.Price and txtAmount.Tax both conform to the hierarchical naming convention described in Chapter 4. Acrobat sees both of these text fields as belonging to the txtAmount group.

When summing them together for the txtTotal field, we need only put the group name into the field box, as in Figure 7.20. Acrobat will calculate the sum of *all* text fields whose names begin with txtAmount. This can be especially useful when a large number of fields must be added together.

| ⊙ Value is the | sum (+) ▼ | of the following fields: |
| txtAmount | | Pick... |

Figure 7.20 Acrobat's hierarchical naming system will add together the values of all form fields that begin with the specified prefix, in this case txtAmount.

Exercise: Creating Text Fields

Now that we've seen how to make text fields, let's continue assembling our Job Application form.

Looking back at Figures 7.1 and 7.2, we will add a total of 11 text fields to the first page of our form and two text fields to the second. On the first page, we shall place the following text fields:

- Simple, one-line text fields over the blank lines for the Name, Address, City-State-ZIP, Previous Employer, and Position Held. (Note that we are not doing the Citizenship field yet; we will do that field later as a Combo Box field.)
- Telephone-formatted fields for Telephone and Fax.
- Numeric-formatted fields for Salary and Bonus.
- A calculated field for Total Income.

On the second page, we shall place:

- A large, multi-line text field for the Essay.
- A date-formatted field for the Date.

When we are finished, our form, front and back, will look like Figures 7.21 and 7.22 when the Form tool is selected.

The plain text fields

So, let's start by creating our unformatted, plain text fields. I'll describe in some detail how to make the Name field, and then you can do the other plain text fields on your own.

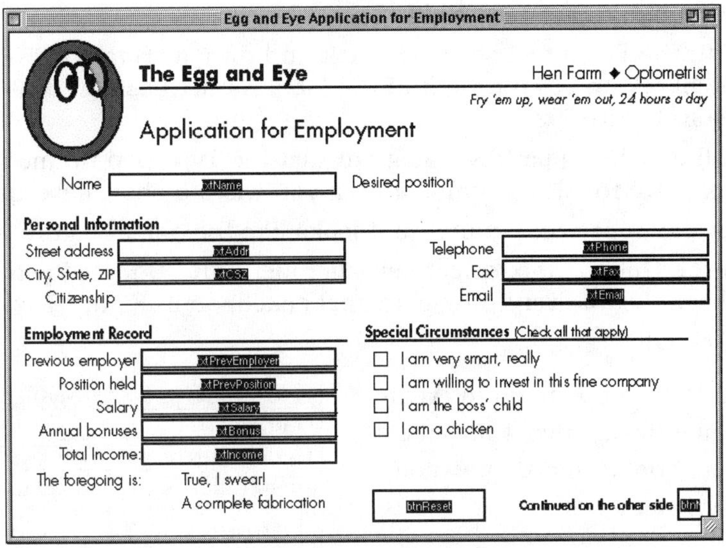

Figure 7.21 Here are the text fields and buttons that should be on Page 1 of our form when you are done with this chapter. This includes six plain, unformatted text fields, two telephone fields, two numeric fields, and a calculated field.

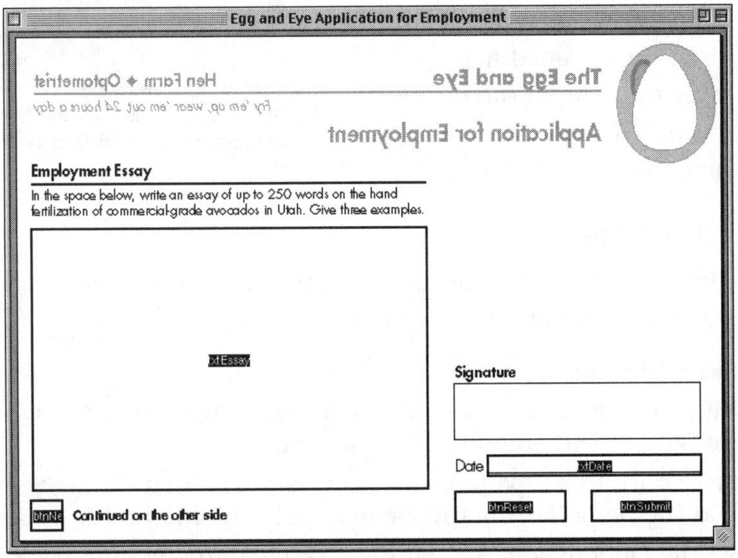

Figure 7.22 Here are the text fields and buttons that should be on Page 2 of our form when you are done with this chapter. We have a multi-line text field and a date-formatted field.

To make the Name text field:

1. With the Form tool selected, click and drag a rectangle over the blank line to the right of the label Name. Position it as you see in Figure 7.21.

2. In the Field Properties dialog box, set the Type pop-up menu to Text; give the field a name and, if you wish, a short description.

3. Set the Appearance panel so it looks like the one in Figure 7.23.

4. In the Options tab, select Left alignment and Do Not Spell Check. Leave everything else unchecked, as in Figure 7.3.

5. Click OK.

That's all we need to do to create the Name field, since it doesn't need actions, formatting, validation, or calculation.

Now make the other four plain text fields for address, City-State-ZIP, Previous Employer, and Position Held. If you wish, you can start each new field by copying and pasting the name field: Just drag each pasted field to its proper position on the page, double-click it, and give it a new name and description.

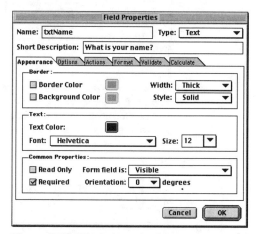

Figure 7.23 This is how the Appearance panel should look for your plain text fields.

The numeric fields

Next, let's make the two fields that gather numeric information, the Salary and Annual Bonus fields.

To make the Salary field:

1. With the Form tool selected, click and drag a rectangle where the Salary field should go (see Figure 7.21).

2. Make sure the Type pop-up menu is set to Text, and give the field the name txtAmount.Salary. Note the hierarchical name.

3. Set the Options and Appearance panels to match Figures 7.3 and 7.23, respectively.

4. Click on the Format tab and select Number as the field's format.

5. Set the Category Options controls as in Figure 7.24.

6. Click OK.

We have now made a form field whose contents will automatically be formatted as a monetary value.

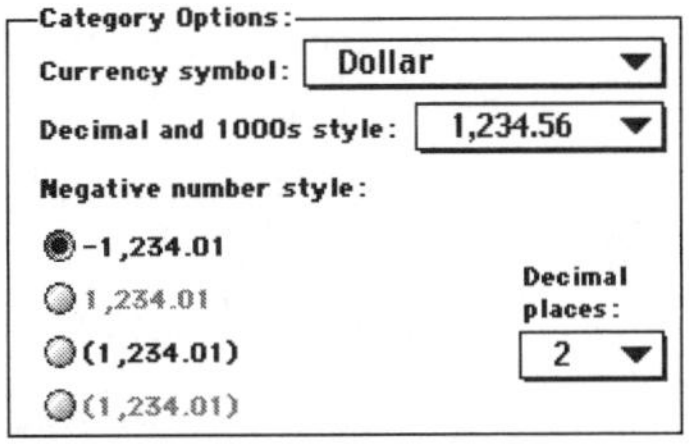

Figure 7.24 Here are the settings for your Salary field's numeric formatting.

Now do the same thing for the Bonus field. Give the bonus field the name "txtAmount.Bonus."

The calculated field

We have one calculate field in this form, the Total Income field.

To make the Total Income field:

1. Make a numeric field, following steps 1 through 5 from "To make the Salary field," above. Give the form field a different name from the earlier buttons. (Do *not* use the txtAmount prefix.)

2. In the Appearance tab, select the Read Only check box. Since this is a calculated field, we don't want users typing in their own text.

3. Click on the Calculate tab.

4. Click on the second radio button ("Value is the...") and select Sum in the pop-up menu.

   If this radio button isn't visible, then you have not set the text field's format to Number. Go back to the Format tab and do so.

5. Now do one of the following:

   Click on the Pick button and, in the resulting Select Field dialog box (Figure 7.18), select the txtAmount.Salary and txtAmount.Bonus fields.

   Or click in the text box just below the Sum (+) menu and type in the name "txtAmount". Acrobat will calculate the sum of all fields that have the hierarchical prefix "txtAmount." In our case, this would be the Salary and Bonus fields.

   I prefer the latter, myself.

6. Click OK.

The Total Income field will always show the sum of the salary and bonus fields. Note that, since we made it read-only, clicking on this field has no effect.

The telephone fields

We have two form fields whose data we shall format as telephone numbers, the Telephone field and the Fax field.

1. Start out by making a plain form field to the right of the "Telephone" label.

    You may wish to follow steps 1 through 4 of our earlier plain text fields procedure. Don't forget to give your field a different name from the other fields.

2. Click the Format tab.

3. Select Special for the format.

4. In the category options, select Phone Number.

    The controls in your Format panel should look like those in Figure 7.25.

5. Click OK.

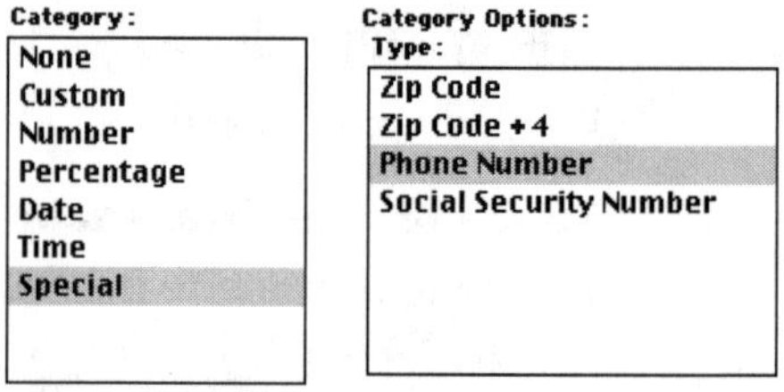

Figure 7.25 Our telephone fields should use Phone Number formatting. Note that this correctly formats only American and Canadian telephone numbers.

Your telephone field will reformat whatever you type into it as a seven-digit telephone number plus area code.

Now copy and paste this form field and turn the pasted version into the Fax field.

The essay field

With the Form tool selected, copy one of the plain text fields (the Name field, say) and then paste it onto Page 2 of our form. We shall turn this into our Essay field.

1. Drag the pasted text field into the Essay rectangle; reposition and resize it so that it exactly fills the rectangle on the page.

2. Double-click the text field to get to its properties.

3. Give the field a new name ("txtEssay" comes to mind) and, if you wish, a short description.

4. In the Options tab, select the Multi-line checkbox. The Options panel should now look like the one in Figure 7.26. If you wish, you could uncheck the Do Not Spell Check button; this lets users run the Acrobat spelling checker on their essays.

5. Click OK.

Field Properties	
Name: txtName	Type: Text ▼
Short Description: What is your name?	

Appearance \ **Options** \ Actions \ Format \ Validate \ Calculate

Default: [   ]

Alignment: [Left ▼]

☑ Multi-line
☐ Do Not Scroll
☐ Limit of [   ] characters
☐ Password
☐ Field is used for file selection
☑ Do Not Spell Check

[Cancel] [OK]

Figure 7.26 Here are the text field options for your multi-line Essay field.

The date field

Finally, let's create a text field for the date on the second page. I'll let you do this one mostly on your own. Here's an overview of what you'll do:

1. Create a text field however you wish: from scratch or copy and paste. Give it an appropriate name and set the Appearance and Options tabs in a way that makes sense to you for a date field.

2. Finally, go to the Format panel and select Date for the format. Pick whichever of the Category Options appeals to you (Figure 7.27).

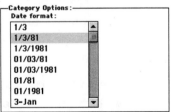

┌─Category Options:─
│ Date format:
│ ┌──────────────────┐
│ │ 1/3   ▲ │
│ │ 1/3/81   ▤ │
│ │ 1/3/1981   │
│ │ 01/03/81   │
│ │ 01/03/1981   │
│ │ 01/81   │
│ │ 01/1981   │
│ │ 3-Jan   ▼ │
│ └──────────────────┘

Figure 7.27 Acrobat provides a very large number of date formats. For our exercise, pick whichever one strikes your fancy.

Done!

Congratulations! We have put all of the text fields in place in our form. Our Job Application is mostly done.

8 Check Box Fields

So many of life's questions are yes or no: Do you have health insurance? Are you a licensed driver in the state of California? Does your ancestry include non-flying waterfowl? These questions are referred to as Boolean questions; their yes-or-no, true-or-false answers are Boolean values.

In a form, questions such as these are best posed using check boxes. The label of the check box presents a statement that the user can affirm or deny with a checkmark.

In this short chapter, we shall see how to make check box fields, and then continue the constructing our Job Application form.

☑ I'm just not good enough to have an inferiority complex.

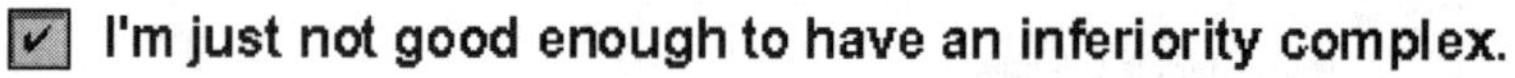

Figure 8.1 Check box fields are used to answer yes-or-no questions or affirm true-or-false statements, as in this example.

This Chapter's Exercise

The previous chapter left our Job Application form with buttons and text fields in place. We'll add our check boxes in the lower left area of Page 1, as in Figure 8.2.

Creating Check Box Fields

Check boxes are the simplest of the form fields. They have the same Appearance and Actions panels as the other field types and have a very simple Options panel.

Drag out a rectangle with the Form tool. Acrobat will present you with the Field Properties dialog box (Figure 8.3). Select Check Box in the Type pop-up menu and give the field a name. Set the Appearance panel properties as you wish. Note that in the Appearance panel, the only font available is Zapf Dingbats; the check box field uses this font for its checkmarks.

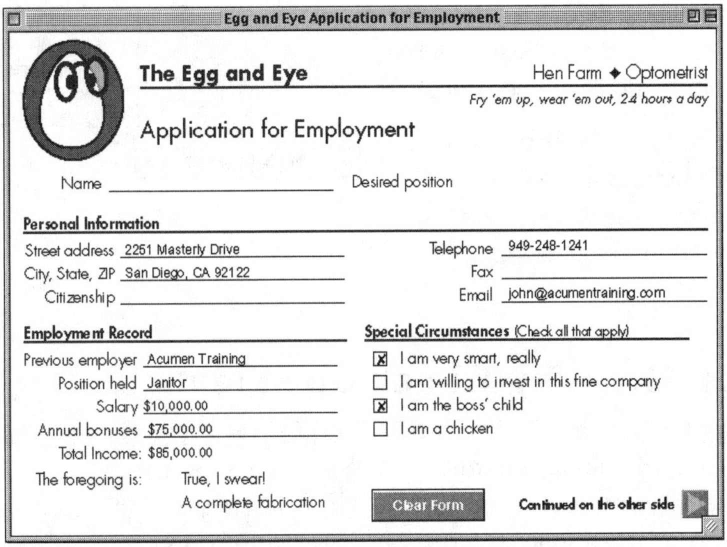

Egg and Eye Application for Employment

The Egg and Eye   Hen Farm ✦ Optometrist
                                        Fry 'em up, wear 'em out, 24 hours a day
Application for Employment

Name _____   Desired position

Personal Information
Street address 2261 Masterly Drive   Telephone 949-248-1241
City, State, ZIP San Diego, CA 92122   Fax _____
       Citizenship _____   Email john@acumentraining.com

Employment Record   **Special Circumstances** (Check all that apply)
Previous employer Acumen Training   ☒ I am very smart, really
      Position held Janitor   ☐ I am willing to invest in this fine company
         Salary $10,000.00   ☒ I am the boss' child
Annual bonuses $75,000.00   ☐ I am a chicken
  Total Income: $85,000.00
The foregoing is: True, I swear!
               A complete fabrication   [Clear Form]   Continued on the other side ▶

Figure 8.2 We'll add four check box fields to our form. They will indicate special circumstances that affect our Job Application.

Check Box Options

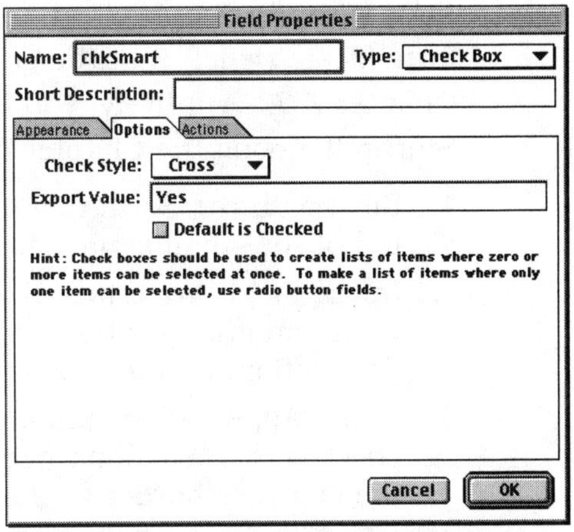

The Options panel in the Field Properties dialog box (Figure 8.3) lets you specify three properties specific to check box fields: the Check Style, the Export Value, and whether the box should be checked by default.

The **Check Style** menu lets you choose among six different checkmarks, as in Figure 8.4. There is no practical difference among these; pick whichever looks best with your design and layout.

The **Export Value** is the text that will be reported, if the check box is selected, to the program processing the form data. This can be any short piece of text; it must match the text that the remote processing program expects for the

Figure 8.3 The Options panel for check box fields is pretty simple. Indicate the checkmark you want to use, the text that should be reported for the field's value, and whether that text should be checked when the user opens the form.

selected check box field. The default value for this property is Yes, which works well for almost all occasions.

Check Style:
Check
Circle
Cross
Diamond
Square
Star

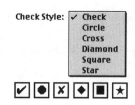

Figure 8.4 You can choose among six different checkmarks for your check box field.

The **Checked by Default** property is every bit as obvious as it seems: If it is selected, your check box field will be checked when the user opens the form file.

Exercise: Creating Check Box Fields

Our Job Application has four check box fields that let the applicant indicate special circumstances to the human resources folks (Figure 8.5). In this chapter's exercise, you will create the four check boxes.

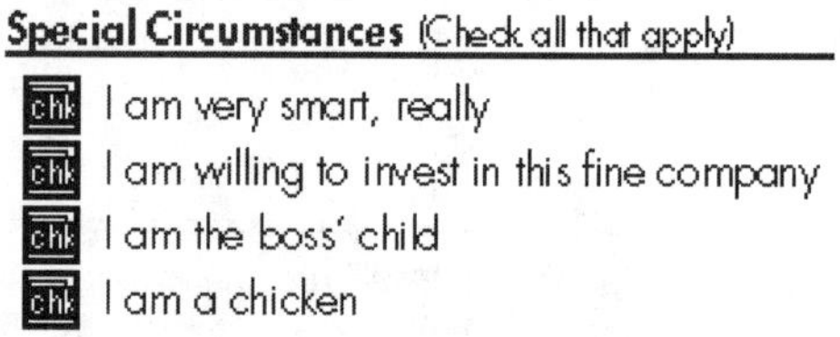

Special Circumstances (Check all that apply)
chk
I am very smart, really
chk
I am willing to invest in this fine company
chk
I am the boss' child
chk
I am a chicken

Figure 8.5 We shall add these four check boxes to our Job Application form.

Start with the Job Application form file as we left it at the end of Chapter 7. Alternatively, you can open the file form.Chapter 8 Start.pdf among the Chapter 8 files on the Acrobat Forms Web site.

1. Start with the Form tool selected; click and drag a rectangle on top of the small square to the left of the "I am smart..." label.
2. In the Field Properties dialog box, select Check Box in the pop-up menu and give the form field a name. Also give it a short description, if you wish.
3. In the Appearance panel, turn off the border and background check boxes. We don't need these because we've already drawn the control's border in the static art.
4. In the Options tab, select whatever shape you want for your checkmark; leave the export value at Yes; leave the Default field unselected. Your Options panel should end up looking like the one in Figure 8.3.
5. Click OK.

That's all there is to it. Check box fields are easy!

You might want to return to the Acrobat Hand tool to make sure your check box field looks as you expected. In particular, you may need to try different text sizes in the Appearances tab to get the checkmarks looking the way you want.

Now do the other three check box fields.

When you are finished, the first page of the Job Application, viewed with the Form tool selected, should look like Figure 8.6.

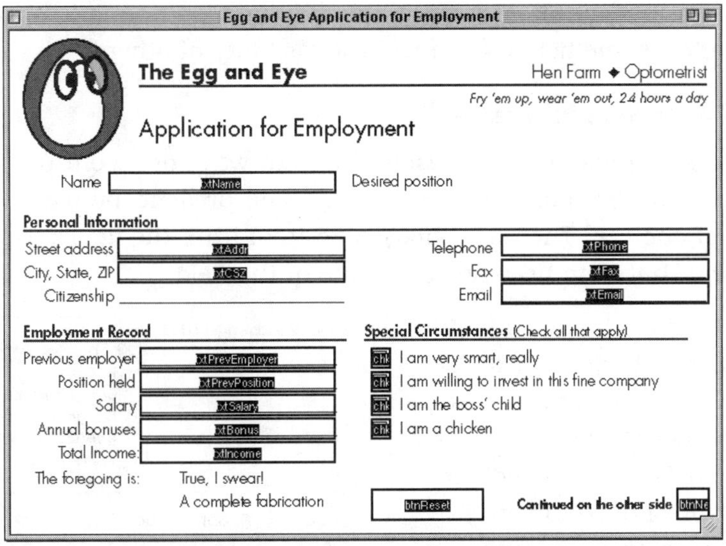

Figure 8.6 Our form now has check boxes and is almost ready to use.

Our Job Application is close to being fully functional—only three more sets of controls left to add. In the next chapter, we'll add the combo box and list box fields so that our applicants can tell us their nationalities and the job for which they are applying.

9 Combo Boxes and Lists

Nearly every online form asks you to select from a list of choices. You might be required to pick your country of residence from a pop-up menu, choose the year in which your credit card expires, or select the kind of pet you want emailed to you.

Acrobat offers two types of form fields that let the user select from lists of items: combo box fields and list fields. In this chapter, we shall see how to construct and use these two field types. We shall also take this opportunity to build some dynamic features into our form that allow some fields to control the visibility of others.

Combo Boxes vs. List Fields

Combo boxes and list fields represent different ways of accomplishing the same purpose in a form: They each present the user with a list of choices. The user chooses an item from the field's list of items, and that item becomes the value of the field.

An Acrobat combo box field (Figure 9.1) is implemented as a text field with an attached menu. The text field part shows the currently selected item. When you click on the field, it presents you with a pop-up menu with items that you may choose. A combo box may also let the user type text directly into the field, in case the user's choice is not listed in the menu.

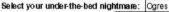
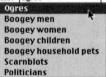

Figure 9.1 A combo box field in Acrobat is a combination of a Text field and a pop-up menu. You can select items from the menu or, in some cases, type your own text directly into the field.

A list field (Figure 9.2) is a scrolling list of items from which users must choose. Users cannot directly enter text into the field; they can only select items from the list. Unlike with a combo box, a user can pick more than one item from a list, as in Figure 9.2. Lists are also more useful than combo boxes for presenting long lists of items.

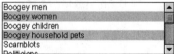

Figure 9.2 A list field presents a scrolling list of choices to the user. A list box can accept more than one selection, if you wish.

On the other hand, they occupy much more of the page than combo box fields.

Hence, use a combo box if screen space is tight, or if you want to let users type in their own text because their choice is missing from the standard choices. Use a list field if you want to allow users to pick more than one item at a time, or if the list of items is very long. You will probably use combo box fields more often than lists.

Item text and export values

Each item in the menu of a combo box or the list of a list field has two pieces of text associated with it: item text, which actually appears in the menu or list, and an export value, which becomes the value of this field if the user selects this item.

When you submit the form data to an external processing program, the export value will be reported as the value of the list or combo box; the text you pick for the export value must therefore be something that the external program expects. The item text, on the other hand, should be descriptive, since this is what the user will be actually selecting.

This Chapter's Exercises

In this chapter, we shall add two combo boxes and a list field to our Job Application. One combo box, the one showing the word "Son" in Figure 9.3, will be visible only if the "Boss' child" check box is selected.

The starting point for this chapter is the form as we left it at the end of Chapter 8. Alternatively, you may start with the file form.Chapter 9 Start.pdf.

Combo Box Fields

Combo boxes are familiar to anyone who works even a little bit with computers. As we said earlier, a combo box is, at its root, a text field with an attached menu. When you select an item from the menu, that text is entered in the text box. Some combo boxes let you type in your own text if nothing on the menu matches what you want.

The Egg and Eye   Hen Farm ✦ Optometrist

Fry 'em up, wear 'em out, 24 hours a day

Application for Employment

Name _____   Desired position   Lens Fitter
                                                    Shoveler
Personal Information   Egg Collector

Street address 2251 Masterly Drive   Telephone 949-248-1241
City, State, ZIP San Diego, CA 92122   Fax _____
     Citizenship United States   ▼   Email john@acumentraining.com

Employment Record   **Special Circumstances** (Check all that apply)

Previous employer Acumen Training   ☐ I am very smart, really
     Position held Janitor   ☐ I am willing to invest in this fine company
           Salary $10,000.00   ☒ I am the boss' child   Son   ▼
Annual bonuses $75,000.00   ☐ I am a chicken
   Total Income: $85,000.00
The foregoing is: True, I swear!
                       A complete fabrication   [Clear Form]   Continued on the other side ▶

Figure 9.3 In this chapter's exercise, we shall add two combo box fields and a list field to our Job Application.

Combo boxes don't actually exist in the Macintosh operating system (neither Classic nor OS X), and so combo boxes, more than any other form field type, look very different on Windows and Macintosh systems. Viewed on a Windows system, the combo box is just a standard Windows combo box; on the Mac, it is a text field that, when you click on it, presents you with a pop-up menu, as in Figure 9.4. The fields work the same way in both environments, however.

Figure 9.4 Combo box fields look very different on Macintosh (left) and Windows (right) machines.

Creating Combo Box Fields

You create a combo box field just as you do any other field in Acrobat: Click and drag out a rectangle and then fill out the properties in the resulting Field Properties dialog box. Include a field name and type, as well as values for the controls in the various panels. You will notice, if you examine Figure 9.5, that all the tabs are identical to those for regular text fields; with the exception of the Options panel, the contents of all the Properties panels are identical to those for text fields.

Here, we shall only discuss the properties available in the Options panel, since the others are absolutely identical to a Text field's controls, and the settings you choose will be identical to those you would pick for a text field. Check out Chapter 6 if you want a refresher on text field properties.

Combo box options

Most of the combo box Options panel (Figure 9.5) specifies the item text and export value for each of the menu items. Setting up the menu is mildly tedious but not difficult: You type in the item text and the export value in the appropriate text boxes in the Options panel, and then click the Add button.

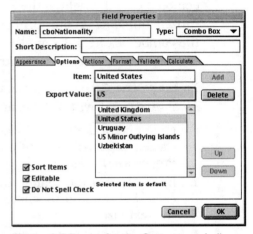

The buttons down the right-hand side of the Options panel let you manage the items in the combo box menu; you can delete an item from the list or move an item up or down in the menu.

Figure 9.5 Except for the Options panel, all of the panels in the combo box field's Field Properties dialog box are identical to those for a text field.

On the left side of the Options panel are three check boxes that affect the characteristics of the combo box:

Sort Items places items in the menu alphabetically. This can be enormously convenient if you need a sorted list.

Editable lets the user type text directly into the combo box text field, rather than just selecting items from the menu. This is important if users' choices are potentially open-ended: You might supply a list of email addresses, but may want to let users enter an address that is not on the list.

Do Not Spell Check instructs Acrobat to ignore the contents of the combo box when it checks spelling.

Exercise: Adding Combo Boxes

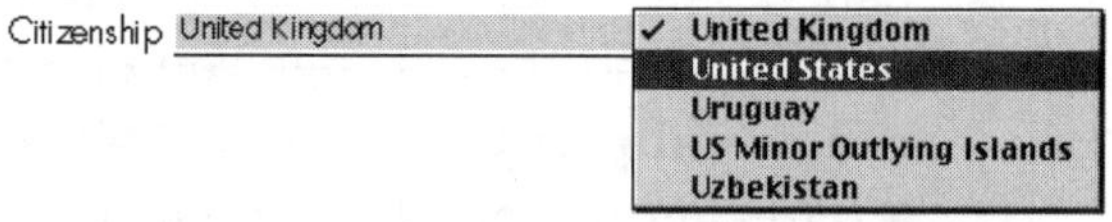

Let's add to our Job
Application a combo box
field that asks users for
their country of citizenship.
We shall place this editable
combo box to the right of the

Citizenship United Kingdom

✓ United Kingdom
United States
Uruguay
US Minor Outlying Islands
Uzbekistan

Figure 9.6 The Citizenship combo box is an editable combo box field. Put the names of whatever countries you wish into this field.

Citizenship label on our form (Figure 9.6). When the user clicks on the combo box field, he or she will be able to pick from a menu of country names or type a country name directly into the field.

To make the Citizenship combo box:

As always, start with the Form tool selected.

1. Click and drag the rectangle immediately to the right of the Citizenship label. Select Combo Box for Type in the Field Properties dialog box and give the field a name, as in Figure 9.5.

2. In the Appearance panel, turn off background color and border color. Set the font to whatever you wish, and select Auto for the text size.

3. In the Options panel, type a country name into the Item box and an abbreviation for that country into the export value box.

   It doesn't matter what you choose for your export value, although there are standard two-character codes for all the nations. What really dictates your choice here is what is required by the remote processing program that will eventually receive your form data. You should consult on this matter with the programmer who writes that remote program. If you will be emailing the form data or otherwise manually processing the data, then it doesn't matter what you choose here.

4. Click the Add button. This adds the item's text and export value to the combo box menu.

5. Repeat steps 3 and 4 for each nation you want to add to the combo box menu.

   Among these items, please include "United States" with "US" as its export value. We will use these entries in an example later in the chapter.

6. Select the Sort Items, Editable, and Do Not Spell Check check boxes. Note that the list of countries sorts itself when you click on the Sort check box.

At this point, your Options panel should look like something like the one shown in Figure 9.5.

7. Click OK.

Now go back to your Hand tool and try out your new combo box field. Note that you can select an item from the menu or type in a country name not in the menu.

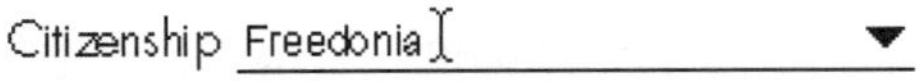

Citizenship Freedonia⟦   ▼

Figure 9.7 We made our Citizenship combo box editable, so you can type your own text directly into the field without using the attached menu.

The "Son/Daughter" combo box

Now, on your own, add the combo box field that is located to the right of the check box field labeled "I am the boss' child," as in Figure 9.8. The menu items for the combo box are the words "Son" and "Daughter"; you may use anything you wish for your export values. This combo box field should not be editable.

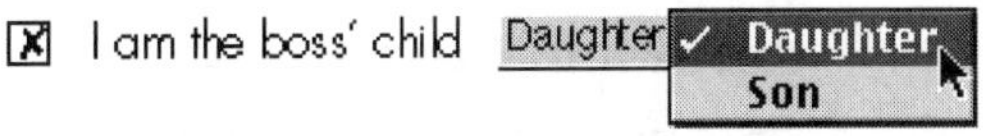

☒ I am the boss' child Daughter ✓ **Daughter**
                                     Son

Figure 9.8 The "Son/Daughter" combo box field goes just to the right of the "Boss' child" check box label.

Note that this combo box is different from other form fields we have created in that it will draw its own border (the blank underline stroke); all our other form fields had their borders drawn in the form's original Illustrator artwork.

Why would you want a form field to draw its own border? Normally, you wouldn't. However, it is not unusual to think of a field that needs to be added after the form is halfway finished. Rather than go back to the original Illustrator file, add the new field's border, and then regenerate the PDF file, it is often easier to just have the field draw its own border. You should eventually go back and add the new border to the original artwork, as well, but doing the border in Acrobat often means the difference between making a deadline or not.

You specify the field's border in its Appearance panel by selecting the Border Color check box and selecting Underlined for the Border Style (Figure 9.9).

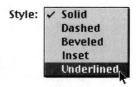

Style:

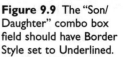

Figure 9.9 The "Son/ Daughter" combo box field should have Border Style set to Underlined.

Later in this chapter, we shall tie this combo box field to the "Boss' child" check box so that it's only visible when the check box is selected.

List Fields

You create list fields nearly the same way you create combo box fields: Drag out the field's rectangle with the Form tool, supply a name and type (List Box, in this case), and then specify the properties for the field. In particular, you specify the item text and export value for each item that should appear in the scrolling list.

List Field Properties

The Field Properties dialog box for a list field has four tabs, including the common Appearance and Actions panels. The two panels specific to the list field are the Options panel, as usual, and the Selection Change panel.

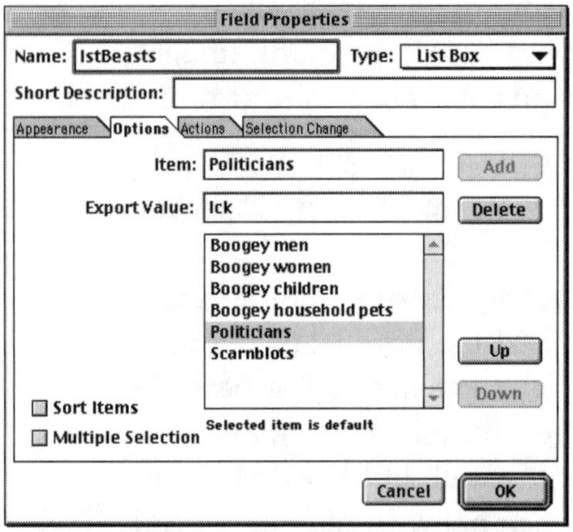

The Options panel (Figure 9.10) presents a set of controls nearly identical to those of the combo box field. As with the combo box Options, you specify the item text and export value of each item you want in the list. You can also have Acrobat automatically sort the list.

Figure 9.10 The Options panel for a list field is nearly identical to the that of the combo box field. Only the Editable and Do Not Spell Check buttons are missing.

The Selection Change panel lets you supply a JavaScript that Acrobat will execute anytime the user clicks on a new item in the list. This JavaScript allows you to do things like list prices, scheduled dates, or other information associated with the item on which a user clicks (Figure 9.11).

We'll discuss JavaScripts associated with this kind of dynamic form field later in this chapter.

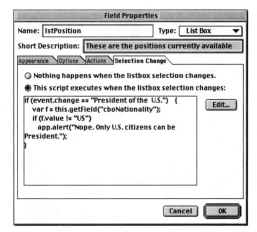

Figure 9.11 The Selection Change panel lets you specify a JavaScript that will be executed when the user clicks an item in the list.

Exercise: Creating the Jobs List

Now let's place a list of available positions in our Job Application form. This is the list field located toward the upper right of the Job Application in Figure 9.3. This is how our user indicates the job for which he or she is applying.

Here, too, we shall let the field draw its own border; I didn't draw the border in the static artwork. Again, this is mostly to offer some practice doing borders using Acrobat's tools; usually, you will have included the border in the original artwork.

We'll let people apply for the President of the U.S. position (Figure 9.13) only if they have also selected "United States" as their country of citizenship.

To make the Desired Position list field:
Start with the Job Application file open and the Form tool selected.

1. Click and drag out the rectangle for the List field; this should be just to the right of the label "Desired Position," as in Figure 9.3. Select List Box from the Type menu and give your form field a name.

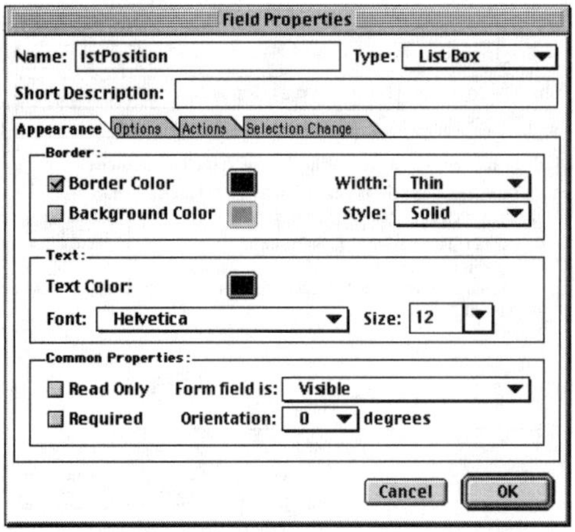

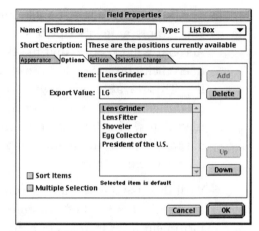

Figure 9.12 Our Desired Position list field will draw its own border. Set the Appearance properties as they are here: Turn on the Border Color control and set the Width menu to Thin.

Figure 9.13 The Options properties for our Desired Position list need to supply the text item (the name of the job) and export value for each item in the list.

2. In the Appearance panel, select a black border color and a thin border width. Select what you wish for the font and size. Your Appearance panel should look like Figure 9.12.

3. In the Options panel, set the item text and export values for all the current job openings. Be creative.

   The jobs I listed are visible in Figure 9.13, but feel free to improvise. Do make sure that you include "President of the U.S.," so that our JavaScript in the next step works correctly.

4. Go to the Selection Change panel (see Figure 9.11) and click the "This script executes..." button.

5. Still in the Selection Change panel, click on the Edit button, and type the following script into the resulting JavaScript Edit dialog box:

```
if (event.change == "President of the U.S.") {
   var f = this.getField("cboNationality");
   if (f.value != "US")
   app.alert("Nope. Only U.S. citizens can be President.");
}
```

   The text "cboNationality" in the code above must match whatever name you gave to the Citizenship combo box field. Also, the job title "President of the U.S." must exactly match what you typed in for that list item's item text.

6. Click the OK button, which returns you to your PDF file.

Now you can give your list a try. Return to the Hand tool and click on different items in the list. Note that if you click on "President of the U.S." you may get a warning dialog box (Figure 9.14), depending on whether or not you also claim to be a U.S. citizen.

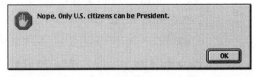

Figure 9.14 If the user clicks on the "President of the U.S." item in the list field, our JavaScript checks to see if "United States" is selected in the Citizenship combo box. If it is not, our JavaScript displays an alert.

Dynamic Forms

A dynamic form is one that changes what it presents to the user in response to the user's selections. If the user clicks on an item in a list, perhaps you can show them some information about that item, as in Figure 9.15. A user's choices early in the form could change the set of form fields we display later in the form.

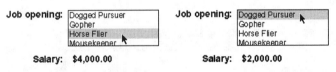

Figure 9.15 A dynamic form can cause a list to display information (salary, in this case) about the current selection. We shall see how to do this particular example in Chapter 13.

Lets look at a simple example of how to implement dynamic features in a form.

Showing and Hiding Form Fields

An important goal in user interface design, including the design of forms, is to not present anything to the user that he or she doesn't really need. We break this rule in our Job Application form because the "Son/Daughter" combo box field is always visible, even if the user is not the boss's child; clearly, if the "Boss' child" check box is not checked, there is no reason the user needs to see the "Son/Daughter" combo box.

Let's add a Show/Hide Field action to the "Boss' child" check box that lets the "Son/Daughter" combo box become visible only if users click on the check box.

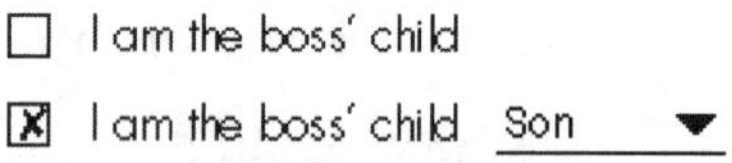

☐ I am the boss' child

☒ I am the boss' child   Son   ▼

To add the Show/Hide Field action to the check box field:

Start with Page 1 of the Job Application visible and the Form tool selected; the form should look like Figure 9.17.

1. Double-click on the "Son/Daughter" combo box field to get to its properties.
2. In the Appearance panel, select Hidden in the Form Field is pop-up menu (Figure 9.18); we'll start out with our combo box invisible.
3. Click OK, returning to the Job Application page.
4. Double-click on the "I am the boss' child" check box field. This will give you access to its properties.
5. Go to the Actions panel, select the Mouse Up event, and click the Add button; you will now see the Add an Action dialog box (Figure 9.19).

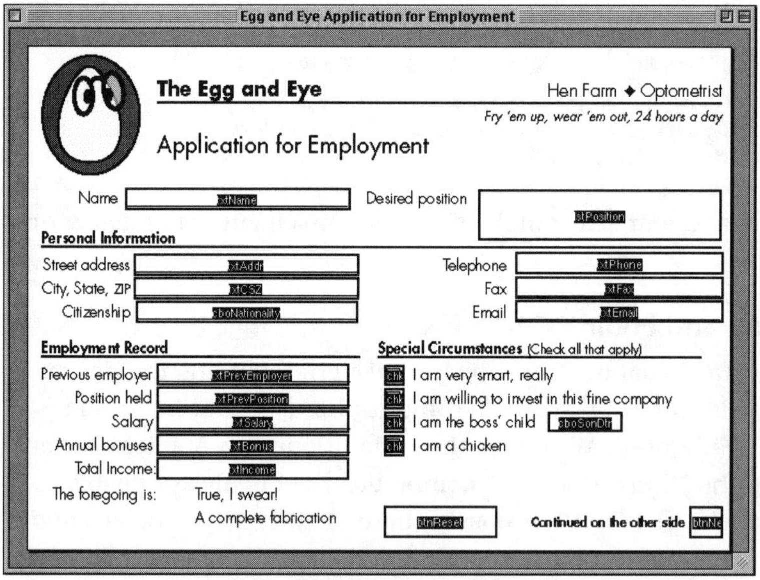

Figure 9.17 At the end of our exercise, we'll have all the form fields in place for our Job Application except for the radio buttons.

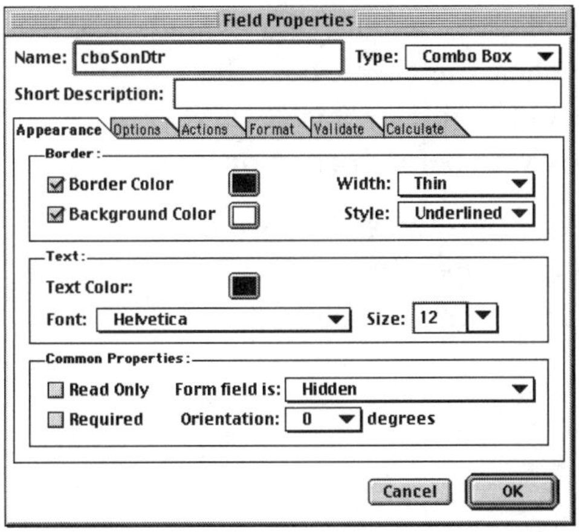

Figure 9.18 In the Appearance panel, we shall mark our "Son/Daughter" combo box as Hidden, so that it is initially invisible. Our "Boss' child" check box will make it visible with a Show/Hide Field action.

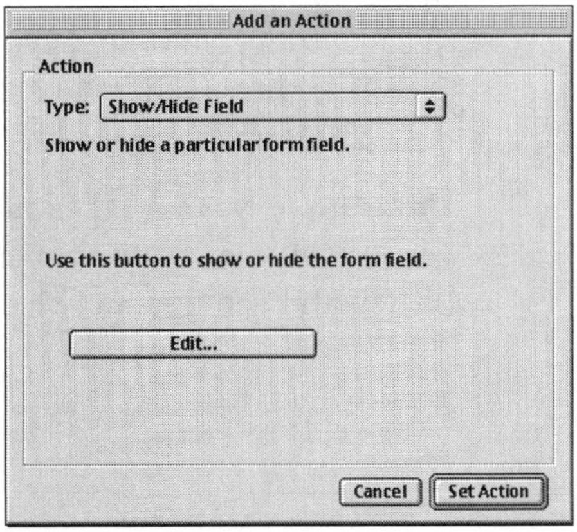

Figure 9.19 In this exercise, we want to add a Show/Hide Field action to the "Boss' child" check box field.

6. In the Add an Action dialog box, select Show/Hide Field in the Type menu and then click on the Edit button. You will now see the Select Field dialog box.

7. Select your Son/Daughter" combo box in the list of form fields and click on the Show radio button, as in Figure 9.20.

8. Exit out of all the dialog boxes until you are back at the form page.

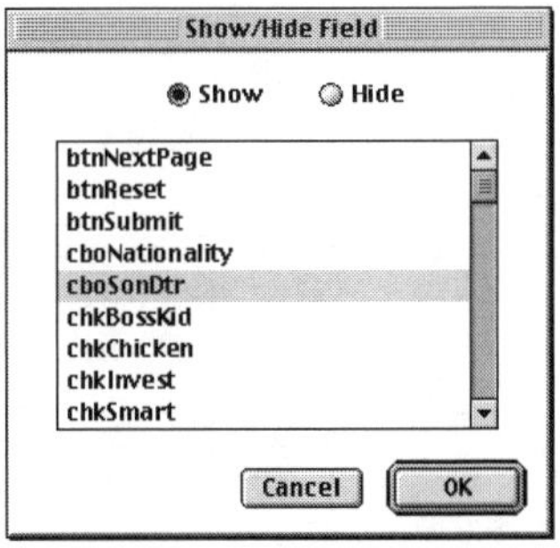

Figure 9.20 Our Show/Hide Field action will make the "Son/ Daughter" combo box visible.

That should be it. Select the Hand tool and try it out. The combo box should be initially invisible, but when you click on the "I am the boss' child" check box, the Son/Daughter choice should magically appear. This will amaze the user, impress your friends, and hold your enemies at bay for a bit.

However, there is one serious problem with using the Show/Hide Field action to make our combo box visible: it only works in one direction. When we first select the "Boss' child" check box, the combo box becomes visible; if we click on the check box again, unselecting it, the combo box remains visible, instead of obligingly disappearing again. Ideally, when you click the check box, the Son/Daughter combo box should become visible or invisible, depending upon whether the check box was being turned on or off.

Unfortunately, this takes more JavaScript prowess than we have yet. We will return to this example in the appendix on JavaScript basics and see how to solve this problem more completely.

Radio Buttons   10

Radio button fields are a common way of presenting the user with a set of mutually exclusive choices. Because all the choices are visible on the page, radio buttons take up a lot of screen real estate and are most appropriate for cases where the number of selections is small.

Radio buttons are unique in that they only have meaning in a group; you never have one radio button. Within a set of radio buttons, the individual controls need to know about each other, so that when you select one button, the others will deselect themselves.

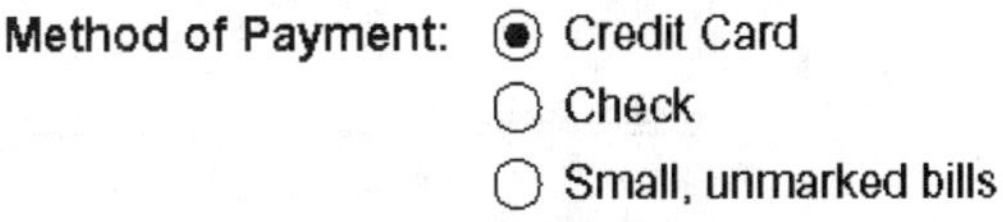

Method of Payment: ● Credit Card
                    ○ Check
                    ○ Small, unmarked bills

Figure 10.1 Radio buttons allow the user to select from among a set of mutually exclusive choices.

How do the radio button fields know which fields on the page belong to their particular set? In Acrobat, all the radio button fields in a set have the same name but different export values. Having the same name identifies them as belonging to the same set. The value of the set, as reported when you submit the form, will be the export value of the selected radio button.

Radio button fields do not have labels. You must create the labels for the individual buttons with your design software, along with all the other static elements of your form.

This Chapter's Exercise

In this chapter, we shall finish our Job Application form, adding two radio buttons to the bottom of the form (Figure 10.2). As always, you can start where you left off at the end of the previous chapter, or go to the Acrobat Forms Web page and get form.Chapter 10 start.pdf.

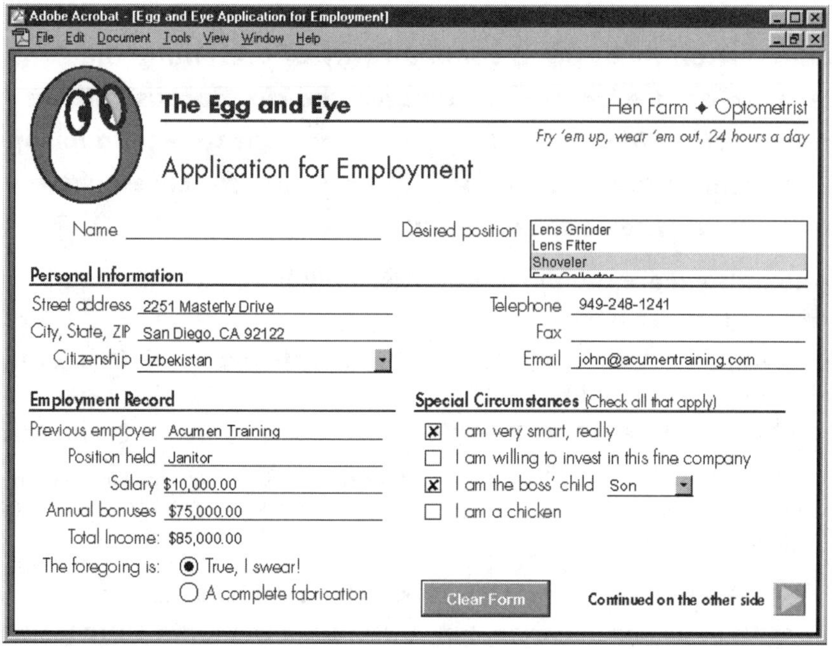

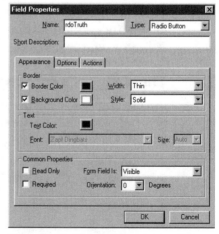

Figure 10.2 In this chapter, we shall add two radio buttons to the bottom of the page. This will complete our Job Application form.

Creating Radio Button Fields

You create radio button fields exactly the way you create other form fields: Drag out a rectangle with the Form tool and fill in the resulting Field Properties dialog box.

A radio button's Field Properties dialog box presents you with the Appearance, Options, and Actions tabs (Figure 10.3). As always, the Appearance and Actions properties are identical to those for other form fields; only the Options panel is unique.

Figure 10.3 The Field Properties dialog box for radio button fields has three tabs: Appearance, Options, and Actions.

With regard to the Appearance panel, radio buttons, more than other controls, should draw their own borders. Make sure that Border Color is chosen in the Appearance panel. Also, I think Thin or Medium are the best choices for the Width menu.

Actions for a radio button are relatively rare, most often used for dynamic effects, such as making other fields appear or disappear when you choose particular radio buttons.

Radio Button Options

The only field properties that require much discussion are those in the Options panel (Figure 10.4). Here you will pick styles and export values for your radio buttons. You will also indicate which of the buttons in the set should be selected by default.

The three controls in this panels are:

Radio Style. You have your choice of six possible styles for your radio buttons, as in Figure 10.5.

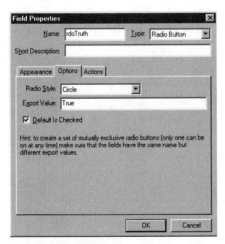

Figure 10.4 The Options panel lets you specify the type of radio button that Acrobat will use, the export value for each individual button, and whether a particular button should be selected by default.

Figure 10.5 Acrobat lets you choose among six different styles of radio button.

Export Value. Allows you to give each radio button its own export value. This value is reported as the submission value for the radio button set if that particular button is selected.

Default is Checked. One of the radio buttons in a set should have this option selected; that radio button will be the default selection when the user opens the PDF file.

Exercise: Add Radio Buttons

Now let's finish the Job Application we've been working on over these last five chapters. We need to add a pair of radio buttons at the bottom of the first page, to the right of the label "The foregoing is" (Figure 10.2). The two labels for the individual radio buttons are already in place.

I won't walk you through this exercise in detail, since you have done several similar exercises already. Just make sure you give the two radio buttons the same name but different export values, and all will go well.

This completes our Job Application. Go back to the Acrobat Hand tool and try out all the controls.

Signature Fields   11

*One of Adobe's goals when it released Acrobat 4 in 1999 was
to make it possible for a PDF file to be a legally binding document. To this end, they included support for digital signatures
in Acrobat 4. Adobe intended that eventually contracts and
other legal documents could be signed and stored electronically,
eclipsing ink signatures on paper. To a large extent, Adobe has
achieved its goal: Acrobat digital signatures have allowed many
companies to accept Acrobat files as legal documents. At
this point, many corporate and government organizations—
including the U.S. and British governments and the U.S. Navy—
accept Acrobat files in just this way.*

The Signature tool in Acrobat 4 and 5 lets a user place a signature
anywhere on a document's page. As a form designer, however, you
can create a signature field that serves as an electronic "sign here"
space; when a user clicks on the field, Acrobat places his or her
electronic signature inside the field's boundaries.

Acrobat signatures are not available in Acrobat Reader, by the
way. Signers and recipients of a signed form must use either
Acrobat Approval or the full Acrobat.

In this chapter, we'll look at how Acrobat signatures work, how you
create a signature field, and what a user must do to sign an Acrobat
form. We'll also examine how to set up the computers of both signers and recipients so that they can use Acrobat signatures.

This Chapter's Exercise

In this chapter, we'll add a signature field to the form pictured in
Figure 11.1. This form has two fields: a Text field for the signer's
name and a signature field for the signature (Figure 11.2). Your
starting point is the file form.Chapter 15 Start.pdf on the Acrobat
Forms Web page.

Figure 11.1 The signature field in the lower-right corner of this form is a placeholder for an Acrobat digital signature. By default, this signature appears on the page as the signer's name, along with some additional information in fine print.

Figure 11.2 This form has two fields in it: a text field for the signer's name and a signature field for the signature.

Acrobat Signatures

The purpose of a signature, whether electronic or ink, is to signal that a particular person has seen, agreed to, or otherwise acknowledged the contents of a document. For this to work, two things must be true of the signature and the document: First, it must be possible to establish that a person's signature was, indeed, placed on the document by that person; second, it must be possible to verify that the document has not been altered since it was signed.

The Acrobat signature mechanism fulfills both these requirements. A signature placed on a PDF page is a set of encrypted data embedded in the PDF file that enables a link between that signature and a particular person. This signature also signals if the Acrobat file is changed after the signature is affixed.

The Acrobat signature mechanism is modular: Companies such as Lexign and Cyber-SIGN® can write Acrobat plug-ins that implement signature handlers appropriate to particular situations. This chapter will examine Acrobat's default signature system, Adobe Self-Sign Security.

Adobe Self-Sign Security

Signing an electronic document is not cripplingly complicated, but it's not quite as easy as putting a pen to paper. Some work must be done to set up signers' and recipients' Acrobats so that they can use digital signatures. In a corporate environment, the company's Information Technology (IT) department will do much of this set-up work, so users can remain pleasantly unaware of what is happening in the background.

User profiles and user certificates

Adobe's Self-Sign Security mechanism is built around two concepts: the user profile and the user certificate.

A user profile is a set of data maintained by the signer's copy of Acrobat that identifies the signer to the Self-Sign Security mechanism. Among other things, this user profile contains a password, chosen by the signer, that must be provided when an Acrobat file is signed.

A user certificate is a file that identifies the signer for the benefit of the recipient of a signed document. It is, in effect, an exported version of the signer's information that Acrobat embeds in a signature. The recipient of a signed document must have installed the signer's user certificate into Acrobat. When the recipient opens a signed document, Acrobat can compare the data in the signature with the information in the user certificate for that signer; if they match, the signature is considered valid.

The first step in signing a document is the one-time process of creating a user profile for the signer. In a corporate environment, this would probably be done for each person by the IT staff. The staff would probably also install signers' user certificates into the Acrobats of the people who will be receiving signed documents. If a signer doesn't have a user profile, Acrobat will let them create one the first time they try to sign a document.

CertExchange JohnDeubert.fdf

We'll see how to create user profiles and certificates later in this chapter.

Signing a Form

We'll place a signature field in this chapter's sample form. To sign the form, the user has to do very little beyond clicking the signature field.

To sign a signature field:

1. Log in to the Self-Sign Security mechanism by selecting Tools > Self-Sign Security > Log In. Acrobat presents a dialog box; the user picks a user profile from the pop-up menu and enters a password (Figure 11.3).

2. Click in the signature field.

   Acrobat will ask for the signer's password again (Figure 11.4). This dialog box also provides a Show Options button, which lets you change some of the user-specified characteristics of the signature (we'll discuss these later).

3. Type in your password.

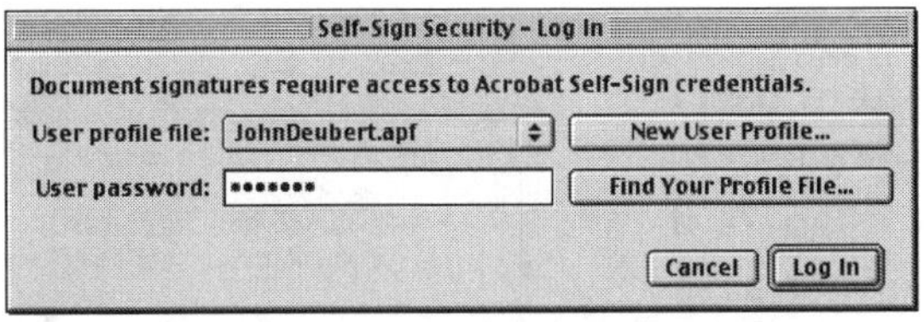

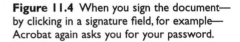

Figure 11.3 Before you can sign a document, you must log in to the Self-Sign Security system. Choose your profile from the pop-up menu and type in your password.

Self-Sign Security - Sign Document

Signing requires saving the document. Click 'Save As..' to place this signature onto a new document or 'Save' to save the current document.

Confirm Password: ●●●●●●   [Show Options]

[Save] [Save As...] [Cancel]

Figure 11.4 When you sign the document— by clicking in a signature field, for example— Acrobat again asks you for your password.

The final signature will appear on the page as a graphic of some sort. By default, this is the signer's name in large letters as well as some additional information in smaller type, as in Figure 11.5.

The default small-font information in the signature graphic consists of the name of the signer; the organization to which the signer belongs; the date, time, and location of the signature; the reason for signing.

Figure 11.5 By default, your signature appears on the page as your name in large text, as well as some additional information in small print.

Once signed, a PDF file becomes an append-only document. Any further changes to the document will be internally added to the PDF file; the old contents will not be removed. If the form is altered after it is signed, Acrobat will announce that fact in the Signature panel (see Figure 11.6); furthermore, Acrobat can revert to the earlier, signed version of the document (we'll see how to do this later).

Tip

A signer can change the information that appears in the signature graphic and even replace the default graphic with a picture of his or her choosing. This is done in the Signature Appearance panel of the User Settings dialog box (Tools > Self-Sign Signature > User Settings).

The Signature Field

A signature field provides a place for a user's electronic signature. When the user clicks in this field, Acrobat asks the user to sign in, if necessary, and then asks for his or her password. Upon receiving the password, Acrobat enters the user's electronic signature into the space provided, as at the bottom of Figure 11.1.

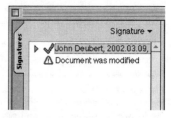

Figure 11.6 The Signature panel, among the panels along the left edge of your Acrobat window, will indicate if a file has been changed after it was initially signed.

You create a signature field as you would any other form field: drag out a rectangle with the Form tool. In the resulting Form Properties dialog box, you select Signature for the field type (Figure 11.7).

Signature Field Properties

The Appearance and Actions panels for the signature field are the same as for all other field types. Interestingly, there is no Options panel; in Acrobat 5 there is a panel named Signed that specifies what should happen when the user signs the document (Figure 11.8).

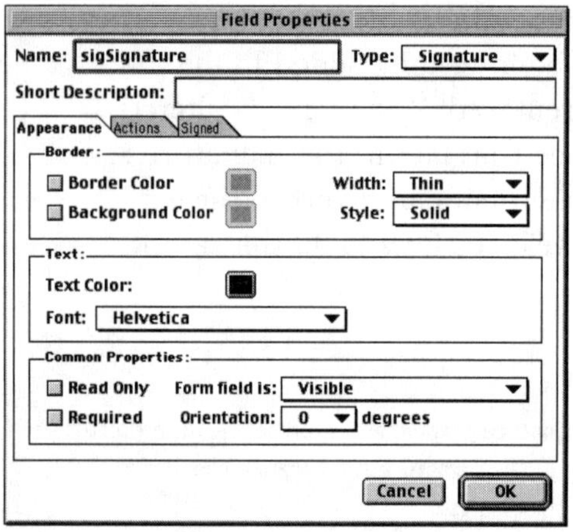

Figure 11.7 The Appearance panel for a signature field is identical to that of all other form fields.

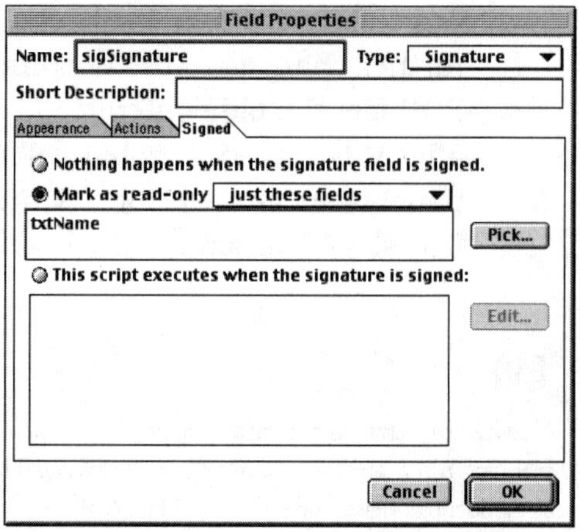

Figure 11.8 The Signed panel specifies what should happen when a user signs your form. You can execute a JavaScript or make one or more additional fields read-only.

You have three choices here: In the first option, nothing happens. The signature graphic is placed in the signature field and that is all. In the second option, some form fields are marked as read-only. In Figure 11.1, for example, you may want to lock the Name field when the form is signed. You have your choice of locking all the fields in the form, some of the fields, or all except certain fields (Figure 11.9). If the user removes the signature (by right/Control-clicking on the signature and selecting Clear Signature from the resulting pop-up menu), the fields will become unlocked again. Finally, in the third option, a JavaScript is executed. This would allow you to do such things as lock and "gray out" certain fields (see Appendix B for a JavaScript that does these things).

The Signed panel doesn't exist in Acrobat 4; the Field Properties dialog box has only the Appearance and Actions panels.

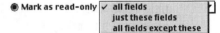
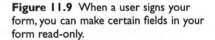

Figure 11.9 When a user signs your form, you can make certain fields in your form read-only.

Submitting Signed Form Data

If you have a signature field in your form, you must keep two things in mind when deciding how your form data should be submitted.

First, the form data must be submitted in FDF format, since HTML doesn't support signature data. Just make sure you select FDF in your Submit button's Submit Form action (Figure 11.10).

Second, whoever ultimately receives the form data must have a user certificate for the form's signer; without this, the recipient cannot confirm the validity of the signature. Unfortunately, there is no way to automate this; the user or a system administrator must create a user certificate and send it to the receiver of the form data.

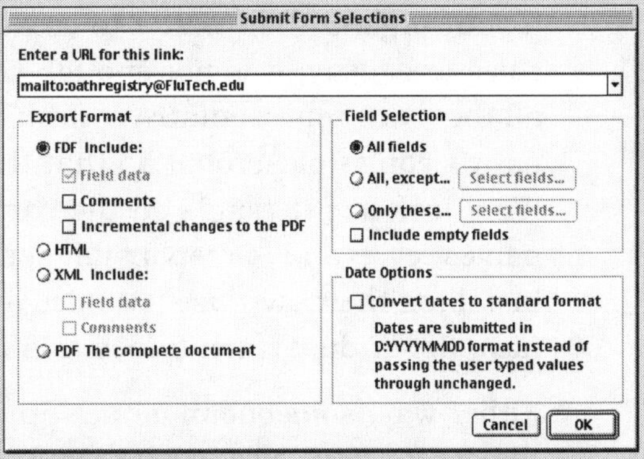

Figure 11.10 If you have a signature field in your form, then you must submit your form data in FDF. HTML doesn't support digital signatures.

Exercise: Create a Signature Field

Your assignment in this exercise is to add a signature field to the form pictured in Figure 11.1. The field should go in the rectangle in the lower-right corner of the form (as in Figure 11.2). Your starting file, form.Chapter 15 Start.pdf, has everything in place except the signature field.

I am not too concerned at this point with the details of your field. The Appearance properties should have Background Color and Border Color turned off; your Appearance panel for the field should look like Figure 11.7.

It would be a good idea to have the Signed panel make the name field read-only. The Signed panel should look like the one shown in Figure 11.8.

Note that once you have made this field, you cannot place a signature in it until you have created a user profile for yourself. In the next section, we'll see how to do this.

Setting Up for Signatures

If your organization wants to create a series of signed forms for its sales force, say, it is not enough that you place a signature field in all the sales representatives' forms. You must also set up the company's copies of Acrobat so that they can use digital signatures. Who does this depends on the corporate situation. In some companies, everyone is responsible for making, distributing, and installing their own user profiles and certificates; in other companies, the IT department does this for everyone.

Either way, *someone* must set up everybody's computers to use the digital signature mechanism; it's not hard, but it can take a while if there are a lot of computers involved.

To set up for digital signature use, someone (let's assume it's you) will need to do the following tasks:

- Create a user profile for each person who will be signing forms.
- Create a user certificate for each potential signer.

- Install all signers' user certificates into each receiver's copy of Acrobat.
- Teach the people who will receive the signed forms how to validate signatures within those forms.

Remember that everyone signing or receiving signed documents must have Adobe Approval or the full Adobe Acrobat; the Reader doesn't create or validate digital signatures.

Let's look at how to do each of these tasks.

Creating a User Profile

This must be done once for everyone who will be signing forms. If you try to sign a form without having a profile, Acrobat will prompt you to create one.

To create a user profile for a form signer:

Start with Acrobat launched.

1. Go to Tools > Self-Sign Security > Log In.

   Acrobat will present you with the Log In dialog box (Figure 11.11).

```
┌─────────────────────────────────────────────────────────────┐
│                  Self-Sign Security - Log In                  │
├─────────────────────────────────────────────────────────────┤
│ Document signatures require access to Acrobat Self-Sign credentials. │
│                                                               │
│ User profile file:  [ JohnDeubert.apf      ◆ ]  [ New User Profile... ] │
│                                                               │
│ User password:  [                    ]  [ Find Your Profile File... ] │
│                                                               │
│                                    [ Cancel ]  [ Log In ]     │
└─────────────────────────────────────────────────────────────┘
```

Figure 11.11 To create a new user profile, start by selecting Tools > Self-Sign Security > Log In, and then clicking on the New User Profile button.

2. Click the New User Profile button.

   Acrobat will present you with the Create New User dialog box (Figure 11.12).

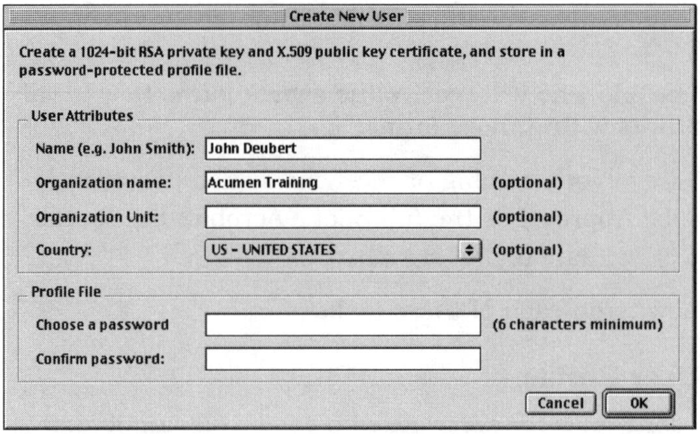

Create New User

Create a 1024-bit RSA private key and X.509 public key certificate, and store in a
password-protected profile file.

User Attributes

Name (e.g. John Smith):   John Deubert

Organization name: Acumen Training   (optional)

Organization Unit: (optional)

Country: US – UNITED STATES   ⬍   (optional)

Profile File

Choose a password   (6 characters minimum)

Confirm password:

Cancel   OK

Figure 11.12 Your user profile requires two pieces of information:
your name and a password.

3. Fill in the form, supplying at least a name and a password,
    then click OK.

    Acrobat will ask you to save the user profile in a file. Save this
    file (suffixed .apf for Acrobat Profile File) somewhere reason-
    ably stable on your hard disk. I save mine in a Profiles folder
    I made in my computer's Documents folder.

That's all there is to it. In the future, you can sign in by
simply selecting your profile from the pop-up menu in the
Sign In dialog box. (If your profile file gets moved, so that
Acrobat can't find it, you can click the Find Your Profile
File button and tell Acrobat where the file has gone.)

JohnDeubert.apf

Creating a User Certificate

Before the signer can usefully send a signed form to someone else,
a user certificate for that signer must be installed into the recipient's copy of Acrobat. The certificate, an FDF file, is created in the
signer's copy of Acrobat and then sent (by email, disk, foot, or
horse) to the receiver. This needs to be done only once; from then
on, the receiver's computer will recognize that signer's signatures.
In the following steps, we'll assume that you are making a user
certificate for yourself as a signer.

Signature User Settings

Creating and importing user certificates takes us to the Self-Sign Signatures User Settings dialog box (Figure 11.13), which presents numerous options to the signer. In addition to the User Information and Trusted Certificates panels discussed in this chapter, the User Settings dialog box has the following panels:

- **Password Timeout,** wherein the user can specify the duration of a password entry. That is, should Acrobat ask for a password every time the user signs a document or should entering a password be good for all the user's signatures for the next hour, two hours, day, or other time period. Acrobat defaults to "always ask for a password," which I think is decidedly the best choice.

- **Change Password,** where the user can change his or her password.

- **Signature Appearance,** which lets the user define a picture or handwritten signature that can be used as the user's signature graphic. If you have a little time on your hands, it is great fun coming up with entertaining signature graphics.

By and large, these are not things that you, as the form designer, will find yourself doing often.

To create a user certificate:

Start with Acrobat running on your computer.

1. Log in to the Self-Sign Security system, if necessary. (Do this by selecting Tools > Self-Sign Security > Log In.)

2. Select Tools > Self-Sign Security > User Settings.

   Acrobat will present you with the User Settings dialog box (Figure 11.13).

Self-Sign Security - User Settings for Antimony Beddoes-Smythe

User Information
Password Timeout
Change Password
Signature Appearance
Trusted Certificates

User Information

Name: Antimony Beddoes-Smythe

Distinguished name (DN):
cn=Antimony Beddoes-Smythe, o=Lame Dick Enterprises, c=US

Certificate Issuer's distinguished name (DN):
cn=Antimony Beddoes-Smythe, o=Lame Dick Enterprises, c=US

Certificate:
Details...   Export to File...   E-mail...

Profile File:
Whoozy:Documents:Profiles:AntimonyBeddoes-Smy   Backup...

Close

Figure 11.13 To create a user certificate, go to Tools > Self-Sign Security > User Settings and then, in this dialog box, click Export to File. You can instead click the E-mail button to create a user certificate and email it to someone in one step.

3. Click User Information in the list on the left side of the dialog box.

   This will reveal a summary of information taken from your user profile. The Distinguished Name (DN) and Certificate Issuer's DN fields are strings made up of your name, organization, and country—information taken your user profile. The Certificate Issuer's DN is intended for other signature mechanisms that might have some central authority that issues certificates.

4. Click the Export to File button.

   You will get a standard Save As dialog box that lets you save the certificate to disk.

5. When you save the certificate file, Acrobat will present you with a pair of long numbers (Figure 11.14) that you should save somehow: write them down or copy and paste them into a text file. These numbers serve as a fingerprint for the certificate.

Figure 11.14 These two long numbers are the fingerprint for your user certificate. Someone who installs your certificate into Acrobat will see this same fingerprint.

When this certificate is installed into a recipient's Acrobat, the software reports the fingerprint values. The recipient can call you up and ask you what the fingerprint numbers were when you made the certificate. If the fingerprint of the newly installed certificate doesn't match your original numbers, the certificate may have become damaged (or someone may have substituted their certificate for yours, allowing them to sign documents in your name). You should resend the certificate if there is a fingerprint mismatch; it would also be worth finding out *why* the fingerprint changed. This can be a serious problem; the possibility of forgery in some environments is quite real.

Tip

If writing down and comparing the fingerprint numbers seems like a nuisance, that's because it *is* a nuisance. Most people using Self-Sign Security do not go to the trouble of matching the sender's and receiver's fingerprints. If a question arises later, a recipient can always get to the fingerprint numbers by clicking the Details button in the User Settings dialog box (see Figure 11.16).

Automatically emailed certificates

If you examine the dialog box in Figure 11.13, you will notice there is a button labeled E-mail. If you click this button, Acrobat will ask you for an email address and then create a user certificate and email it in one step (Figure 11.15). This is very convenient if you are making a certificate that you will send to only one person.

Most of the time, however, I recommend that you make a certificate file, as outlined in the numbered steps. This gives you a file that you can send to as many recipients as you wish.

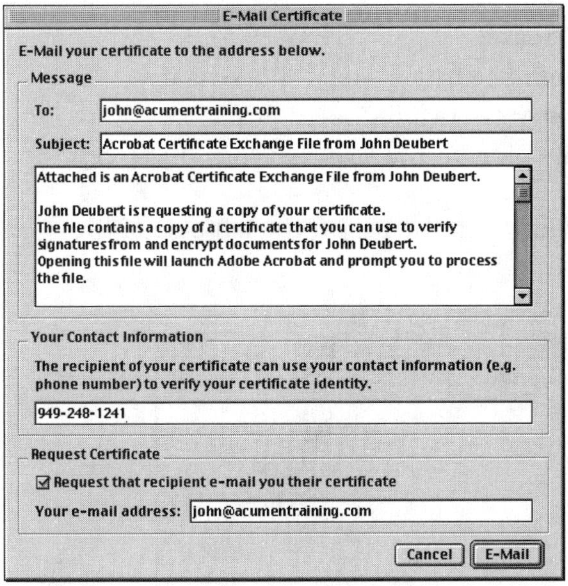

Figure 11.15 Type an email address into the To box and click the E-mail button: Acrobat will create a user certificate and email it in one step. Everything except the To address is taken from your user profile, although you can change anything you wish.

Installing a User Certificate

Before you can verify the validity of a signed document, you must install the signer's user certificate into your copy of Acrobat. An installed user certificate is referred to in Acrobat as a Trusted Certificate; "trusted" in the sense that you are confident that the certificate actually came from the signer. (Perhaps you called them on the telephone and asked if they just now emailed you a certificate file.)

In the instructions below, I'll assume that you are installing someone else's user certificate into your copy of Acrobat. You have received that certificate file as an email attachment and have moved it to some convenient temporary place on your hard disk.

Again, in many corporate environments, it is the job of the IT department to distribute and install user certificates into each employee's copy of Acrobat.

To install a user certificate:

1. Log in to the Self-Sign Security system, if necessary.
2. Select Tools > Self-Sign Security > User Settings.

   Acrobat will present you with the User Settings dialog box (Figure 11.16).
3. Click Trusted Certificates in the list on the left side of the dialog box.

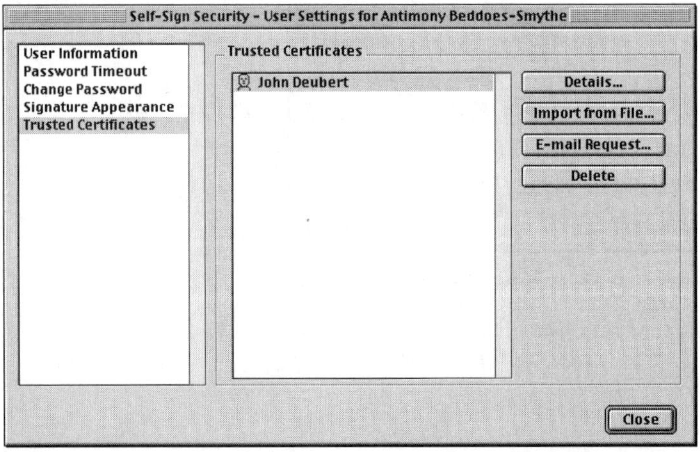

Figure 11.16 Among a form receiver's user settings is a list of Trusted Certificates that have been installed into Acrobat. The Self-Sign Security system recognizes the digital signatures of all the people listed here.

4. Click the Import from File button and select the certificate file in the resulting Open dialog box.

Acrobat will present you with the fingerprint numbers for the certificate (Figure 11.17).

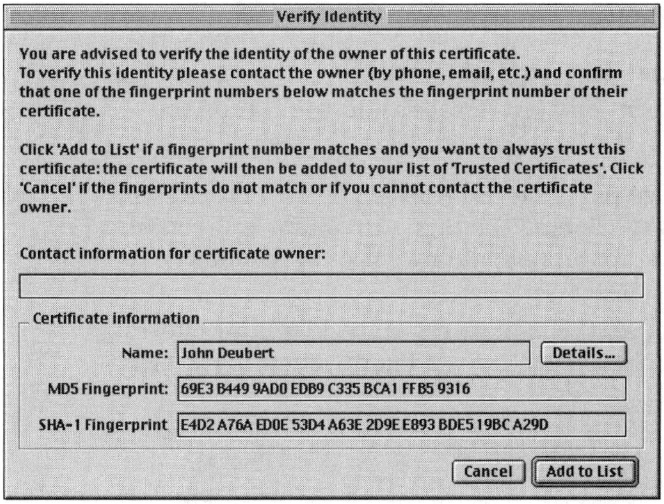

Figure 11.17 When a recipient installs a user certificate, Acrobat reports the fingerprint numbers for that certificate. If these numbers don't match the fingerprint numbers reported when the sender first made the certificate, there may be a problem with the certificate.

5. If possible, compare the fingerprint numbers with those that the sender saw when the certificate was created.

If there is a mismatch, then there is a problem with the certificate: it may be corrupted somehow, or someone other than the person it claims to represent may have sent it. In the latter scenario, all the signatures from that person then become suspect. In either case, the signer should resend the certificate.

As noted earlier, this comparison step is routinely ignored. If the question ever arises, you can always get to the fingerprint numbers later by selecting the certificate in the User Settings dialog box (see Figure 11.16) and clicking the Details button.

6. Click the Close button in the User Settings dialog box.

This copy of Acrobat will now recognize the signer.

It's a good idea to store the user certificate file somewhere safe, in case you ever change your copy of Acrobat. This lets you reinstall the certificates without having to contact all the signers.

Verifying Signatures

The whole object of a digital signature is to verify that a particular person signed a particular document. After receiving the signed PDF file and installing a trusted certificate from the signer, you can now have Acrobat look at the form and verify that the signatures it contains are valid.

To verify the signatures in a signed form:

Start with the signed form open in Acrobat and the Hand tool selected.

1. Expose the Signature panel on the left side of the Acrobat window (Figure 11.18) by clicking the Signatures tab. You can also open this panel as a floating palette by selecting Window > Signatures.

    You will see a list of all the signatures embedded in the form. Each unverified signature will have a big question mark next to it.

Figure 11.18 The Signature panel lists all the signatures in the current document. Any unverified signatures have question marks next to them.

2. From the "Fly-out" menu attached to the Signature panel (Figure 11.19), select Verify All Signatures. You can also do this from the Tools menu (Tools > Digital Signatures > Verify All Signatures).

Acrobat will scan all the signatures in the form, checking each against the corresponding user certificate. Those signatures that

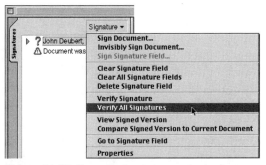

Figure 11.19 To verify the signatures in the form, select Verify All Signatures from the Signature panel's drop-down menu.

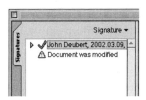

Figure 11.20 A verified signature has a big checkmark next to it. Notice that this form was modified after it was signed.

pass the verification will have a large checkmark placed next to them in the Signature panel (Figure 11.20). If the document has been changed since the signature was placed on the form, that will be noted in the Signature panel.

What if the document has been changed?

If the Signature panel indicates that the form was changed after it was signed, you can ask Acrobat to revert to the earlier, signed version. Simply click the arrow in the Signature panel and select View Signed Version from the drop-down menu (Figure 11.21). Acrobat will open the signed version of the document as a new PDF file.

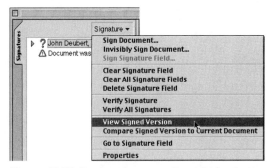

Figure 11.21 If a document was changed after it was signed, you can select View Signed Version in the drop-down menu. Acrobat will open a new document window that displays the Acrobat file as it was when it was first signed.

You can also have Acrobat compare the signed version with the current version and indicate any differences it discovers. To do this, select Compare Signed Version to Current Document in the drop-down menu. The use of Acrobat's Compare feature is quite beyond the scope of this book, but if you have never seen it before, it's a marvel.

Working with Forms

three

12 Acrobat Design Tools

Creating a form with Acrobat—or with any software, for that matter—can be tedious without tools to help with routine tasks. The tools that Acrobat supplies for this purpose are the subjects of this chapter. They are available whenever the Form tool is selected and exist in both Acrobat 4 and 5, unless I note otherwise.

This Chapter's Exercise

In this chapter, we shall add form fields to a timesheet form, pictured in Figure 12.1. This form will give us a very good opportunity to use the shortcuts described in this chapter.

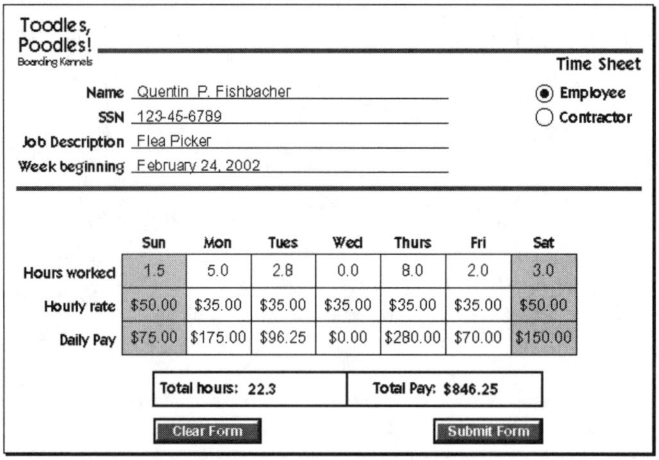

Figure 12.1 We shall create a timesheet form in this chapter.

The starting point for this timesheet is the file form.Ch 12 start.pdf; as usual, this file is available at www.acumentraining. com/AcrobatForms. This initial file has several form fields already in place, as in Figure 12.2. If you wish, you can make these form fields yourself; the file form.Ch 12 blank.pdf is the same PDF file with no form fields at all, though all the static elements are in place. If you choose to do this, see the sidebar for a list of fields you will need to create.

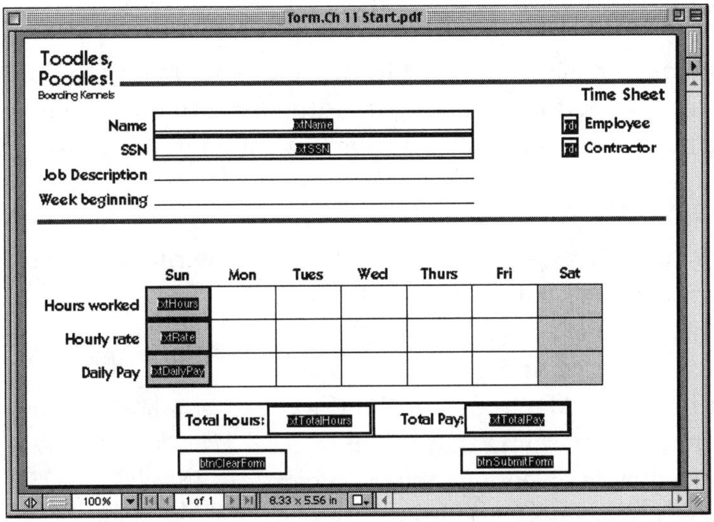

Figure 12.2 The starting file for our timesheet has some form fields in place already. If you want to create these initial fields yourself for practice, the Acrobat Forms Web page also has a blank PDF file with no form fields.

Creating the Initial Form Fields

If you want the practice, you can create all of initial form fields for this chapter's exercise. You will need to start with the file form.Ch 12 blank.pdf from the Acrobat Forms Web page and then add the following fields:

- Text fields for the name and social security number. The SSN field should have the Social Security Number format selected.

- A text field for Sunday's hours worked; this should use Number format.

- Text fields for Sunday's hourly rate and daily pay, both formatted as numbers with Dollar Sign chosen for the currency symbol.

- Two calculated text fields that indicate the total hours and pay for the week. Leave the Calculate panel for these two fields untouched for the moment—we'll fill them in later.

- Two button fields, one each for Clear Form (using the Reset Form action) and Submit Form (using the Submit Form action).

- Two radio button fields for the Employee vs. Contractor choice.

Refer to Chapters 6 through 10 if you need a review of how to make these fields. We shall add the remaining fields over the course of this chapter.

Duplicating Form Fields

The most basic design aid in Acrobat is its ability to duplicate a form field and then modify that duplicate to create a new form field. This chapter will describe several such duplication methods.

Copy and paste

We have already used copy and paste in earlier chapters, but for completeness, I'll mention it here. When the Form tool is active, you can cut, copy, and paste form fields in the usual Macintosh or Windows manner. Something that is not immediately obvious is that you can copy and paste between PDF files. If you are making a form that uses form fields identical to those in another form, you can copy and paste form fields from the original.

> ### Tip
>
> There are two ways of selecting multiple form fields for copy and paste or other actions. You can, of course, hold down the Shift key and click on the fields you want to select. Alternatively, you can hold down the Shift key and drag a marquee that selects the fields; any form field that the marquee encloses or touches will be selected.

Ctrl/Option-drag

A handy way of duplicating a form field is to Ctrl- or Option-drag the field. To do this, click on the field to select it, hold the mouse button down (this is the left mouse button for Windows users), and then hold down the Option key (Mac) or the Ctrl key (Windows). The cursor will become a double-arrowhead in Windows; on the Mac, it gains a little plus sign. With the Option/Ctrl key held down, drag the form field's outline to the desired location, as in Figure 12.3 Holding down the Shift key will constrain the drag direction to horizontal or vertical. When you release the mouse button, Acrobat will create a duplicate of the original form field.

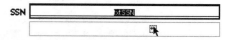

Figure 12.3 When you hold down the Option (Mac) or Ctrl (Windows) key and drag a form field, Acrobat makes a copy of that form field. The Shift key constrains the direction of the drag.

The Duplicate command

The Duplicate command is extremely handy for multi-page forms. It allows you to create duplicates of a form field on a selected range of pages in the PDF file. The duplicates are placed in the same position on each page as on the original page. This eliminates an enormous amount of tedium in creating such things as Next Page buttons and other navigation tools that recur on each page.

To use this command, select the form fields you want to duplicate and then go to Tools > Fields > Duplicate. Acrobat will let you specify the range of pages onto which you want to duplicate the fields (Figure 12.4). By default, Acrobat will duplicate the fields on all pages in the document. When you click OK, Acrobat will duplicate the fields on the pages you specify.

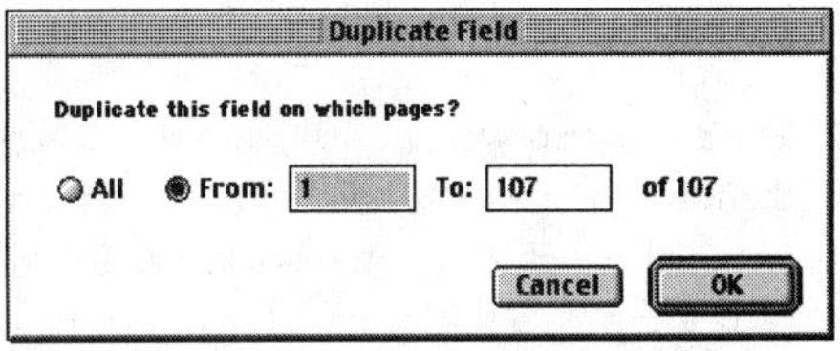

Figure 12.4 Acrobat lets you duplicate a form field onto any of the pages in your PDF file—a big time-saver.

Tip

You can get to the Duplicate command and the various alignment commands we shall discuss later by selecting the fields in which you are interested and then Control-clicking (Mac) or right-clicking (Windows) on one of the form fields. You can select Duplicate or other commands from the resulting pop-up menu, as in Figure 12.5.

Figure 12.5 Right-clicking or Control-clicking on a set of selected form fields gives you convenient access to the Duplicate and Alignment commands.

Deleting Duplicate Fields

It can be risky to delete duplicate fields created with any of the methods we discuss in this chapter. Since the duplicates and the original all have the same name, Acrobat regards them as instances of the same control. When you select one of the fields and press the Delete key, Acrobat asks you if you want to delete all form fields with this name, as in Figure 12.6.

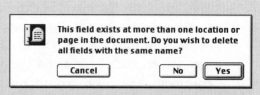

Figure 12.6 When you delete a duplicate of a form field, Acrobat asks if you want to delete all of the fields with that name. Tell it No, unless you are sure you want to do this; it is irreversible.

The correct answer is usually No. If you click on the Yes button, Acrobat will, indeed, delete all of the form fields with this name, original and duplicates alike. Undo doesn't work here, so there is no way of recovering from this action, short of reverting to an earlier saved version of the document.

Notice in Figure 12.6 that Yes is the default response. Be careful not to reflexively hit the Return key when this dialog box comes up; you can easily wipe out an hour of work this way.

Exercise: Option/Ctrl-drag

Let's get a little practice with the Option-drag technique. At the top of our timesheet form (see Figure 12.2) is a text field named txtName; this is where the employee will enter his or her name. Using Option/Ctrl-drag, let's make this field the starting point for creating our Job Description and Week Beginning fields.

To create the Job Description and Week Beginning fields:

1. With the Form tool selected, click and hold down the mouse button on the txtName field.

2. Hold down the Option or Ctrl key, then drag a copy of txtName directly downward to the blank line next to the Job Description label. (You may want to also hold down the Shift key so your drag is constrained to the vertical.) Acrobat will create a copy of the txtName field.

3. Double-click on the duplicate and change its name (I used txtJob, if you are curious).

4. Now Option/Ctrl-drag a copy of txtName to the line next to the Week Beginning label.

5. Double-click on the new duplicate and give it a new name; it would also impress people if you changed its format (in the Format panel) to Date.

Creating Tables

One common feature in forms is a table of text fields that collect periodic or repeated data, such as the three rows of fields in our timesheet that collect the daily hours worked, hourly rate, and daily wage for the week (see Figure 12.1). Clearly, the first step is to create an initial form field for each of these rows (as we have done in our starting timesheet file, Figure 12.2), but then what? You could Option-drag each of the starting fields six times and then change the names of each of the duplicates. This works fine, but Acrobat 5 provides a much easier way.

Acrobat 5 has a little-known feature that makes creating a table of individually named fields fast and painless. This feature is much more easily demonstrated than described, so let's use it to turn our three initial timesheet fields into a full week's worth of individually named text fields. You may want to follow along in your copy of the timesheet.

Again, this feature is not available in Acrobat 4. (Alas!)

To create a table of daily time and pay entries:

Start with the timesheet PDF file open and the Form tool selected.

1. Hold down the Command key on the Mac or the Shift key in Windows and drag a marquee around the three fields in the Sunday column on the timesheet.

   The Command/Shift marquee tells Acrobat that you are selecting these fields for the purpose of creating a table. Acrobat draws a dotted line, including handles at the sides and corners, around the set of selected fields (Figure 12.7).

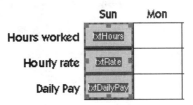

Figure 12.7 To create a table, Command-drag (Mac) or Shift-drag (Windows) a marquee around the fields that you want to duplicate.

2. Hold down the Command key (Mac) or Ctrl key (Windows) and click and drag the middle handle on the right side of the selected fields, expanding the selection rectangle until it encompasses the entire week.

   When you release the mouse button, Acrobat shows you where the new form fields will go, as in Figure 12.8.

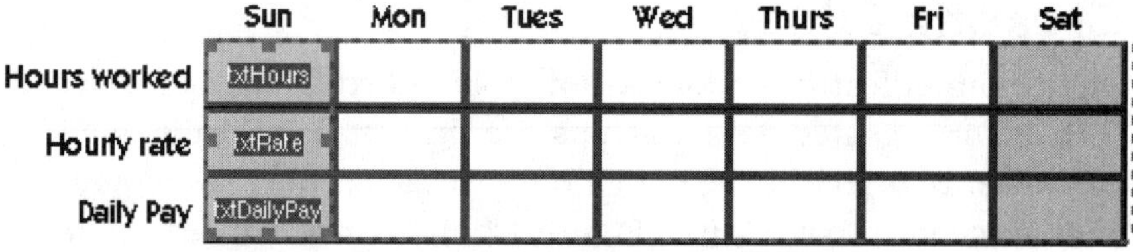

	Sun	Mon	Tues	Wed	Thurs	Fri	Sat
Hours worked	txtHours						
Hourly rate	txtRate						
Daily Pay	txtDailyPay						

Figure 12.8 Command- or Ctrl-drag one the handles on the dotted outline. Acrobat shows you where it will put the new form fields.

3. Press the Enter or Return key on your keyboard.

Acrobat will create all the new form fields (Figure 12.9). It will also rename all of the fields, including your originals. The renaming scheme is simple: Acrobat adds a period and a numeral to the original fields' names; thus the txtHours field becomes a row of fields named txtHours.0, txtHours.1, and so forth. Note that this conforms to Acrobat's hierarchical naming convention; this will be convenient later, when we perform calculations with the values of these fields. (We'll return to this shortly.)

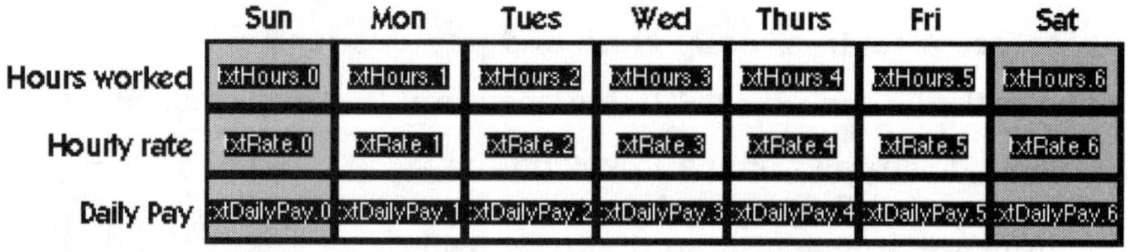

	Sun	Mon	Tues	Wed	Thurs	Fri	Sat
Hours worked	txtHours.0	txtHours.1	txtHours.2	txtHours.3	txtHours.4	txtHours.5	txtHours.6
Hourly rate	txtRate.0	txtRate.1	txtRate.2	txtRate.3	txtRate.4	txtRate.5	txtRate.6
Daily Pay	txtDailyPay.0	txtDailyPay.1	txtDailyPay.2	txtDailyPay.3	txtDailyPay.4	txtDailyPay.5	txtDailyPay.6

Figure 12.9 Finally, press the Return or Enter key. Acrobat will create the new form fields. It will also rename all of the fields, applying names consistent with the Acrobat hierarchical naming convention.

Calculation fields within the table

One important thing that the table-creation feature does *not* do for you is change your calculations to accommodate the changed field names. If you examine the original Sunday Daily Pay field in our starting file for this chapter (the field named txtDailyPay in Figure 12.2), you'll find that it's a Calculate field whose value is the product of txtHours and txtRate (Figure 12.10).

Acrobat has now renamed txtHours and txtRate to txtHours.0 and txtRate.0. The calculation in the newly named txtDailyPay.0 should be changed to the product of txtHours.0 and txtDailyPay.0. Unfortunately, Acrobat won't make this correction for you. Each calculated txtDailyPay value needs to become the product of the txtHours and txtRate in its particular column. Thus, the value of txtDailyPay.0 becomes the product of txtHours.0 and txtRate.0, the value of txtDailyPay.1 becomes the product of txtHours.1 and txtRate.1, and so forth.

Unfortunately, there are no shortcuts for this. You will need to double-click on each txtDailyPay field and make the appropriate change in its Calculate panel (Figure 12.10).

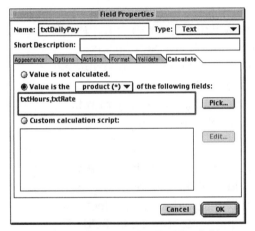

Figure 12.10 The original txtDailyPay field Calculated its value by multiplying the values of the txtHours and txtRate fields. After making the table, you will need to change the calculation to use the new field names.

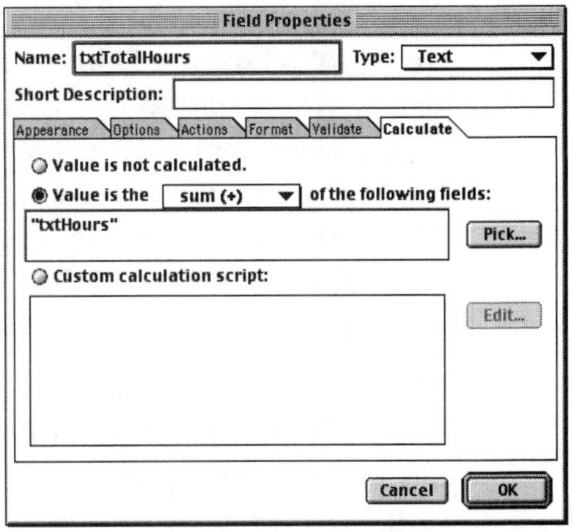

Figure 12.11 The value of the txtTotalHours field is the sum of txtHours. This causes Acrobat to add the values of all fields that start with this name—in our case, txtHours.0 through txtHours.6.

Basing calculations on table entries

The fact that the names assigned to the new fields conform to the Acrobat hierarchical naming convention yields a benefit when we want other fields to carry out calculations based on the table entries.

For example, our timesheet has a Total Hours field whose value should be the sum of txtHours.0 through txtHours.6. Since these are hierarchically named, however, the Calculate panel for txtTotalHours needs only to specify that its value is the sum of txtHours, as in Figure 12.11. Acrobat will calculate the sum of all fields whose names start with txtHours.

Similarly, the txtTotalPay field needs only calculate the sum of txtDailyPay. Acrobat will correctly sum all of the txtDailyPay fields.

Alignment Tools

Creating forms often involves spending considerable time nudging form fields into place next to each other and getting them to be the same size. Acrobat provides commands for these tasks, which can make life much cheerier.

These are all available in a submenu buried deep in the menu hierarchy; you get to the submenu by going to Tools > Forms > Fields. The submenus below this lets you align, center, distribute, and match the sizes of the currently selected form fields (Figure 12.12). By the way, these actions are all undoable, so if you mistakenly center a set of fields, you can quickly revert them to their original positions.

When you select multiple form fields in Acrobat, the first item you select will be colored red; the other fields will be colored blue as you select them. The red field will not change when you select one of the Align/Center/Distribute/Size commands; the other fields will alter their positions or sizes to match the red field.

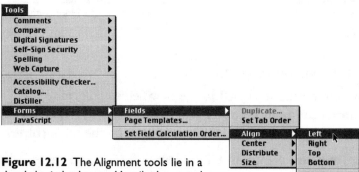

Figure 12.12 The Alignment tools lie in a deeply buried submenu. Happily, they are also available by right- or Control-clicking on the selected fields.

These fields all work the same way.

To align or center several form fields:

1. Select the form fields you want to align. Most of the Alignment commands take the first field you select as the key field; the other fields will be moved so they line up with this field.

2. Select the appropriate alignment menu item; for example, to align the fields' left edges, you would select Tools > Forms > Fields > Align > Left (Figure 12.12).

Aligning, centering, matching sizes

The submenus that align or center the currently selected form fields (Figure 12.13) line those fields up with the first-selected field. Notice from the menus shown in the figure that you have a broad choice of exactly what parts of the fields should line up.

The commands in the Size submenu (Figure 12.14) change the widths or heights of the selected fields to match the first-selected field.

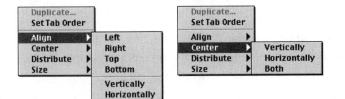

Figure 12.13 The Align and Center commands align the selected form fields with the first-selected field.

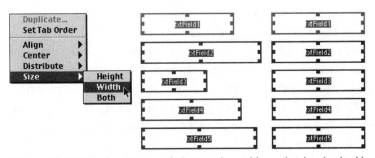

Figure 12.14 The Size command changes the widths or heights (or both) of the selected fields to match the first-selected field. Note that the first-selected field is outlined in red; the others are outlined in blue.

Distributing fields

The Distribute submenu (Figure 12.15) will distribute the selected form fields vertically or horizontally, placing them so that they are evenly spaced. If you distribute the fields vertically, the fields will be evenly spaced between the topmost and bottommost of the selected form fields. Horizontal distribution will distribute the selected fields between the leftmost and rightmost fields.

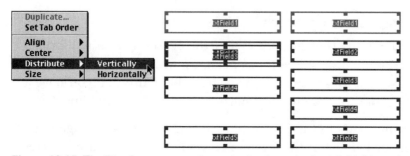

Figure 12.15 The Distribute commands evenly distribute the form fields. Vertical distribution spaces the fields between the top and bottom selected fields; horizontal, between the leftmost and rightmost selected fields.

Note that, unlike the other alignment tools, the Distribute commands do not pay attention to the order in which you select the form fields; the first-selected field is not the key field for distribution.

Setting Tab Order

While filling out a form, the user can move from one form field to another by pressing the Tab key. By default, the order in which Acrobat moves the user through the fields is the order in which those fields were created. This may not be the most useful order for filling out the form. For example, in our timesheet, we would like the Tab key to take us through the Name, SSN, Job Description, and Week Beginning fields before taking us to the daily hours and payment fields; this is true regardless of the order in which we happened to create the fields.

You can change the order in which the Tab key moves the user through the form fields by selecting Tools > Forms > Fields > Set Tab Order. (Again, you must have the Form tool selected.)

Acrobat will number the form fields on the current page, identifying the order in which the Tab key accesses the fields (Figure 12.16). To change this order, simply click on the fields in the order you wish the Tab key to follow. Acrobat will renumber the fields as you go, indicating the current Tab order. When you have the fields numbered to your satisfaction, simply click on the Form tool.

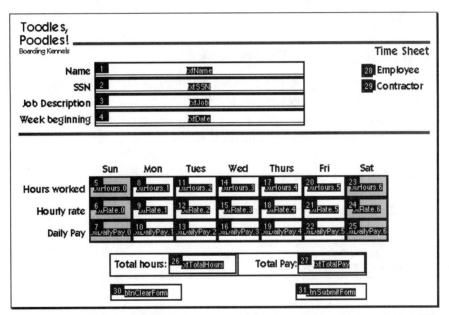

Figure 12.16 With the Set Tab Order command, Acrobat numbers the form fields in Tab order. You can change this order by simply clicking on the fields in the desired order.

You do not need to start your Tab order renumbering at the first field. Hold down the Option key (Mac) or Ctrl key (Windows) and start clicking wherever you wish to begin creating a new Tab order sequence. For example, if only fields 8 through 15 need renumbering, just Option/Ctrl-click on field 7 and then continue clicking on the later fields in the proper order.

13 Form Extras

In this chapter, we shall discuss some features that can add polish to your forms and give them a more professional feel.

- **Rollover help** is help text that appears when the mouse moves over a form field.
- **Templates** let you dynamically add sets of controls or whole pages to your form when the user clicks a button.
- **Document Properties** let you control what the user will see upon opening the form file.
- **Security settings** prevent users from modifying your form in ways other than entering data into the fields.

This Chapter's Exercises

In this chapter, we shall add these features to our timesheet form. Start with the timesheet as we left it at the end of Chapter 12 (Figure 13.1) or, if you wish, you can get the file form.Chapter 13 start.pdf from the Acrobat Forms Web page.

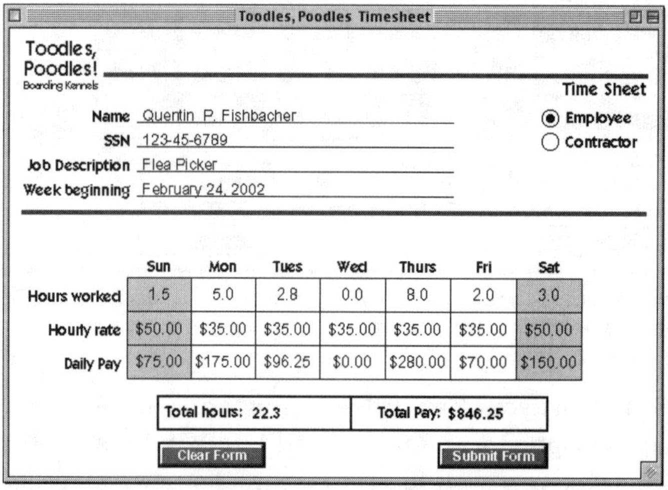

Figure 13.1 Here is the timesheet as we left it at the end of the previous chapter. We will add rollover help and password protection to the file, as well as specify how it should look when it's initially opened.

Rollover Help

I'm sure you have seen rollover help in a variety of Web pages and applications: When the mouse pointer moves over a button, a snippet of text appears that tells us what the button does, as in Figure 13.2.

Why would you use rollover help instead of tool tips? (Remember that the short description in a field's properties becomes the tool-tip text.) The choice is purely one of aesthetics—how you want your form to "feel" as the user is filling it out. With tool tips, the user must move the cursor over a form field and leave it there for a half-second before the text appears; rollover help appears as soon as the cursor moves over the field. Both mechanisms achieve the same end.

Creating Rollover Help

We will add rollover text to our timesheet's Clear Form button, as pictured in Figure 13.2.

Figure 13.2 Rollover help text is initially invisible (left). The help text appears when the mouse pointer moves over the button (right).

Text for the rollover help resides in a text field that is initially hidden. It can be made alternately visible and invisible by two actions attached to the form field that the help text describes: a Mouse Enter action that makes the help text field visible, and a Mouse Exit action that makes the help text field invisible again.

To make rollover help for the Clear Form button:

Start with your form file open and the Form tool selected. The page should look something like the one shown in Figure 13.3.

1. Click and drag out a new text field to the left of the Clear Form button, as indicated in Figure 13.4.

2. In the text field's Properties dialog box, set the Appearance panel's controls to match those in Figure 13.5.

   It is most important that the field is hidden and read only, and that the Border Color and Background Color check boxes are selected. (For background color, I find that pale, pastel shades work best.)

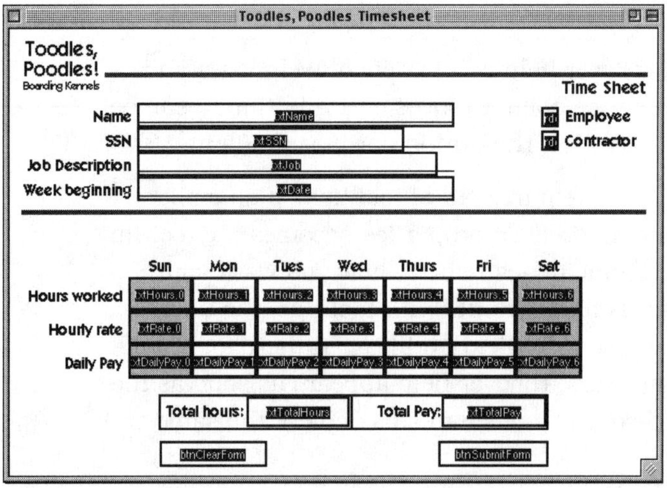

Figure 13.3 Our timesheet starts out with these highlighted form fields defined. We'll add rollover help to the btnClearForm and btnSubmitForm buttons. Both reside at the bottom of the window.

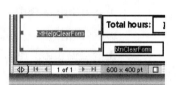

Figure 13.4 Our help text will reside in a new text field that we'll create to the left of our Clear Form button.

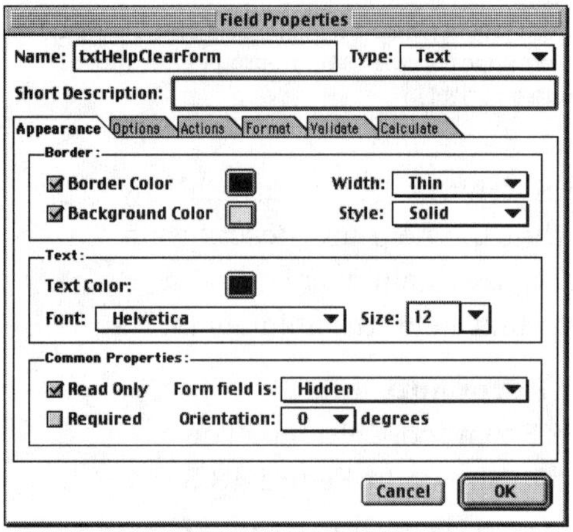

Figure 13.5 Here are the Appearance settings for our help text field. Note in particular that the field is hidden and read only, and that both Border Color and Background Color are turned on.

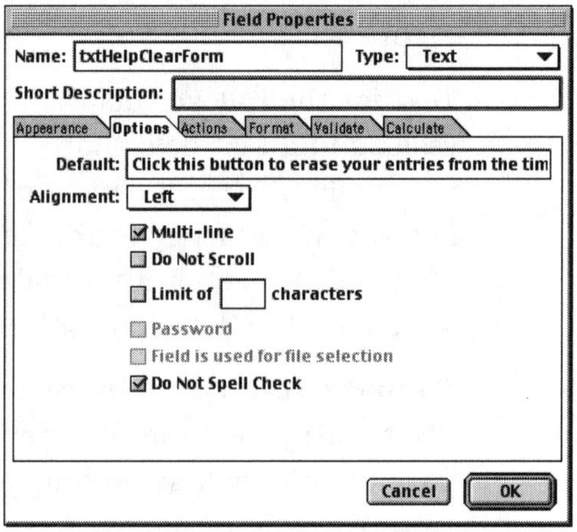

Figure 13.6 In the Options controls for our help text field, select the Multi-line check box and type the help text into the Default field.

3. Set the text field's Options controls to match those shown in Figure 13.6.

   The Default text field contains the actual help text; you can make this any helpful note that you wish. You will also want to check the Multi-line check box.

4. Click OK to return to your form page (shown in Figure 13.3).

5. Double-click the Clear Form button to gain access to its properties.

6. In the Clear Form button's Actions panel (Figure 13.7), select the Mouse Enter event and click the Add button.

Acrobat will present you with the Add an Action dialog box.

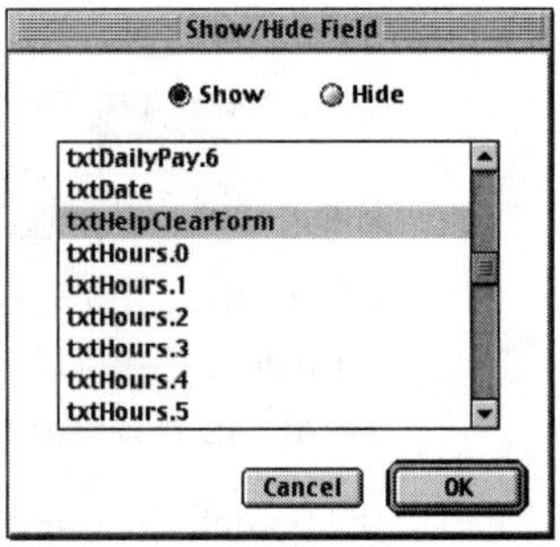

Figure 13.8 The Clear Form button's Mouse Enter action should show the text field that contains your help text.

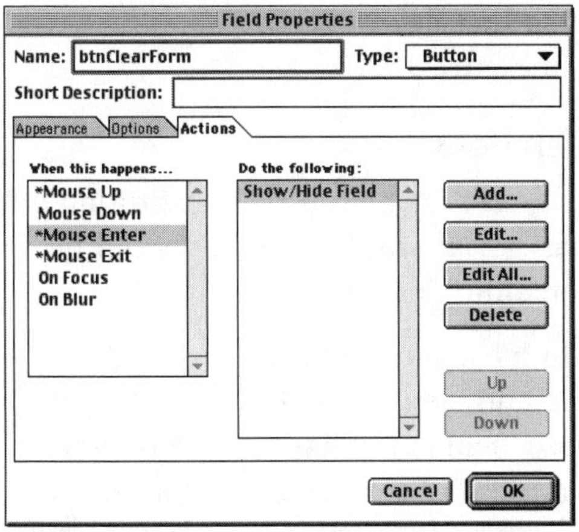

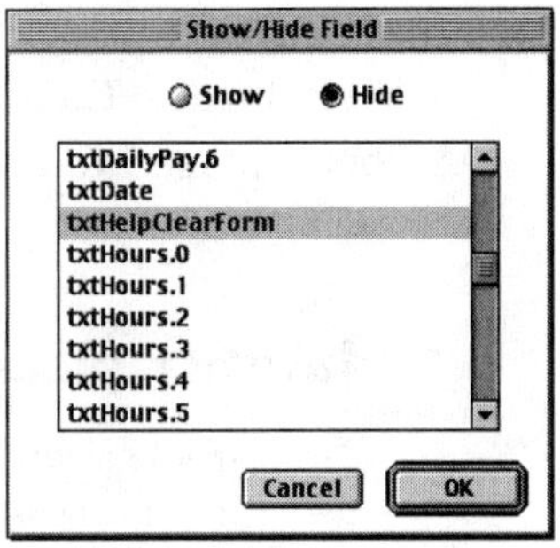

Figure 13.7 We will assign two Show/Hide Field actions to our Clear Form button: A Mouse Enter action that shows the help text and a Mouse Exit action that hides the text again.

7. Select Show/Hide Field for the action type and click the Edit button.

Acrobat will present you with a dialog box that lets you choose a form field to show or hide (Figure 13.8).

8. Click the name of your help text field and click the Show radio button, as in Figure 13.8.

9. Click OK in the Show/Hide Field dialog box and again in the Add an Action dialog box. This will return you to the Actions panel.

Figure 13.9 The Clear Form button's Mouse Exit action should once again hide the text field that has your help text.

10. Choose the Mouse Exit event and click the Add button again.

11. Repeat steps 7 through 9, with one change: select the Hide button, rather than the Show button, in the Show/Hide Field dialog box (Figure 13.9).

12. Click OK, which returns you to the Acrobat page.

That should do it. Click the Hand tool and try it out. When you move the mouse pointer over the Clear Form button, your help text should appear in a box to the left of the control, as in Figure 13.2.

Figure 13.10 Your next assignment—should you choose to accept it—is to create rollover help for the Submit Form button.

Try adding similar rollover help to the Submit Form button. Place the help text field near the Submit Form button, as in Figure 13.10.

Help text design considerations

I find that a gentle touch is best for help text: background colors should be pale, rather than garish, and text size should be as small as possible while remaining easy to read.

It is perfectly acceptable to have your help text field overlap other controls and elements on the page. While the help text field is hidden, it will not have any impact at all on the use of any underlying form fields, or on the visibility of any static elements. If we desired, our help field for the Clear Form button could have been placed to the right of the button, as it is in Figure 13.11.

Figure 13.11 Your rollover help text field can obscure lower-lying elements on the page; this will not interfere with the operation of your form.

JavaScript and Rollover Help

An alternative method of implementing rollover help employs JavaScripts to modify the value of the help text field. This method adds less to the size of the PDF file than the Show/Hide method we discuss here.

I'll discuss this alternative method in the JavaScript appendix at the end of the book.

Templates

In Chapter 9, we examined a technique for making individual controls visible when a user clicks on another form field. (Recall that we made a combo box visible when the user clicked on a check box.) Templates are a mechanism with which you can make sets of controls or entire pages visible when the user clicks on a form field.

A template starts out as just a regular page in your form file. It contains all the elements that you want to have dynamically appear in response to a user clicking on a button (or other form field event). After creating the page and placing form fields on it, you command Acrobat to turn it into a template by selecting Tools > Forms > Page Template.

Adding a template page

To examine how this works in detail, let's add a template to our timesheet form so that, at the click of a button, the user can add blank timesheet entries for an additional week. (This way, the user could submit payment requests for two weeks at a time.) We shall make it initially invisible and then "spawn" a copy when the user clicks the New Week button, visible in Figure 13.15 on page 163.

If you wish to follow along, the starting file is form.Chapter 13 Template.pdf on the Acrobat Forms Web page.

To add a template to a form:

1. Create a page that contains the static art and form fields that make up your template (Figure 13.12).

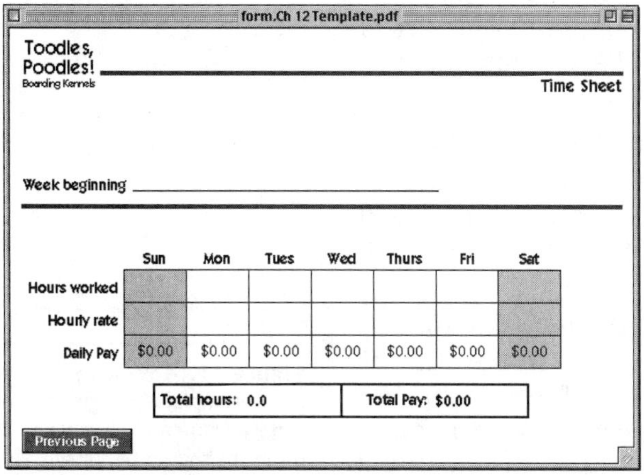

Figure 13.12 This page will be the template for a second week of timesheet entries in our form.

Figure 13.13 shows the page that we shall turn into a template in our timesheet form. It contains everything needed for an additional week of timesheet entries, including the form fields we need to gather the time data. This page exists as Page 2 in our sample file.

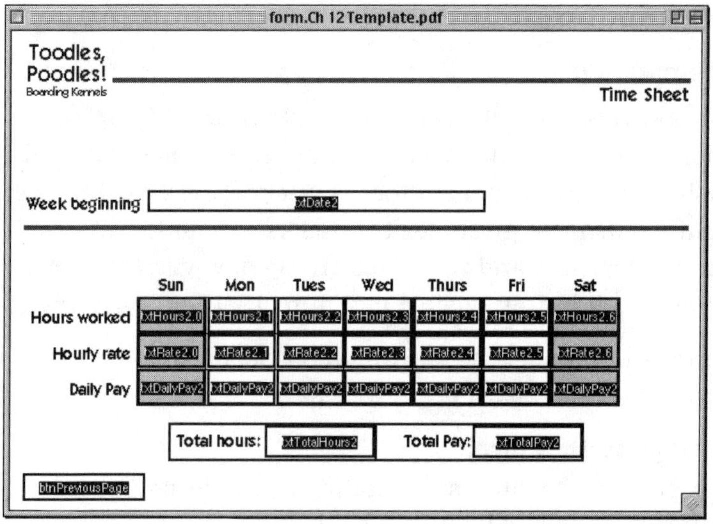

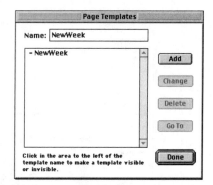

Figure 13.13 The template page has all the static elements and form fields that we need for adding an additional week of entries.

2. With the form document displaying the prospective template page, select Tools > Forms > Page Templates.

    Acrobat will present you with the Page Templates dialog box (Figure 13.14).

3. Type a name for the new template (anything you wish, but I recommend it be something descriptive) and click the Add button.

    Acrobat will add the template name to the list of templates in the current PDF file. To the left of each name is an icon that indicates whether the template will be initially visible or not. When you click this icon, it toggles between visible (•) and invisible (–). Note that in Figure 13.14, our New Week template will start out invisible.

Figure 13.14 When you turn a page into a template, you give the new template a name and specify whether the template should be initially visible.

4. Click the Done button.

Your page is now a template in the PDF document. You will notice that the timesheet has become a one-page document; our new template was marked as invisible, so we can't see it until we create a copy of the template—a process called "spawning."

Spawning a template

Creating the template page is only half the task. We also need to provide some trigger that tells Acrobat to create a new page based on the template. This is referred to as "spawning the template." When you spawn a template, you are not making the template visible; Acrobat actually creates a copy of the template's contents and then makes *those* visible.

Spawning a template is done with a relatively simple JavaScript attached to a button or other form field. To see how this is done, let's add a New Week button to our timesheet (Figure 13.15). We shall attach our spawning JavaScript action to this button's Mouse Up event. This button is already in place on the first page of our timesheet sample file.

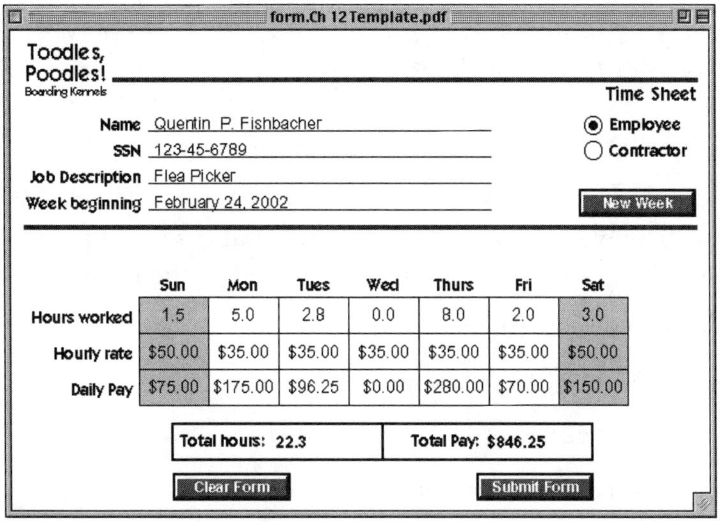

Figure 13.15 We shall add a New Week button to our original timesheet. This button will have a JavaScript action attached to it that will spawn our New Week template.

To spawn a template from a button action:

Start with the timesheet form open and the Form tool selected.

1. Double-click the Button field to gain access to its properties.

2. In the Actions panel (Figure 13.16), add a JavaScript action to the Mouse Up event.

   The JavaScript is pictured in Figure 13.17; we'll discuss it in more detail in a moment.

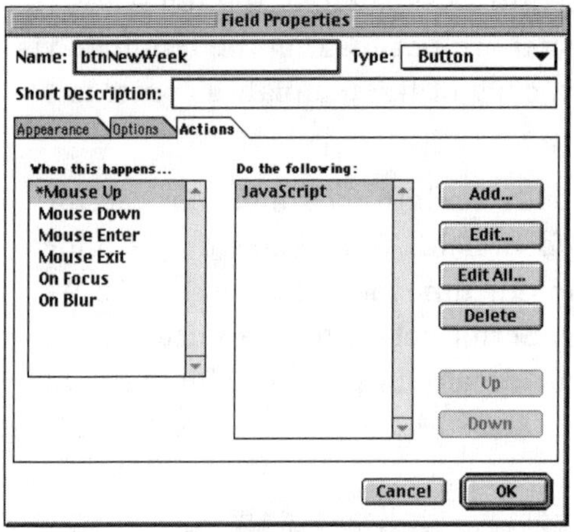

Figure 13.16 Our New Week button will have a JavaScript action attached to its Mouse Up event.

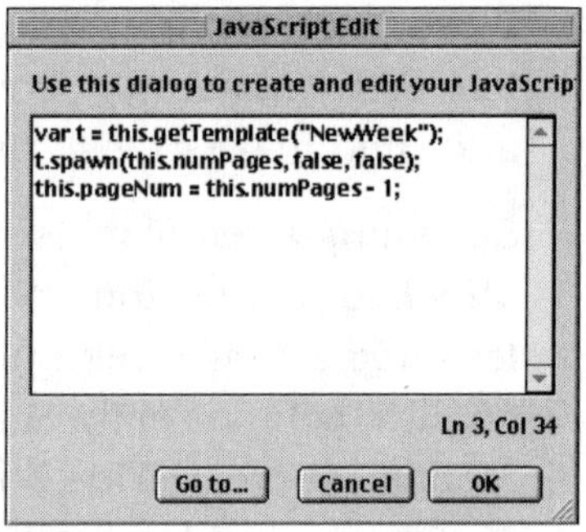

Figure 13.17 This JavaScript gets our "NewWeek" template, spawns it as a new page, and then turns the user's view to that new page.

3. Repeatedly click OK to get back to the Form page.

That's all there is to it. When you return to the Acrobat Hand tool and click the New Week button, you will find that a second page that looks just like our template has been added to the form.

The JavaScript that does the deed is this:

```
var t = this.getTemplate("NewWeek");

t.spawn(this.numPages, false, false);

this.pageNum = this.numPages - 1;
```

For a detailed description of what's going on here, refer to the Acrobat JavaScript Object Specification. In overview, however, here's what this JavaScript does.

The first line announces that we shall be doing something with the template named "NewWeek." Within our JavaScript, we shall refer to this template by the name "t."

The second line spawns a copy of the template, placing it at the end of this document. The two "false" values tell Acrobat to add the template to our form as a new page and to keep all of the template's form field names unchanged.

The final line moves our view of the document so that we are looking at the new page.

Limitations of our example

Our template example is a useful addition to our timesheet, but it has a severe limitation. Every time we click the New Week button, we get another spawned copy of the template. Every time we spawn a new copy of our template, we get a new page with form fields whose names are identical to those in every other spawned copy of that template. (In every spawned New Week page, the Sunday Hours Worked field is named txtHours2.0.)

The result is that we cannot usefully add more than one additional week to our template. If we add a third week, all of its time values will flow into the identically named form fields in the other spawned weeks.

The spawning mechanism can generate new names for the form fields on a spawned template page, but using those renamed fields requires JavaScript skills far beyond what we can describe here. (If you want to try it, change the second "false" in our New Week button's JavaScript to "true":

```
t.spawn(this.numPages, false, true);
```

Spawn a copy of the new template and look at the names of the fields in the resulting new page.

Document Properties

The Acrobat Document Properties submenu (in the File menu, Figure 13.18) has two items that are important to the look and feel of a form file:

Open Options let you specify such details as what page should be presented to the user when the form file is opened.

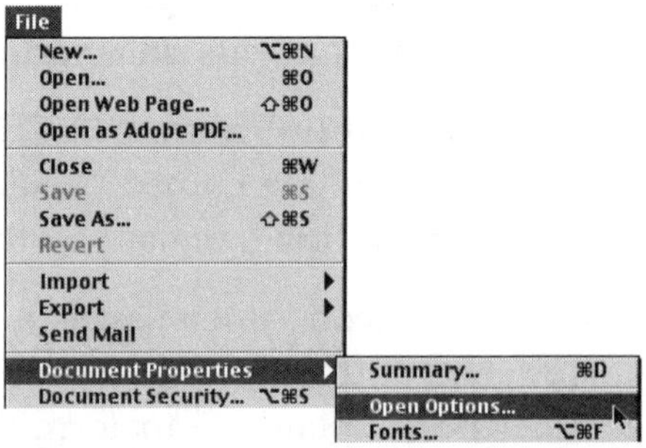

Summary properties let you specify the document's name, as distinct from the name of the file in which the document resides. This name will be displayed in the title bar of your form window, regardless of the name of the form's PDF file.

Figure 13.18 The Document Properties submenu gives you access to the Document Open Options and the Summary controls, both of which are important to your final form.

Paying attention to these sets of properties will add considerably to the professional feel of your form.

These same sets of controls are also available in Acrobat 4, though the submenu is File > Document Info.

Open Options

What should a user see upon opening your form? In particular, what page should be visible when the form first opens? At what magnification should your form be displayed? How big should the form's window be?

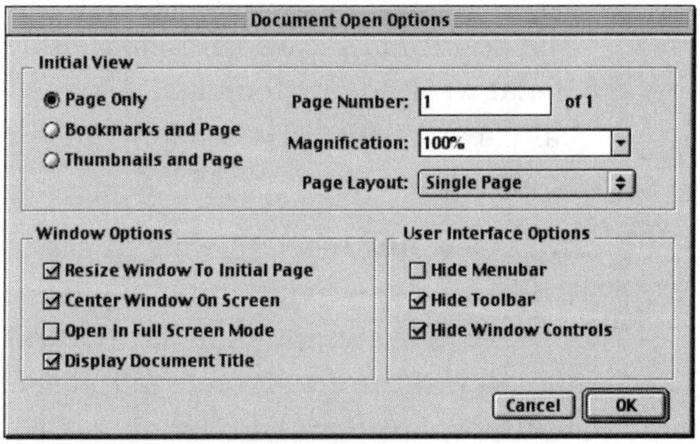

Figure 13.19 The Document Open Options control how your form appears when the user first opens it.

Acrobat gives you a full set of controls that define how your form should look and behave when opened. You gain access to these controls by selecting File > Document Properties > Open Options (in Acrobat 4, it's File >

Document Info > Open). Acrobat will present you with the Document Open Options dialog box (Figure 13.19), whose controls specify how your form will be initially presented to the user.

Let's discuss these controls and the settings appropriate to an Acrobat form.

Initial view controls

The top half of the Open Options dialog box is occupied by a set of controls that specify what view of the document Acrobat should initially present to the user.

Page Only/Bookmarks/Thumbnails let you specify whether the Bookmarks panel or Thumbnails panel should be open when the user first opens the document, or if the user should see only the document's pages. For a form, you will usually want to choose Page Only; most forms make no use of either thumbnails or bookmarks.

Page Number specifies which page should be visible when the PDF file is opened. In most documents, the first page is the intended initial page, so 1 is the usual default value for this control.

Magnification lets you select the initial magnification at which your document should be displayed. One hundred percent is the usual choice for a form. You will need to set this control explicitly, since Acrobat files otherwise inherit the previous document's magnification.

Page Layout picks whether the document should be displayed one page at a time or with some other layout (see Figure 13.20). For forms, Single Page (the default) is invariably the best choice.

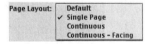

Figure 13.20 You have four choices for how your form's pages should be arranged on the screen. Only Single Page is useful for a form.

Window option controls

These four check boxes let you specify options that apply to the Acrobat window when the form is first opened.

Resize Window to Initial Page tells Acrobat to match the size of the initial window to the page size of the document, as in Figure 13.1. This is an excellent thing to do for an Acrobat form; it makes your document look much more professional on first impression.

Center Window on Screen does just what it says. You should select this check box—it just looks better.

Open in Full Screen Mode makes your document fill the screen and erases everything else from the screen. This is fine for marketing presentations or kiosk displays, but it doesn't work well for forms. Turn this control off.

Display Document Title (Acrobat 5 only) will cause Acrobat to display the title of the PDF file in the Window's title bar. This is usually what you want, so turn this check box on. Unselect this control only if you want one of the graphic elements in your form to be the only visible title.

User interface options

Finally, the Open Options let you hide some of Acrobat's interface if you wish.

Hide Menu Bar hides all of Acrobat's menus whenever this document is the frontmost window.

Hide Toolbar hides the Acrobat toolbar.

Hide Window Controls hides the set of small controls that line the bottom of an Acrobat window (Figure 13.21) as well as the tabs (Bookmarks, Thumbnails, and so on) running down the left side of the window.

Figure 13.21 The Window Controls referred to among the Open Options are these small controls at the bottom of an Acrobat window and the tabs running down the left side.

I generally hide the toolbar and window controls and leave the menu bar visible. This is purely a matter of aesthetics; I find that hiding the toolbar and window controls reduces distractions for the user. However, most users find it a little alarming to have the menu bar disappear, since this leaves them with no obvious way to quit the program. If you insist on hiding the menu bar, you should supply an Exit button that executes a Menu Item action (specifically, File > Quit).

If you hide the toolbar, remember that you are also hiding the built-in Acrobat navigation controls (Next Page, Previous Page, and so on); make sure you supply buttons for all the necessary navigation actions in your form.

The end result

I usually end up setting the Open Options as they are in Figure 13.19. The resulting form page then looks like Figure 13.1: It's centered on the page, with no toolbar visible. (Note also that the window controls are missing from the bottom and left side of the window.)

Document Properties Summary

The other Document Property dialog box that's useful to form design is the Document Summary dialog box, available from File > Document Properties > Summary in Acrobat 5 (File > Document Info > General in Acrobat 4).

The only thing that's extremely important in this dialog box (Figure 13.22) is the Title box. This is the name that Acrobat will place in the title bar of your form's window. If you do not enter a title in

```
┌─────────────────── Document Summary ───────────────────┐
│                                                          │
│      File:  Wheezy:Acumen Training:...form.Ch 12 Help v 1.1.pdf │
│                                                          │
│     Title: [Toodles, Poodles Timesheet              ]   │
│   Subject: [                                        ]   │
│    Author: [Klepton C. Orp                          ]   │
│  Keywords: [                                        ]   │
│   Binding: [Left Edge          ⬍]                       │
│                                                          │
│   Creator:  Adobe Illustrator 10                        │
│  Producer:  Adobe PDF library 5.00                      │
│   Created:  2/27/2002 11:46:26 AM                       │
│  Modified:  3/2/2002 3:26:28 PM                         │
│  File Size: 213.1 KB (218,256 Bytes)                    │
│  Security:  None                                        │
│                                                          │
│  PDF Version: 1.4 (Acrobat 5.x)      Fast Web View:  Yes │
│   Page Size: 600 pt x 400 pt          Tagged PDF:  No   │
│ Number of Pages: 1                                       │
│                                                          │
│                            [ Cancel ]  [  OK  ]          │
└──────────────────────────────────────────────────────────┘
```

Figure 13.22 The text you enter for the Document Summary Title line will be displayed by Acrobat in the title bar of your form's window; this will be true regardless of the name of the PDF file in which your form resides.

Document Properties, Acrobat simply places the name of the file in the title bar. (Note that in Figure 13.1, the form window is titled "Toodles, Poodles Timesheet", despite the fact that the PDF file is named "Form.Ch 13 Start.pdf". You may also want to enter your name in the Author field so people know whom to blame.

The other fields in this dialog box are optional from the standpoint of an Acrobat form.

Document Security

Although you want users to fill in the form fields you provide, you don't much want them using Acrobat editing tools to change your labels and other static artwork. Happily, you can password protect your file so that only people who know the Magic Word can make actual changes to your form.

Acrobat's security mechanism is open-ended: A programmer can write a plug-in that adds any security mechanism desired, usually to match the security used by a particular corporate or government organization. However, Acrobat also provides a default security mechanism, Acrobat Standard Security, which will serve us quite nicely.

Applying Acrobat Standard Security

Acrobat Standard Security lets you password protect the opening of a PDF file and also apply a variety of restrictions on printing and other activities a user might carry out with that file. You can supply up to two passwords for a PDF file, one that is needed to open the file and another that allows the user to change the restrictions placed on file activities.

Adding this security to a file differs between Acrobat versions 4 and 5,

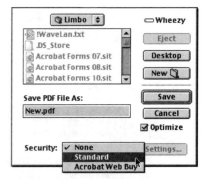

Figure 13.23 In Acrobat 4, you apply security to your file by going to File > Save As, and then selecting Standard from the Security menu.

although the security settings themselves are substantially the same.

In Acrobat 5, you choose File > Document Security. In Acrobat 4, you choose File > Save As and then select Standard in the Save As dialog box's Security pop-up menu (Figure 13.23).

Acrobat 5 presents you with a dialog box that lets you specify what kind of security you want to apply to this file (Figure 13.24). Select Adobe Standard Security from the pop-up menu and click OK.

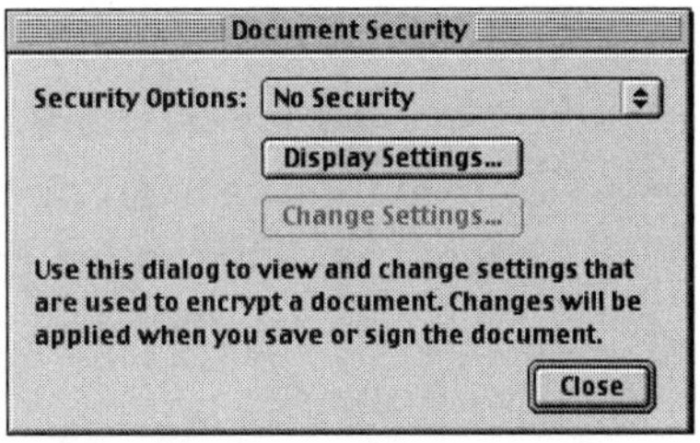

Figure 13.24 In Acrobat 5, selecting File > Document Security leads you to this Document Security dialog box. Choose Acrobat Standard Security from the Security Options menu.

In either version of Acrobat, you will now be looking at the Standard Security dialog box (Figure 13.25). This lets you specify the security settings you want to apply to the form. (The Acrobat 4 version has nearly the same set of controls, but they aren't laid out quite as nicely.)

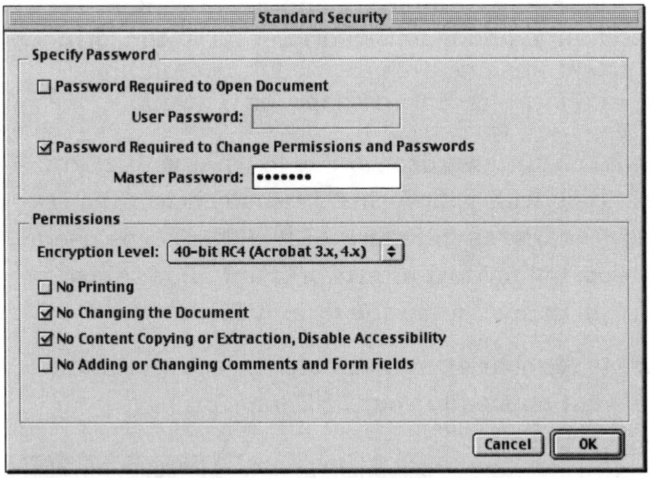

Figure 13.25 The Standard Security dialog box allows you to specify two passwords and a set of restrictions that will apply to your document.

Standard Security Settings

The controls in the Standard Security dialog box (Figure 13.25) allow us to assign one or two passwords to the form, and to specify a list of activities the user is forbidden to do with this file. We can also specify the level of encryption that Acrobat should use with the file.

Restriction controls

Let's start by looking at the usage restrictions. The set of check boxes in the lower half of the Standard Security dialog box specify the restrictions that apply to this file. Most of these are pretty self-explanatory.

- **No Printing.** The user is not allowed to print the document.
- **No Changing the Document.** The user is not allowed to change any of the static elements in the form, but can still fill in the form fields.
- **No Content Copying.** The user cannot copy text or graphics; this keeps him or her from pasting your text or artwork into another application.
- **No Adding or Changing Comments and Form Fields.** The user cannot add annotations to the form or fill in the form fields; as you might imagine, this restriction is stunningly inappropriate in a form (except, perhaps, as a prank).

You will need to make your own decision as to what your users should be allowed to do with your forms. I usually select the second and third check boxes, as in Figure 13.25. This keeps users from changing or copying my text or artwork, but allows them to print the form and, of course, fill in the form fields.

In Acrobat 5 (but *not* Acrobat 4), you can also select what level of encryption you want applied to your PDF file. You have your choice between 40- and 138-bit encryption (Figure 13.26). Acrobat 4 doesn't support 138-bit encryption, so I recommend you stay with the 40-bit encryption unless you

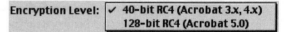

Figure 13.26 Acrobat 5 lets you choose between two types of encryption. The 138-bit encryption is more effective, but it will prevent Acrobat 4 from opening your form.

are certain you will be sending this form only to people who have Acrobat 5.

Passwords

You can specify two passwords for your PDF file.

The first password will be required to open the Acrobat document. If the user doesn't know the password, he or she cannot open the document. I don't usually specify an Open Document password, but you may need to do so if your form contains confidential material.

The second password is required to change the restrictions you applied to this form. If you do not supply a password, the restrictions still apply (the user still won't be able to change your text, for example). However, anyone can go to this dialog box and remove the restrictions. If you specify restrictions to the user's activities, you will certainly want to select a Change Permissions password.

Don't make your password too easy. Your own name, the name of your spouse, or your company's telephone number are all easily guessed. Use the name of your neighbor's parakeet that died ten years ago or something else that you will recall, but that no one else is likely to guess.

By the way, *do not forget your password!*

14 Form Data

By this time, you should have a pretty good idea of how to build a form in Acrobat that will collect a variety of information from a user. In this chapter, we shall discuss what to do with the data you collect. Every form must have a button that the user clicks when finished with the form—this button must send the form data to you for processing.

In this chapter, we shall review the different ways that Acrobat can send your form data back to you. In addition, we'll compare HTML and FDF as data formats for transmitting form data. We shall also discuss in detail how to have your form send its information back to you as an email attachment.

One thing to keep firmly in mind through this chapter is that it is you, the form designer, who determines how data is submitted. When the user triggers the data submission by clicking on a button, Acrobat will carry out instructions that you have put into the form; these instructions specify how the data gets submitted, and to whom. It is easy to think of the user as submitting the data and therefore having some say in how that happens. In fact, the user only triggers the action—*you* determine what actually happens next.

Sending Form Data

There are four things Acrobat can do with form data, once the form has been filled out. Two of these are only available if the user is filling out the form with the complete version of Acrobat. Acrobat can:

- Print the filled-out form.
- Export the form data to an FDF file (but not in Acrobat Reader).
- Save the filled-out form as an Acrobat file (but not with Reader).
- Submit the form to a processing program.

Again, keep in mind that it is you who will be providing the user with these abilities. You must place a Print Form or other appropriately labeled button in your form whose Mouse Up action carries out the necessary activity.

You must decide what software your particular users will probably use to fill out your form. In general, you should probably assume that at least some of your users would fill out your form with the Reader, which eliminates the possibility that they can save the form data as an FDF or full Acrobat file. The form data must be submitted to a processing program, which can be done from within all variants of the Acrobat software.

Let's look briefly at each of the four ways of sending data for processing.

Printing the Form

If you give your users a Print Form button, they can print the form to paper and then fax the form to you. This is pretty basic and requires neither a network connection on their part nor any processing software on your server. It is a minimal-tech way of retrieving users' form data. Your Print Form button will work with any of the Acrobat products.

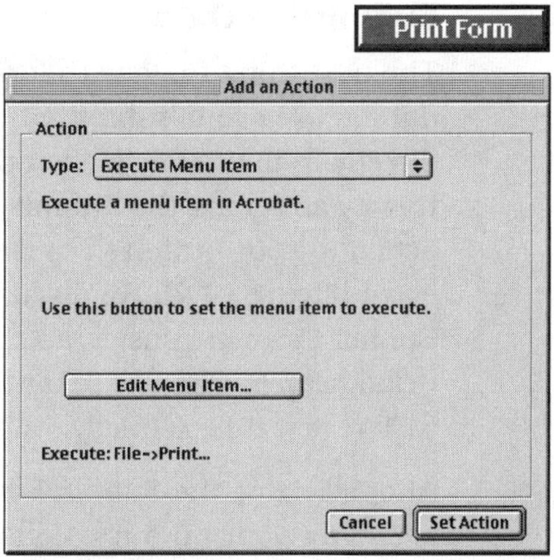

You create a Print Form button by associating the Mouse Up event with the Execute Menu Item action; the menu item is File > Print.

Figure 14.1 You create a Print Form button by assigning an Execute Menu Item action to the button's Mouse Up action.

Export Data and Save Form

These two actions are very similar: They each create a file on the user's hard disk that contains the form data. Export Data creates an FDF file that contains only the form data, while Save Form saves the entire form (with fields filled in) to a new Acrobat file.

These actions are the least effective of the four possibilities: They add an extra step for your users, who must somehow deal with the FDF or Acrobat file that they create: email it to you, send it to you by post on a disk, or perhaps place it on a server for you to retrieve. In any case, this is a bit awkward: It will feel to the user like an imposition, and it gives an unsophisticated impression. However, you may in some cases want to let your user save a copy of the filled-out form (for archival purposes, for example).

If you really want to use these methods, you can add appropriate buttons to your form. Each button will be associated with an Execute Menu Item action: File > Export > Form Data on the one hand, File > Save As on the other.

Submitting Data

The best thing to do with form data is to have it submitted directly from your form. You do this by assigning the Submit Form action to your button's Mouse Up event (Figure 14.2). We discussed Submit Form in considerable detail back in Chapter 5, but we'll review it here briefly.

After selecting the Submit Form action for your button's Mouse Up event, you must click the Select URL button; this presents you with the Submit Form Selections dialog box (Figure 14.3), where you can specify the details of the action.

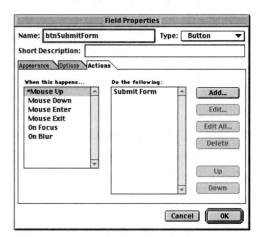

Figure 14.2 The Submit Form action will send data to a remote processing program. Clicking on the Select URL button lets you specify the details of the action.

You must specify four pieces of information:

- The URL where you wish to send the form data, usually the Web address of a processing program written by you or someone you know. This program should receive the form data and do something useful with it, such as add it to a database.
- The format in which the data should be sent, probably either HTML or FDF. In the next section, we will discuss in detail the differences between these formats, and why you would choose one or the other.

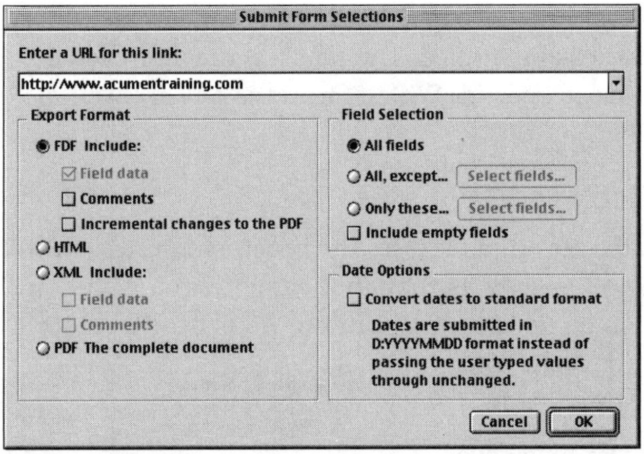

Figure 14.3 In the Submit Form Selections dialog box, you specify the URL to which form data should be sent, the format used for the data, which fields to send, and whether dates should be converted to a standard format.

- Which form fields you wish to send. By default, all the form fields' values will be sent to the processing program, which is nearly always what you want to do.
- The format that should be used for dates in the exported data. Consult with the programmer who is writing the processing program to see if he or she needs this specific format.

HTML vs. FDF

To repeat, the best way to send form data for processing is submission to a data-processing program accessible with a Web address. That program examines the data and extracts the name and value of each field in the form. What it does with these name-value pairs is up to the programmer who writes the remote program.

The programmer who writes the processing program must choose the format in which the data should be submitted from the form. Acrobat can send data in four different formats:

- **Form Data Format (FDF).** Acrobat's native form export format.
- **HTML.** Form data that looks as though it's derived from a Web page.
- **XML.** Form data encoded using XML tags.
- **Acrobat file.** The entire Acrobat form file.

The programmer must choose one of these as the most useful for the form's particular circumstance. The most common choice is HTML, with FDF a close second. Which format is better? Well, as usual, it all depends.

Why send as HTML?

If your form submits its data as HTML, the processing program will receive data that looks exactly as though it came from a Web form. When the user clicks on your Submit button, Acrobat will create an HTML file with the form data embedded in the HTML header.

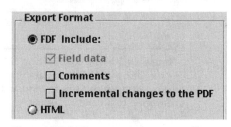

Figure 14.4 The two most common formats for submitting form data are Acrobat's FDF and the Web's HTML.

HTML has some advantages over FDF. First, it is compatible with a very large number of existing, free or cheap form-processing programs written in Perl, C, Visual Basic, and other programming or scripting languages. The CGI Resource Index (http://www.cgi-resources.com) is an excellent source of such programs. (CGI, or Common Gateway Interface, is a standard means by which a programming language can access data in an HTML form.)

Second, many more programmers are familiar with HTML-encoded form data than with its FDF counterpart. Thus, writing a processing program with HTML goes faster and tends to be less troublesome for programmers. This will likely change over time, as more programmers become familiar with FDF.

Although HTML doesn't support the signature field and some of the other features that can exist in a PDF file, it is perfectly capable of handling the vast majority of Acrobat forms.

Why send as FDF?

FDF is Acrobat's native form-data-export format. As such, it is in many ways a more efficient means of transmitting Acrobat form data to a processing program. At this point, far fewer programmers have experience working with FDF files than with HTML files, and relatively few Web servers have installed the software tools that a programmer needs to work with these files.

Still, FDF provides some significant advantages over HTML. First, form data encoded as FDF tends to be more compact than the same data sent as HTML. Second, FDF supports the signature field, which doesn't exist in HTML. Finally, FDF files can contain information about other, non-form-field components that may exist in an Acrobat form, such as comments and embedded files.

Which should you use?

You need to submit your data in whatever format the processing program expects. This decision is made by whoever writes that program. If this is not you, then you must consult with whoever does the programming to see what's required.

When in doubt, pick HTML as the most likely choice of the programmer. If your form has a signature field, however, you must submit your form in FDF.

Submitting Without Programming

If creating a form in Acrobat seems to entail a discouraging amount of programming in order to process your data, rest easy. You do need a processing program if you want completely automated handling of incoming form data. However, if you don't mind doing the data processing "by hand" (for example, manually entering the submitted data in a database), then you don't need to do any programming at all; just have your Submit action email you the form or its data.

Submitting to Mailto:

When you attach a Submit action to a button (as shown in Figure 14.2), the Add an Action dialog box provides a Select URL button that sends you to the Submit Form Selections dialog box (Figure 14.5). To have your form send its data to you as an email attachment, simply enter an email address, preceded by "mailto:" as the URL for the Submit action. You also need to specify the data

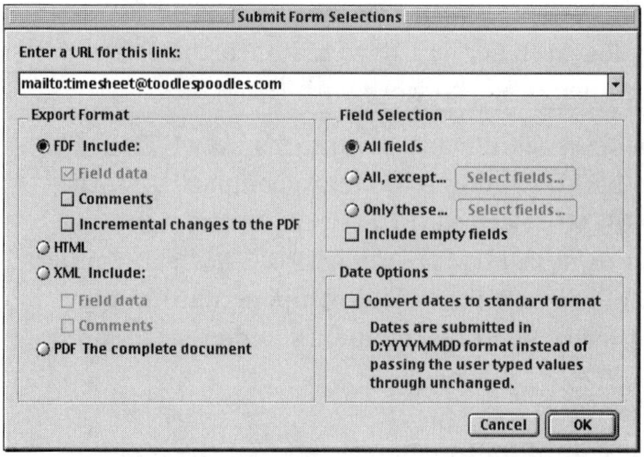

Figure 14.5 The Submit Form action can send the form data as an email attachment if the URL you supply is an email address preceded by "mailto:."

format and other information in this dialog box. I recommend that your form send its data in FDF format—it's the most useful format for mailto: submissions.

When the user clicks on the Submit button, Acrobat will do the following:

1. Create a data file containing the form data.
2. Launch the user's mail client.
3. Create a new email message form addressed to the email address you supplied.
4. Attach the data file to the email message (Figure 14.6).

The user need only click the email form's Send button to send the data on its way. (Note the FDF attachment to the email form in Figure 14.6.)

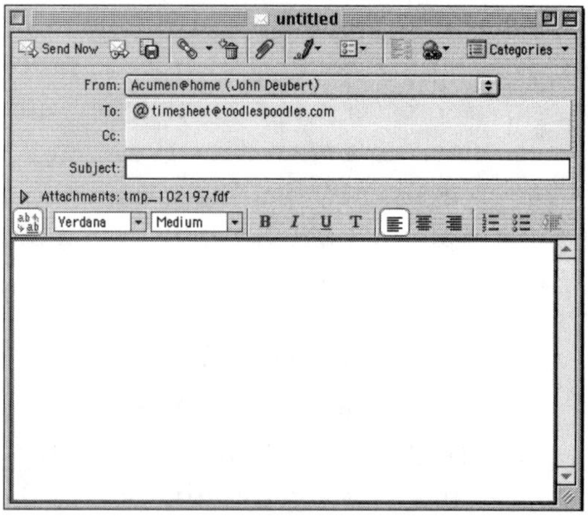

Figure 14.6 If your form submits its data to a mailto: URL, Acrobat will launch the user's mail client and create a properly addressed email form with the FDF file attached.

Receiving the data

When you receive the email with the attached FDF file, you copy the attachment to your hard disk, open your copy of the form in Acrobat, and then import the FDF file by selecting File > Import > Form Data. Acrobat will populate your copy of the form with the user's entries. You can now do whatever you wish with the user's response.

Mailto: pros and cons

Submitting your form's data using mailto has a significant virtue: it doesn't require you to have a data processing program installed on your server. The data is sent to you by email, and you process the data manually by importing it into your own copy of the form. No programming needs to happen.

The problem, of course, is that you will have to handle the incoming data without any automation. If many people will be sending you data, you will sooner or later (sooner, probably) want to have a processing program for handling that data. At worst, the mailto: submission is a reasonable temporary expedient: It lets you use your form while the processing program is being designed, written, debugged, and deployed.

Emailing with JavaScript

Acrobat also lets you email form data from within a JavaScript, rather than with a Submit action, and there are some benefits to doing so. In particular, this method lets you specify a subject for your email, which may be required by your users' email software, as well as the destination email address.

You may want to review JavaScript actions in Chapter 5.

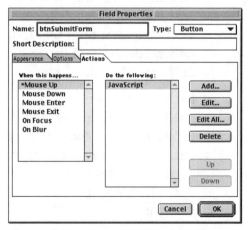

Figure 14.7 You can submit form data with a JavaScript, rather than a Submit action. This allows you to specify both the destination email address and a subject for the resulting email form.

The JavaScript that submits your form by email is relatively simple, if a little cryptic at first:

```
this.mailForm(true,
"timesheet@toodlespoodles.com",
"",
"",
"Timesheet attached");
```

The JavaScript tells this document (our form) to email the form data to the specified email address. The initial "true" tells Acrobat to present the email form to the user before it is sent; this gives the user a chance to cancel the operation, which I consider a good idea. (In principle, an initial "false" would email the data without bothering the user with a dialog box, but I find this fails on some systems. Go with "true.")

The email address and subject lines are pretty evident in the JavaScript; the two empty pairs of quotes in between the address and subject are the Cc and Bcc addresses for your email, if any. In this case, I left these blank.

When users click our form's Submit button, they will see an email form similar to Figure 14.8. Note that both the destination address and the Subject fields are filled in.

I strongly recommend that you use the JavaScript method for submitting your form data by email; otherwise your user may need to manually enter a subject, which will be a minor annoyance.

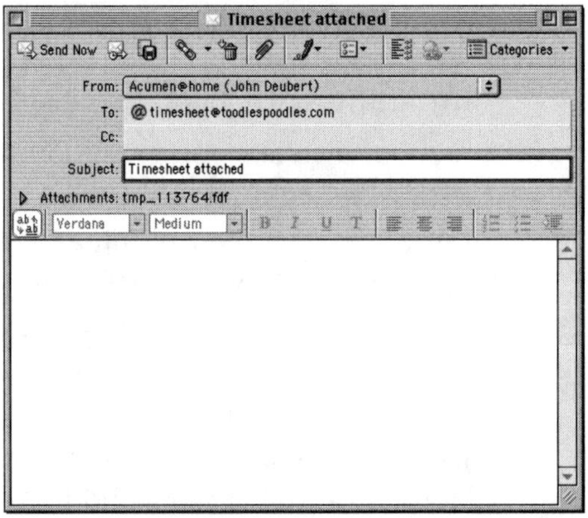

Figure 14.8 The JavaScript we discuss here specifies both destination email address and the subject for the email form.

Unfortunately (and it's a *big* unfortunately), this method will not work if the user fills out your form using Acrobat Reader; it requires either the full Acrobat or Acrobat Approval.

If your users will be using Acrobat Reader to fill out your form, then you should stick with the Submit action, as we described earlier.

Prompting the user

One bothersome characteristic of using mailto: submissions is that the user must carry out one additional action after clicking on your form's Submit button: He or she must click the Send button in the mail client's window. This isn't particularly hard, but the first time users click your Submit button, they will be a little mystified by the sudden appearance of their email software; it would be kinder to let them know what is about to happen. (It's bad form—so to speak—to leave users wondering what to do; always tell them, if you can.)

One very easy way to let users know what to expect when they submit the form is to provide rollover help for your Submit button, as in Figure 14.9. The process for creating this rollover help is described in Chapter 13. This takes little effort and will reduce the self-doubt that so many users experience when their computers do something unexpected.

As an alternative, your Submit Button's Mouse Up action can put up a warning dialog box, but this requires some JavaScript. See the JavaScript appendix for information on how to do this.

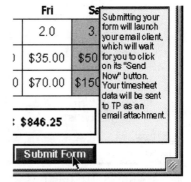

Figure 14.9 You should warn users that the Submit button will launch their mail client software. The easiest way is to attach rollover help to the Submit Form button.

Exercise: Add a Submit Action

In this exercise, you'll add an action to the timesheet's Submit button that will email the form data to timesheet@toodlespoodles.com. (Note that there is no such email location, so your data will come back to you with a No such address message. You could email the data to your own email address if you prefer.)

Start with the timesheet form as we left it at the end of Chapter 13. You can also get form.Chapter 14 Start.pdf from the Acrobat Forms Web page.

The abbreviated steps below lead you through adding a Submit action to the Submit Form button.

To add the Submit action to the Submit Form button:

Start with the form open and the Form tool selected (Figure 14.10).

1. Double-click the Submit Form button (at the bottom of the form page) to gain access to its properties.

2. In the Actions panel (shown in Figure 14.2), select the Mouse Up event and add a Submit action that will email the form data. Your Submit Form selections should match those in Figure 14.5.

3. Exit all dialog boxes until you are once again looking at the Acrobat page.

Now try it out. Choose the Hand tool and click the Submit button. You should see the alert, and then your email client should appear with a properly addressed email window.

At this point, your timesheet is a fully functioning form. It can not only collect data from the user but also can send that data to you for processing.

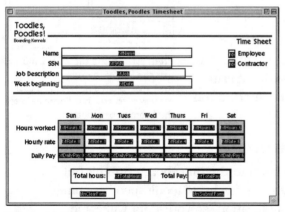

Figure 14.10 In this exercise, you will assign a Submit Form action to the Submit Form button's Mouse Up event.

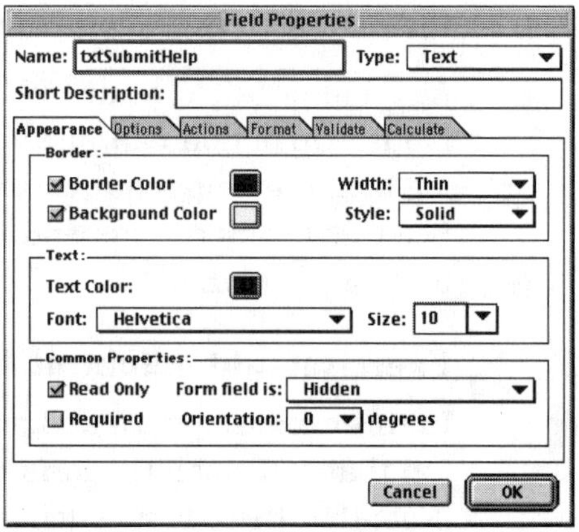

Figure 14.11 Here are the settings for the help text field's Appearance panel. Note that the field is Hidden and both Border Color and Background Color are turned on.

Extra Credit Assignment: Rollover Help

If you wish to augment the Submit button, add the rollover help you see in Figure 14.9. Here are the abbreviated steps:

To add the rollover help to the Submit Form button:

Start with the form open and the Form tool selected (Figure 14.10).

1. Create a text field to the right of the Submit Form button, as in Figure 14.9.
2. Set the Appearance properties of the text field to match those of Figure 14.11. Note that the field is hidden.
3. Set the Options properties of the text field to match those shown in Figure 14.12. In the Default box, write the help text that will appear to the user when the Submit Form button is rolled over.
4. Return to the form page (Figure 14.10).
5. Double-click the Submit Form button and go to its Actions panel (Figure 14.13).
6. Add a Show/Hide Field action for the Mouse Enter event; this action should show the text field you just created.
7. Add a Show/Hide Field action for the Mouse Exit event; this action should hide the text field.
8. Return to the form page and the Hand tool.

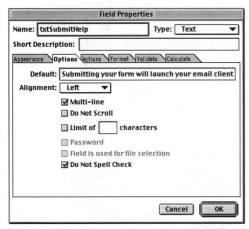

Figure 14.12 This is what the Options properties should be for your help text button. The Multi-line check box is selected and the Default field contains your help text.

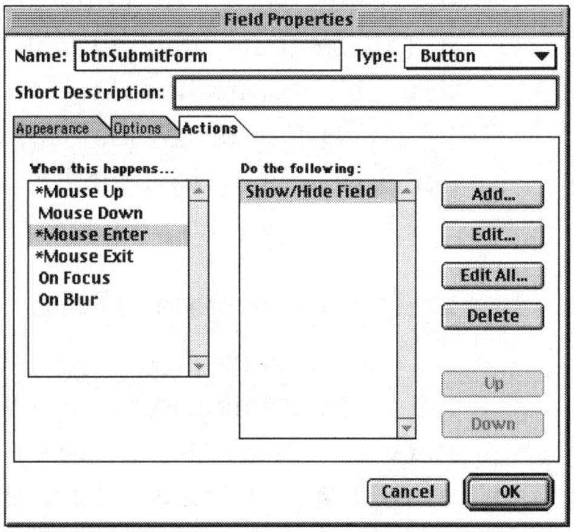

Figure 14.13 In the Actions panel, choose the Mouse Enter event, click the Add button, then choose Show/Hide Field as the action type.

Now see if it works: Move your mouse over the Submit Form button and see if your help text appears.

For extra-extra credit, make the help text field remain visible until you click in it. See the Acrobat Forms Web page to learn how to do this. (Hint: Add a Mouse Up event to your help text field.)

Form Processing

Let's talk about the data submission process in a little more detail. In particular, it would be helpful to look at what happens when the processing program consumes your submitted form data.

A full discussion of how to write a data-processing program is quite beyond the scope of this book; the topic fills hundreds of books on the shelves of your favorite bookstore. Most books on scripting and programming languages, such as ASP and Java, cover this subject extensively. (ASP is a scripting language commonly used on Windows-based Web servers.)

The fact is, you don't really need to know how to write such a program to create perfectly usable forms in Acrobat; just use mailto.

Still, in the long run, it's good to have at least some notion of how data-processing programs work, and that is what we shall discuss in this section. We shall look at how the data-submission process takes place, and how Acrobat handles response pages generated by processing programs. Keep in mind that if your Submit action sends your data to a mailto: address, none of the topics in this section will apply; they become background information.

Data Submission: HTML

Let's start with something familiar: what happens when you fill out and submit a form on a Web page. We've all done this and we know the user's perspective on how it works: You fill out the form in your Web browser and then click a Submit button, the Web browser talks to itself for a moment, and then you get a page thanking you nicely for your order.

What's happening under the hood is this:

1. The browser sends your form data, embedded in an HTML file, to a processing program that resides on a Web server.

2. The processing program—written in C, Java, Perl, or some other language—reads the incoming HTML form data (which consists primarily of the name of each field in the form and the value of that field).

3. The processing program does something with that data: puts it into a database, saves it in a file on the server's hard disk, or whatever is intended for that data.

4. The processing program creates and sends back to the Web browser the HTML code for a Thank You page, which the browser presents to the user.

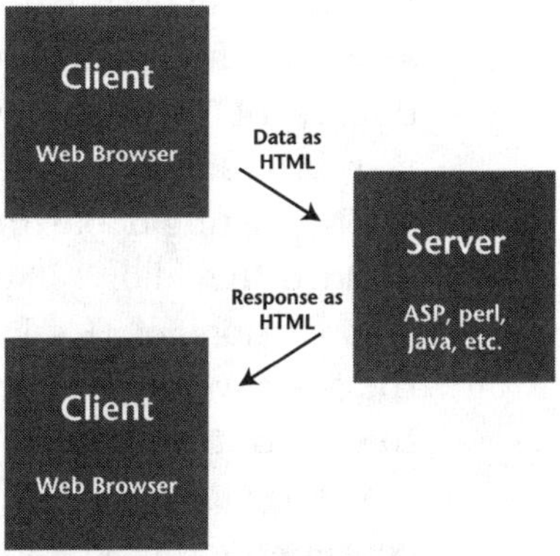

Figure 14.14 In HTML submission, the Web server or Acrobat sends form data, embedded in an HTML file, to a program on a server, which does something with the data and sends back an HTML document for the response page.

Graphically, this looks like Figure 14.14.

The point here is that HTML is sent both directions: to the Web server (the form data) and back to the Web browser (the response page).

So here is the important part: If your Acrobat form submits its data in HTML format, *the submission process is absolutely identical to that of Web form submission.* If you already have a Web form set up, you could replace it with an Acrobat form without having to change any other part of your system. Acrobat can then send HTML-encoded data to the Web server's processing program and accept HTML-encoded response back from the server. Figure 14.14's scheme remains completely unchanged, except that the user is now running Acrobat, rather than a Web browser.

For example, Toodles, Poodles (TP) originally implemented its timesheets as Web forms: Contractors could log on to the TP Web site and fill in their timesheets. A program called timesheet.asp on the TP server handled the Web-based form data. This program sent

the data to the Human
Resources department and
sent back a response page
(Figure 14.15) to the user's
Web browser. Eventually,
the Marketing department
decided they didn't like the
Web versions of TP's forms;
the fonts weren't right and
the layout tended to
rearrange itself. So, they
converted to Acrobat forms.

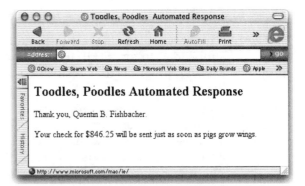

Figure 14.15 The data-processing program on the server generates the HTML code for this response.

Figure 14.16 shows the details of the Submit action for the Submit Form button on the Acrobat version of the timesheet. Note that the Acrobat form submits its data as HTML to the same timesheet.asp program that processed the original HTML form. *This works perfectly well.* We need make no changes at all to timesheet.asp to use it with an Acrobat form. It receives HTML-encoded data (generated by Acrobat, rather than a Web form) and

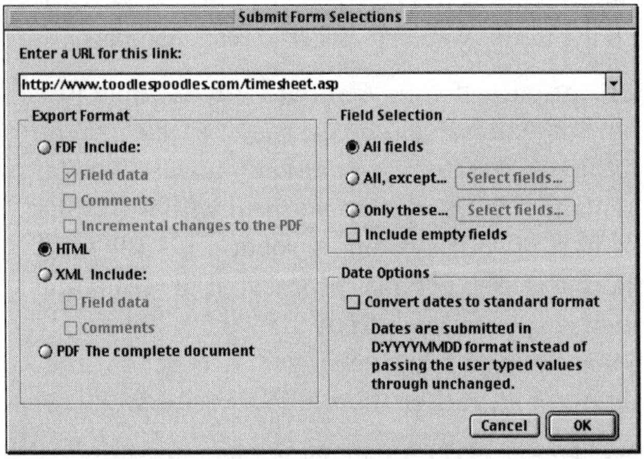

Figure 14.16 Our Acrobat form can submit its data to the same processing program that a Web-based form employs. All that is required is that the data be sent in HTML format. The processing program doesn't need any alterations.

sends back HTML code for a response page. As long as the field names in our Acrobat form match the field names in the original Web form, timesheet.asp will work just fine.

When Acrobat receives an HTML response page from the processing program, it uses Adobe's Web Capture technology to convert the incoming HTML page to an Acrobat page, which Acrobat then displays (Figures 14.17 and 14.18).

Web Capture Status
URL:
http://www.acumentraining.com/cgi-bin/aformTest.asp
Files Downloaded: 0
Stop

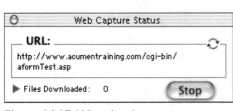

Figure 14.17 When Acrobat receives an HTML response page, it converts the HTML to PDF. Acrobat can then display the PDF response page shown in Figure 14.18.

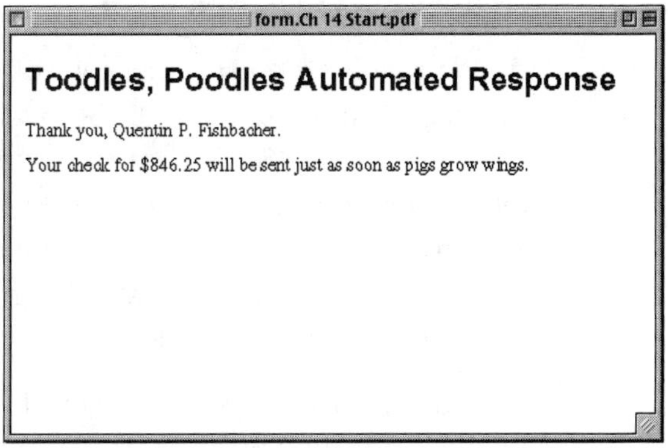

form.Ch 14 Start.pdf
Toodles, Poodles Automated Response
Thank you, Quentin P. Fishbacher.
Your check for $846.25 will be sent just as soon as pigs grow wings.

Figure 14.18 After converting the response page's HTML to PDF, Acrobat can display it to the user.

If you submit your Acrobat form data as HTML, you can use any processing program written to process Web forms. As we saw earlier, there are many free processing programs available on the Web; http://www.cgi-resources.com is a good place to start for a *very* large number of free programs. I should warn you that anything having to do with server-side processing programs is a programmer's task. Even using one of the free, downloadable processing programs entails at least a little programming skill.

Data Submission: FDF

FDF is Acrobat's native format for submitting form data to a processing program and receiving a response back. FDF data submission proceeds exactly like the HTML case we described earlier (steps 1 through 4, above), except that here the data is sent and the response is returned as FDF (see Figure 14.19).

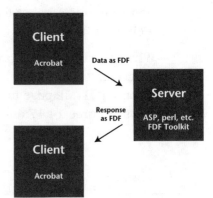

Adobe provides programmers with a software toolkit named the FDF Software Development Kit (SDK) that makes it relatively easy to write a processing program that extracts field names and values from an FDF file, as well as construct an FDF file for the Thank You response.

Figure 14.19 The overall process for FDF data submission is very similar to that for HTML data. Instead of passing HTML code back and forth, the data and the response are both encoded as FDF.

If you are putting together a set of Acrobat forms that don't need to be compatible with HTML, and if you are a programmer (or have one on tap), FDF is in many ways the better medium for submitting Acrobat form data. As I pointed out earlier, FDF is more compact than HTML and has support for signature fields and other PDF features that HTML lacks.

If you are not using signature fields, and you need compatibility with Web-based forms and processing programs, then HTML may be a better choice.

PFN, Paper, and the Web 15

At this point you should be quite adept at making functioning, useful Acrobat forms for a wide variety of purposes. You have experience creating all of the form field types, you can build rollover help and other aids into your form, and you know how to make your form submit the data it collects.

In this final chapter, we'll address a couple short issues that often crop up in Acrobat classes and discussion groups:

- How do you distribute Acrobat files on the Web?
- How can you provide a mechanism that will automatically fill in a user's commonly required information (such as name, address, and telephone numbers)?
- How do you convert paper forms to Acrobat forms?

Distributing Acrobat Forms

Once you have created an Acrobat form, how do you make this form available to users? The full answer depends very much on your situation, of course. Acrobat forms are often distributed on CD-ROMs as part of a software package or other product. (Electronic registration cards are very usefully distributed as Acrobat files.) They may be placed on local area networks for people to download by FTP.

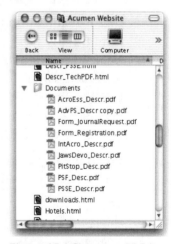

However, Acrobat forms that must be accessible to the public are very often posted on a Web server and made available as a link on a Web page. This is pretty simple to do: you copy the PDF file to the Web server's hard disk, and you add a link to that PDF file on the appropriate Web page.

Exactly where on your Web server you should store your PDF file depends entirely on how your server is organized. The Acumen Training Web server, for example, has a Documents folder where I put all such files.

Figure 15.1 Place your PDF form wherever is useful on your Web server. The Acumen Training Web site keeps its forms and other PDF files in a Documents folder.

Having placed the PDF file on the server, you need to create a link to it in your Web page. You do this with your favorite Web design software: Dreamweaver, BBEdit, or whatever you use to create and maintain Web pages. Simply add to the Web page a descriptive link that is tied to the PDF file wherever it resides on the Web server (Figure 15.2).

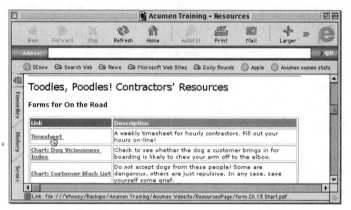

Figure 15.2 You need to create a link on one of your Web pages that is connected to the PDF file for your form.

In-browser viewing

One consideration to bear in mind when you post an Acrobat form (or any PDF file) on the Web is that Internet Explorer and Netscape Navigator both routinely use a "PDFViewer" plug-in (installed as part of the Acrobat package) to display PDF files in the Web browser's window. By default, most users, when they click a Web page's link to a PDF form, will see the form displayed in their browser window (Figure 15.3).

When displayed in the Web browser, the form will behave just as it would when viewed in Acrobat. All of the form fields are fully functional and will behave exactly as normal.

This can be very useful if you are distributing your forms on the Web, because users can fill them out directly in their Web browsers, without the separate steps of downloading a PDF file to their hard disks and then opening it. It provides a nice integration of PDF forms into your Web site.

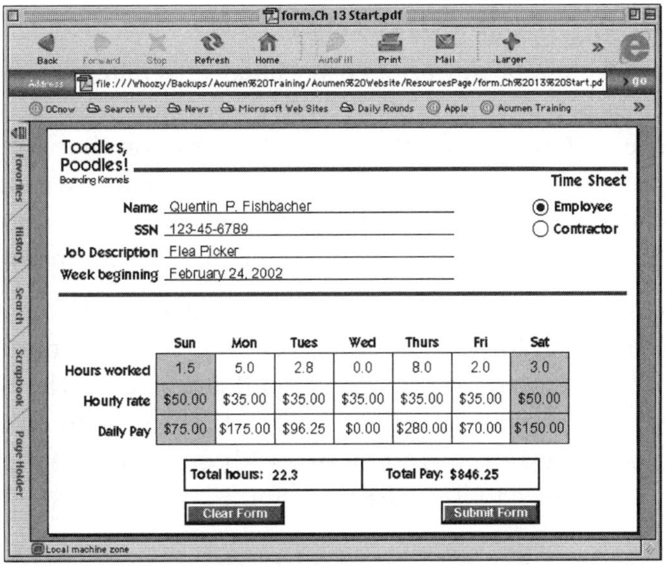

Figure 15.3 Depending on your users' Web browser settings, clicking on a Web page's link to a PFD file may either download the file to their hard disks or display the form in their browsers. If the latter, forms may be filled out in their browser, just as in Acrobat.

Browser Preferences

When users click on a PDF link in a Web page, their browsers may either download the PDF file or display it in a browser window. Unfortunately, the user's Web browser preferences determine which of these alternatives happens, not the form designer. Specifically, the Web browser's Helper Applications preferences determine exactly how PDF links are handled.

The File Helpers panel in a Web browser's preferences will tell you how that browser handles PDF files (Figure 15.4). For PDF files to be viewed in the browser, PDF files must be viewed with the PDFViewer plug-in, as shown in the Handling section of the dialog box. If this is not the case, then clicking on a PDF link in a Web page will cause the browser to download the PDF file; the user can then open it in Acrobat and fill in the form.

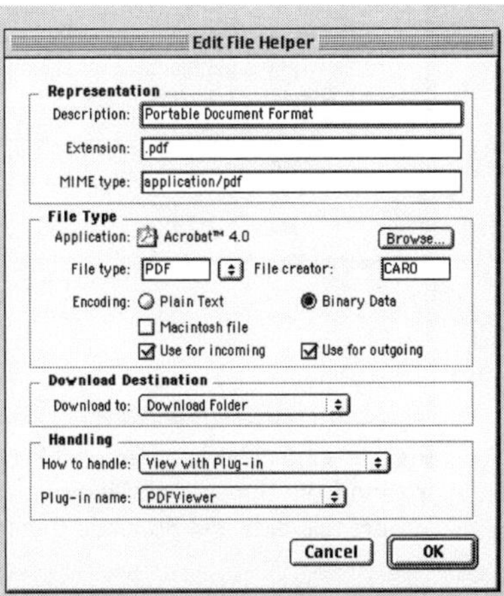

Figure 15.4 A user's Web browser preferences regarding Helper Applications determine how the browser handles Acrobat files. By default, Internet Explorer and Netscape Navigator use the PDFViewer plug-in to display the form in a browser window.

Filling Fields Automatically

One of the minor nuisances associated with filling out forms, electronic or paper, is endlessly retyping your name, social security number, address, and other bits of information that rarely change. It would be very convenient for the user if he or she could supply this information once and then have all future forms supply a button that gets this information and fills in the appropriate fields.

This is easily done using tools we have discussed in this book. You can distribute to your users a "Personal Profile" form that asks them for their personal information (Figure 15.5). The Save Profile button you provide in this form exports the data to an FDF file on the user's hard disk. (You do this with an Execute Menu Item action, executing File > Export > Form Data.)

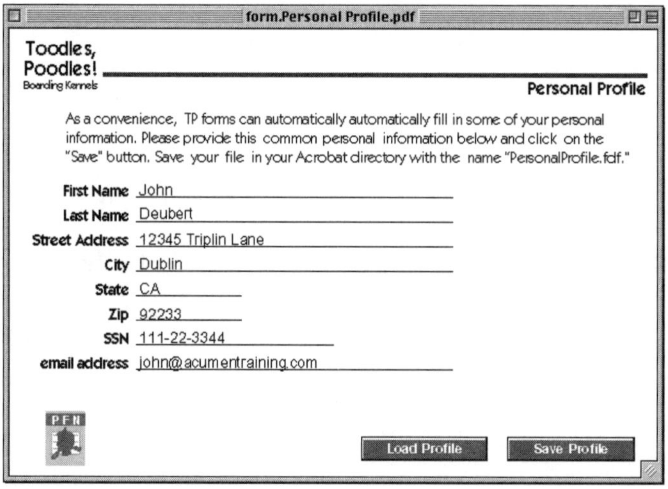

Figure 15.5 This is a Personal Profile form that collects personal information from the user and exports it to an FDF file. Other forms can import this data and populate their fields with the appropriate values.

In all of your other forms, you can create a Load Profile button that imports common data from the previously exported Personal Info FDF file (Figure 15.6); you do this by attaching the Import Form Data action to a Load Profile button. Any form fields whose names match fields in the Personal Profile FDF file will be filled in with the corresponding data; non-matching fields are ignored.

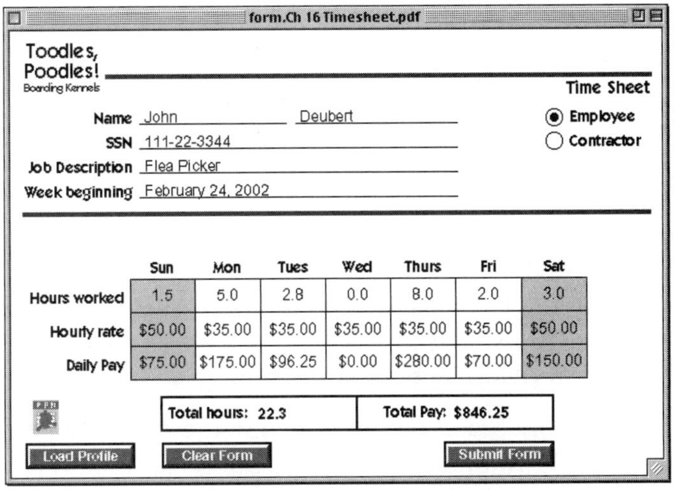

Figure 15.6 Here we have added a Load Profile button to our earlier timesheet form. This button imports form data from the FDF file created by the Personal Profile form.

One fine point to consider is that the Import Data action will look for an FDF file with a particular name that you, the form designer, supply as part of the action. (See Chapter 5 for a review of how Import Data works.) If Acrobat cannot find that file at import time; it will ask the user to browse to an FDF file from which to read data.

Having Acrobat always asking the user to navigate to the FDF file is a little clunky; things would work much more smoothly if you tell the user what file name to use when they save their profile FDF and where to save it, as does the Personal Profile form in Figure 15.5. If Acrobat knows where to find the file, and what it's called, it will open it automatically.

The best place for users to save their data file is in their Acrobat or Acrobat Approval folder; Acrobat always searches those folders when it is carrying out an Import Form Data action. In Windows, Acrobat also searches the Windows folder, the System folder, and folders in the Windows PATH statement. On the Macintosh, it searches the Preferences folder. If the FDF file is located in any of these places, Acrobat will find it without presenting an Open dialog box.

Adobe Personal Field Names

As long as the form field names match, the imported Personal Profile data will be used to fill in the fields in your form. If you have designed both the Personal Profile questionnaire and the forms that use the exported FDF file, you can easily arrange to have all of the form field names match.

In the best of all worlds, however, wouldn't it be nice if there were standard field names for this common personal information? That way, information gathered by your personal info questionnaire could be imported by any form that adheres to that naming standard.

Adobe has defined just such a standard. Documents that adhere to Adobe's Personal Field Names (PFN) specification can import form data from any FDF file that also adheres to the PFN. The naming convention is pretty straightforward. Table 15.1 gives a sampling. The Acrobat Forms Web page has a sample questionnaire, supplied by Adobe, that contains form fields for the complete PFN spec.

Table 15.1 PFN Field Names

FIELD NAME	DATA
name.first	First name
name.last	Last name
name.initial	Middle initial
name.prefix	Mr., Ms., etc.
home.address.line1	First line of the home address
home.address.line2	Second line of the home address
home.address.city	Home address' city
home.address.state	Home address' state

If you are planning on supporting a personal profile from which your users can fill in common form fields, I strongly recommend drawing field names from the PFN standard. The Acrobat Forms Web site contains a document that provides all of the PFN field names.

If you do this, you may want to place the PFN icon on your form pages. Adobe provides this icon as part of the package of PFN information it distributes. Of course, the icon will only puzzle your users, so you should either display it discreetly or supply rollover help that explains it. (On the other hand, if you are looking to make new friends, having thousands of users calling in to ask, "What the heck's 'PFN?'" might just do the trick.)

Converting Paper Forms

Any organization that has been around for awhile has accumulated a set of forms for everything from applying for vacation time to signing out laptop computers for use on the road. Most such organizations are now looking at changing these forms from paper to PDF. It would save enormous time if rather than re-create all of their forms from scratch, they could simply convert their current paper to PDF.

The process is simple:

1. Scan the paper form.
2. Convert the paper form to PDF.
3. Lay your form fields over the PDF page.

Let's examine some of the details.

Scanning and Converting to PDF

Scanning within Acrobat

Acrobat can scan your paper and convert it to directly into PDF if your scanner has a TWAIN driver. (TWAIN is a very commonly used standard for scanner drivers; your scanner probably has such a driver available for it.) This is the most efficient way to convert paper to PDF if you have only a couple of forms; it results in an image-only PDF—that is, a PDF file containing only image data with no editable text or line art—which is what you want for your form (Figure 15.7).

Simply choose File > Import > Scan. Acrobat will ask you what scanner you want to use (Figure 15.8). Select your scanner in the

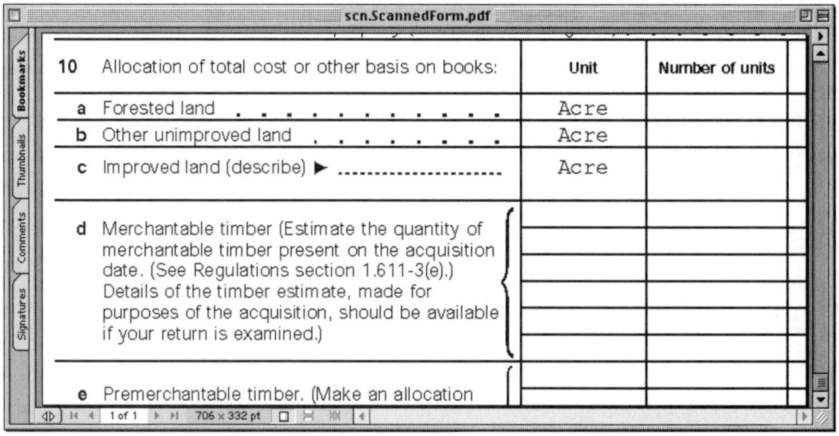

Figure 15.7 Scanning from Acrobat yields an image-only PDF file, containing only image data.

menu and click the Scan button. Acrobat launches your scanner's driver, which lets you pick bit depth and other details of the scan, and then scans the page. (See Scanner Settings, below.) Acrobat captures the image data and stores it in a PDF page.

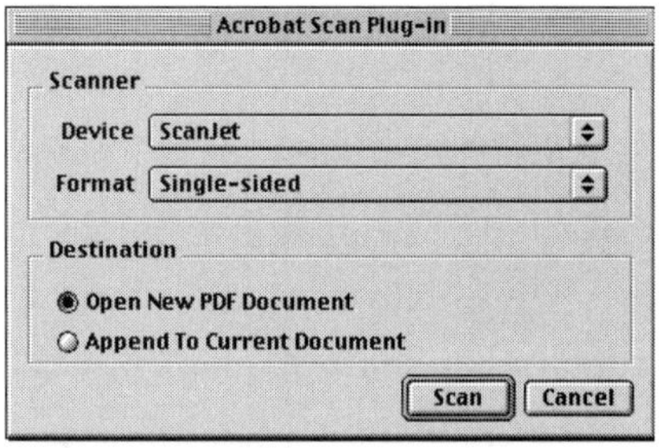

Note that the Scan Plug-in dialog box allows you to specify whether the new scan should be placed in a new Acrobat document or appended as a new page in the currently open document. When dealing with multi-page forms, it is very convenient to just add the new pages to the current document.

Figure 15.8 When you scan your pages from within Acrobat, you must pick your scanner. Then indicate whether your document is one- or two-sided and whether you want to create a new file with the scan or just add the scan to the current document.

If your scanner does not appear in the Scan Plug-in dialog box, you may need to visit your scanner company's Web site to see if they have a TWAIN driver that you can install in your system. If they don't have a driver for your system, then you will need to scan the pages outside of Acrobat and have Acrobat convert the scanned images; this is described in the next section.

Scanning outside of Acrobat

If you have a great many paper forms to convert (some organizations have thousands of forms they need to turn into PDFs), you may want to use a scanner with a sheet feeder that will scan a whole pile of pages at a time, saving them as TIFF files or some other image format. You will then open Acrobat and convert each scanned page to PDF by selecting File > Open as Adobe PDF. Acrobat will ask you what file format you want to show (Figure 15.9); choose TIFF (or whatever format you used in your scanning). Note that you can select several image files on your computer's desktop and then drag them to the Acrobat application; Acrobat will open them all as individual image-only PDF files.

The Settings button in the Open dialog box is extremely important. Clicking it opens the Conversion Options dialog box, where Acrobat presents you with options for converting the TIFF file to a PDF image file (Figure 15.10). It is very important that you pick ZIP for the compression type. ZIP compresses a file without changing its data; JPEG, the other choice, discards data and will severely affect the visual quality of your form.

The net result is exactly what you would have gotten from scanning the pages directly from within Acrobat: a PDF file that contains only a scanned image.

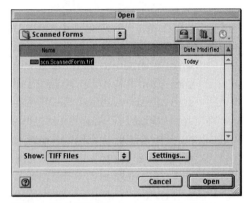

Figure 15.9 When you select File > Open as Adobe PDF, Acrobat lets you pick from a wide variety of file types. You should pick whatever file format you used for your scans. Don't forget to check the settings (click the Settings button) at least once.

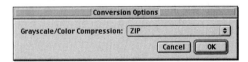

Figure 15.10 The Conversion Options dialog box controls the details of converting of an image to PDF. It is very important that you choose something other than JPEG for your compression. (ZIP is always good.)

Scanner Settings

When you scan your pages, whether within or outside of Acrobat, your scanner software is going to ask you some questions about how you want to scan that page. There are two settings that are particularly important: resolution and bit depth.

Resolution is how many dots per inch there are in your scan. For a printed document, this would be between 200 and 300 dpi. However, your form is going to be primarily viewed and filled out onscreen, so you should scan at a resolution of 72 dpi to match the screen's resolution.

Bit depth refers to the amount of data (expressed as bits per pixel) retrieved for each point on the page the scanner examines. If your form is entirely black and white, with no grayscale or color in it, then you should scan at a depth of 1 bit per pixel. This will minimize the size of the scanned file. If the page contains grayscale artwork, then you should choose 8-bit grayscale for your scan; if the page contains colors that you want to preserve, then 24-bit RGB is your choice. If you don't mind having the form's colors come out as grays, then you have the choice of 8-bit grayscale for the color pages, as well; this will reduce the scan size to one-third what it would be in color.

The settings you choose will have a considerable impact on your file size. The higher the resolution and the greater the bit depth, the greater the file size. Table 15.2 shows the image sizes associated with some combinations of bit depth and resolution.

Table 15.2 File Sizes for a Letter-Size Page

COLOR TYPE	BIT DEPTH	RESOLUTION	SIZE
Black and White	1	72	59 KB
Black and White	1	300	1 MB
Grayscale	8	72	473 KB
Grayscale	8	300	8 MB
RGB	24	72	1.4 MB
RGB	24	300	24 MB

The actual size of your PDF form file will be smaller than those shown in the table, because the image will be compressed. How much smaller the final file will be depends on the individual scanned image; some images compress better than others.

Placing the Form Fields

At this point, you have an Acrobat file that contains your form as a PDF image; open it up in Acrobat and you will be looking at the form, just as it was on paper (see Figure 15.7).

What remains to be done is tedious, but not hard: place form fields onto the page in places corresponding to the spaces on the scanned form (Figure 15.11). The form field types should match the type of space on the original paper form (check box fields placed on check boxes, etc.) and all of your form fields ought to be without borders or background colors.

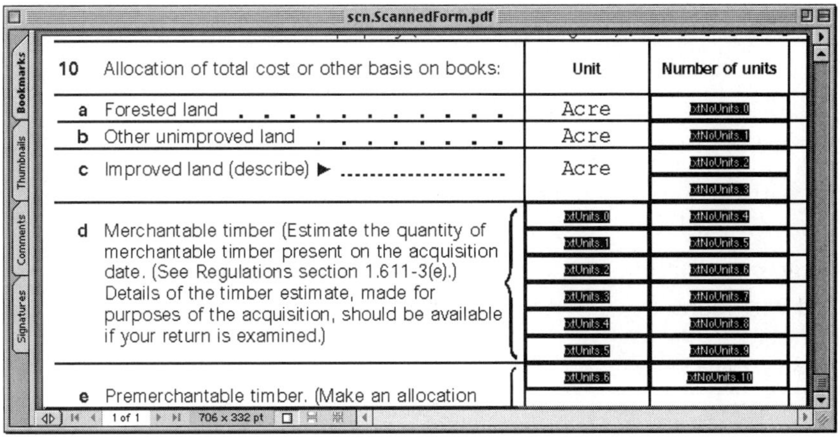

Figure 15.11 Finally, you place form fields over the scanned paper form. Make sure the field types match the data being collected, using text fields, check boxes, and radio buttons as appropriate.

Paper Capture

Acrobat 4 includes a plug-in called Paper Capture that performs Optical Character Recognition (OCR) on image-only PDF files. It scans through the image and converts bitmapped text to real text, doing a magically good job of assigning appropriate fonts. The result is a paper document converted into a PDF file with searchable text; it's very impressive.

Unfortunately, Paper Capture is available only for the Windows version of Acrobat 5. You can get it from http://www.adobe.com:80/products/acrobat/ under the Downloads heading. On the Macintosh, Paper Capture is, all by itself, reason for hanging on to your old version of Acrobat 4.

That said, Paper Capture is not usually worth using to convert paper forms to PDF. It is relatively slow, your form's labels and other text don't particularly need to be editable, and Paper Capture does not in any way make the form more useful for its job, that is, collecting data.

Just scan your pages and be done with it.

Wrapping It Up 16

The creation of Acrobat forms is still a young craft. Until now, Acrobat has been best known for its incredible flexibility and utility as a document distribution format. Increasingly, however, corporations and other organizations are using Acrobat forms to collect and process all manner of data.

This is a beginner's book, an initial how-to to enable you to create useful forms. From here, your assignment is to practice, practice, practice. As you work on more forms in Acrobat, you will become increasingly aware that creating Acrobat forms is not just a useful way of gathering data and, perhaps, making a living. Making Acrobat forms is *fun*.

The control Acrobat gives you over the design, appearance, and behavior of your form is a joy. If you someday learn even a little JavaScript, you will find great vistas of new capabilities opening to you.

I like this stuff a lot, and you will too. It won't be so very long before your perpetual chant (like mine) becomes, "So many forms, so little time."

For More Information

Books

There is a great lack of ready information available on creating Acrobat forms. Most books on Acrobat talk about forms at least briefly, but at the time of this writing, the book you're holding is the only one I know of on this subject.

However, many books exist about more general Acrobat use; I can recommend the following:

PDF with Acrobat 5: Visual QuickStart Guide, by Jennifer Alspach. A very good beginners' introduction into Acrobat use. It provides step-by-step instructions on everything from articles to Web Capture.

Real World PDF with Adobe Acrobat, by Anita Dennis. This is an excellent book on creating PDF files, with an emphasis on pre-press needs.

Acrobat 5 PDF Bible, by Ted Padova. This reference goes into great depth on a wide range of Acrobat-related topics. Not the best book for beginners, but an excellent reference for the more experienced user.

Adobe Acrobat 5.0 Classroom in a Book, by Adobe Systems. This is Adobe's very well written official guide to Acrobat 5.

Your local bookstore or online book source has hundreds of other books on Acrobat. If my favorites above aren't quite what you want, then browse around and pick up something that appeals to you. There are plenty from which to choose.

Web Sites

There are many sites on the Web that provide information about Acrobat forms. These are some of my favorites. Links to all of these are available on the Acrobat Forms Web page (www.acumentraining. com/AcrobatForms).

Acumen Training, my own Web site, posts a free monthly newsletter, the Acumen Journal, each of whose issues has a how-to article on Acrobat. Recent articles talk about the Document Open properties, making your own signature pictures, and fixing hairlines in Acrobat 5 (they're normally too thick). The topics of these articles are mostly drawn from questions that people pose, so they are pretty much guaranteed to be useful.

There is a link to the Journal on the Acrobat Forms Web page, or you can go directly to www.acumentraining.com/AJournal.html.

Planet PDF (www.planetpdf.com) is an excellent Web site with links to plug-in manufacturers and an emailed newsletter full of industry news. It also has many white papers and tutorials available for all manner of Acrobat-related topics, including form creation and JavaScript.

PDFZone (www.pdfzone.com) is similar to Planet PDF: lots of white papers and online tutorials.

Adobe Systems' Web site (www.adobe.com) offers many technical notes, including some that apply to Acrobat. There are also links to plug-in sites and other Acrobat-related companies. Most of the more relevant tech notes are also available on the Acrobat Forms Web page.

Newsgroups

These two quite active newsgroups are worth browsing periodically: comp.text.pdf and list.comp.software.adobe.acrobat.

These are both typical newsgroups: lots of people posting questions and problems, and other people suggesting answers. It is worth browsing these occasionally to see if anyone has asked anything of interest to you. Of course, if you have questions of your own, these aren't bad places to ask.

Appendices

A Job Options For Forms

Despite what you may have heard, PDF files are not quite a one-size-fits-all format. It is perfectly possible to make a PDF file that is not satisfactory for a particular use—in our case, an Acrobat form. The controls that specify how a PDF file is constructed are the Distiller Job Options and the equivalent controls in other applications that make PDF files.

In this appendix, we will look at the Distiller Job Options settings that are best for making Acrobat form files. We shall talk specifically about controls in Distiller, but all applications that make PDF files have at least some of these controls.

In this appendix, as in this book, I assume that you know generally how to make PDF files with Acrobat Distiller or from some other application, such as Adobe Illustrator.

Distiller Job Options

After launching Distiller, you get to its Job Options controls by selecting Settings > Job Options. You will be faced with a five-tab dialog box (Figure A.1) whose options dictate how Distiller creates a PDF file. Most of these controls exist in both versions 4 and 5; I shall point out any controls that are missing from the earlier Distiller.

We shall look briefly at the best settings for making Acrobat forms. I won't completely detail these controls, and I will completely skip any controls that have no bearing on whether a PDF file will work well as a form. The controls that I don't discuss may be set to anything you like, and your PDF file will work just fine as a form.

For full information on the purposes of all the Job Options controls, see the Distiller Help Guide or such books as Anita Dennis' *Real World PDF with Adobe Acrobat 5*, from Adobe Press.

Let us now look at the panels in this dialog box, working from left to right.

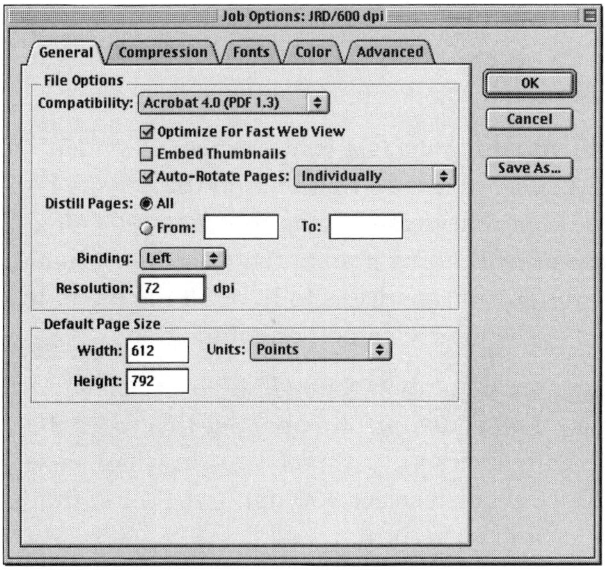

Figure A.1 The Distiller Job Options controls dictate how Distiller should create a PDF file.

General Options

The controls on the General panel (Figure A.1) specify the characteristics of the Acrobat file, as distinct from the PDF code inside that file. The controls that matter to making a form are these:

The **Compatibility** menu lets you specify the minimum, or earliest, version of Acrobat that will be able to open your form: Acrobat 3, 4, or 5. If you know you are sending your form only to people who have Acrobat 5, then select Acrobat 5—your file will often be smaller and will open faster. However, if you don't know what version of Acrobat your users have, then you should probably pick Acrobat 4, as many people are still using this version. Do not pick Acrobat 3: The form mechanism in Acrobat 3 is very incomplete.

Optimize for Fast Web View should be turned on, particularly if you will be placing your form on a Web page. This greatly reduces the time it takes to display an Acrobat file in a Web browser.

The **Embed Thumbnails** control has no great effect on form files. I generally turn it off for forms, since thumbnails add to file size without contributing much to the form.

Auto-Rotate Pages (Acrobat 5 only) is a convenience. When it's turned on, it rotates the PDF pages so that text on the page is horizontal. It saves you a bit of time versus doing this manually after the PDF file has been created. I turn it on and choose Individually from the pop-up menu. (The alternative is to have all the pages in the document rotated to the most common orientation.

Resolution determines the resolution that will be used for TrueType fonts that are embedded as bitmaps. Set this to 72 dpi unless you plan on having users print your forms, in which case 300 dpi is better. (You could also select 600 dpi, but I think that's more than you need for a printed form.)

> ## Tip
>
> **Binding** and **Default Page Size** both sound important, but they usually aren't. Binding only affects how Acrobat displays your document when you select View > Continuous-Facing. Since forms always use View > Single Page, the Binding control has no effect on our form files. The page size is virtually always overridden by the PostScript that Distiller receives, and so has no effect. (In Acrobat 4, the Default Page Size controls are on the Advanced panel.)

Compression Options

The Compression panel (Figure A.2) specifies how the contents of a PDF file should be compressed. Getting compression right is everyone's biggest problem in PDF file creation. Happily, we have a pretty forgiving situation; no one looks at electronic forms with the same critical eye that they apply to pre-press documents.

There are four sets of controls here: a single check box at the bottom, and three sets of controls for color, grayscale, and mono-chrome (1-bit) images. For each of the image controls, there are two items that you must specify: the extent to which images should be downsampled and what kind of compression should be applied.

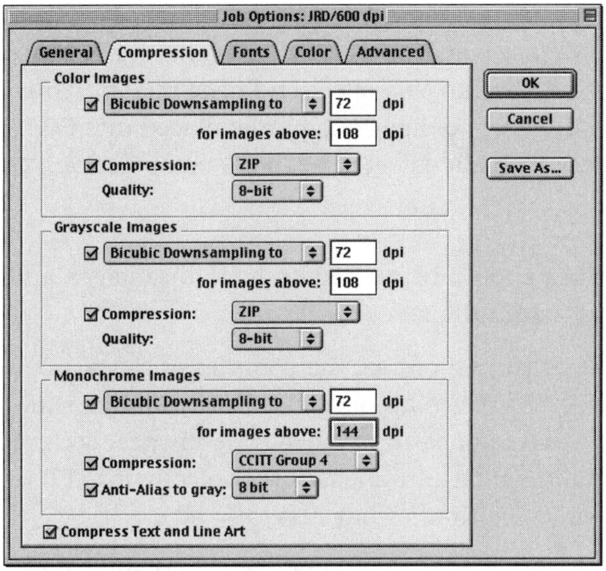

Figure A.2 The compression settings for forms are dictated by the fact that the document will be viewed primarily onscreen.

Downsampling is a technique for removing data from an image until its resolution matches what the printer or display device can actually reproduce. It is intended for use on images whose resolution, including scaling, is very high compared to the capabilities of the display device. (There is no point in maintaining 300 dpi data if you are looking at it on a 72 dpi screen.)

Compress Text and Line Art should be turned on. There is no reason not to do this: The compression method does not discard data (it is "lossless"), so it has no effect whatsoever on the quality of the text or line art.

Color and Grayscale Images

The controls for color and grayscale images are identical, so we shall examine them together here.

Bicubic Downsampling should be selected for both these image types; select 72 dpi as the target resolution. The "For images" above value will automatically set itself to 108 dpi, which is fine.

Compression should be turned on, select ZIP for compression type, and 8-bit for quality. We are being very conservative here: ZIP compression is lossless, so it can have no effect on image quality. This is important because the types of images typically placed into PDF forms tend to be especially badly affected by JPEG compression.

Monochrome Images

Bicubic Downsampling should be turned on for 1-bit images and the resolution should match the screen's 72 dpi.

Compression should be turned on. All the compression types available for monochrome images are lossless. Furthermore, they are all very effective when applied to monochrome images, so it doesn't matter too much which you choose. Technically, CCITT Group 4 is most effective, so that's what I usually pick.

Anti-Alias to Gray (Acrobat 5 only) should be turned on and set to 8-bit. Monochrome images can become extremely ugly when downsampled; this control tells Distiller to convert the monochrome image to grayscale and then downsample that. It looks *much* better, as Figure A.3 demonstrates.

Figure A.3 Downsampled monochrome images usually look pretty awful (left). You should let Acrobat convert the image to grayscale and then downsample it, as at right.

Fonts Options

The Fonts panel (Figure A.4) mostly controls the embedding of fonts in your PDF file.

Embed All Fonts should be selected. Embedding the font definitions into your Acrobat file ensures that your form will look the same on any platform.

Subset Embedded Fonts does not have a simple recommendation. For most forms it should be unchecked; this ensures that fonts used in your form fields (as distinct from the static labels) all display correctly.

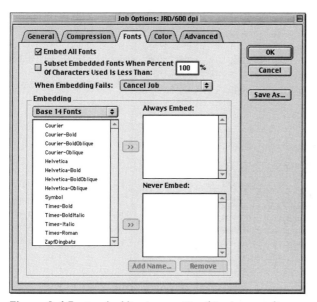

Figure A.4 Font embedding is a positive thing in our culture. It ensures that a PDF file will look reasonably identical on all platforms.

If file size is important, and your form fields use only the base 14 Acrobat fonts (Times, Helvetica, Courier, Symbol, and Zapf Dingbats), then you should check the Subset Embedded Fonts box and set its threshold to 100%; this ensures that when Distiller embeds a font in the PDF file, it only embeds the characters within that font that are actually used in the form. Unfortunately, subsetting also effectively eliminates the editability of text within the form, so it it's important here that your form fields use the standard 14 fonts. (Remember that your form fields' fonts are chosen in the Appearance panel of the Field Properties dialog box.)

The **Never Embed** list should be empty. If there are any fonts here, select them and click on the Remove button.

Color Options

In the Color panel (Figure A.5) there is only one control that has any real impact on a PDF file's fitness as a form.

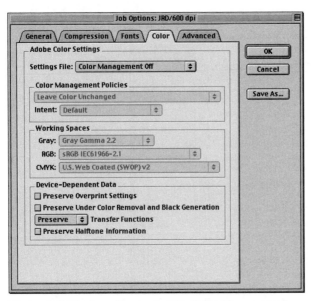

Figure A.5 The best thing to do with Color Management in forms is to turn it off. Color management usually doesn't improve things except under the most carefully controlled settings.

Settings File should be set to Color Management Off. Except in the most rigorously controlled environments, color management is just another gremlin that makes semi-random changes to your color. Turn it off here in Distiller. If you want to do color management, it's better done upstream, in QuarkXPress or Illustrator, say; design software usually has better controls for color management than does Distiller.

In Acrobat 4, select the radio button entitled Leave Color Unchanged.

Advanced Options

Most of the controls in the Advanced panel (Figure A.6) are irrelevant from the standpoint of making a form file.

Convert Gradients to Smooth Shades (Acrobat 5 only) is worth turning on. This makes Distiller convert gradients from QuarkXPress, Illustrator, and other design software into PDF Smooth Shades. These look better, are much smaller, and display faster than the original gradients.

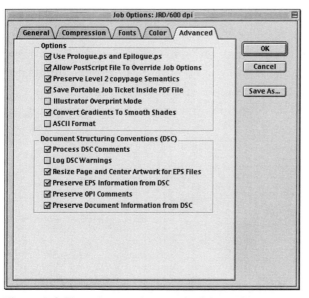

Figure A.6 The only control among the Advanced options that matters to a form file is Convert Gradients to Smooth Shades. In some cases, this can reduce the size of your PDF files that contain gradients, as well as speed up their display.

Application Controls

Most design and page-layout applications allow you to export or save a document directly to PDF. In some cases, the software makes a PostScript file and then launches Distiller in the background, telling it to convert the PostScript to PDF. Other applications actually create their PDF directly.

In either case, most applications give you a set of controls that correspond to some of the Distiller Job Options. Exactly what these controls look like varies from one software package to the next. Whatever they may look like or however they may be labeled, my recommendations for their settings are the same as we discussed above.

For example, when you save a document in Illustrator 10, one of your choices for file format is PDF. When you save to a PDF file, Acrobat presents you with the dialog box in Figure A.7. These controls should look familiar: With the exception of Preserve Illustrator Editing Capabilities, these are all controls taken from the Job Options. (The Embed ICC Profile is the equivalent of turning on Color Management.)

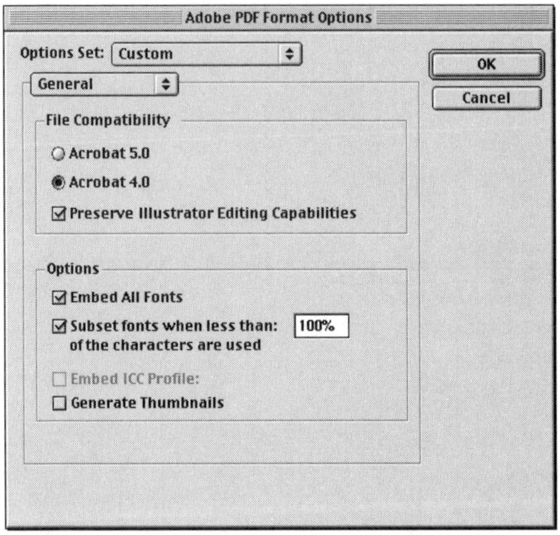

Figure A.7 Applications that can save or export directly to PDF usually give you access to at least some of the same controls that we examined in this appendix.

Sample JavaScripts   B

*JavaScript is the scripting language used by Acrobat forms.
As I have hinted throughout this book, you can do an amazing
array of impressive stuff with JavaScript. In this appendix,
we'll look at four examples of useful JavaScript code. Each
example will augment a form from an earlier chapter.*

This appendix is not a formal tutorial in JavaScript. Rather, it is
a set of examples that you should be able to copy and paste into
your own forms; to make them work, just change the field names
to match those in your form.

This appendix assumes that you are *not* a programmer. If you
are a programmer, this will be annoyingly simple. It is intended to
present the non-programmer with four samples of JavaScript code
that give some feeling for how the language works and provide
"cookbook" code that can be easily modified.

I do warn you that this appendix will not make for very light reading. JavaScript is a powerful scripting language and not quickly
picked up unless you have at least some programming background.

Before beginning, you may wish to reread the section in Chapter 5
on JavaScript actions to remind yourself how to assign a JavaScript
to an event and how to type a JavaScript into Acrobat.

All the forms in this appendix are on the Acrobat Forms Web page.

Acrobat JavaScript Object Specification

Much of what I will briefly present here is documented in detail in the Acrobat JavaScript Object Specification,
which I described in Chapter 5. This document is available directly in Acrobat by going to Help > Acrobat
JavaScript Guide. It provides you with facts such as the word "this" in a JavaScript refers to the current
document, and that you make a field invisible by setting its Hidden property to true.

As I said in Chapter 5, the Acrobat JavaScript Object Specification is a programmer's document—and not
for the faint of heart. Still, if you really want to dig into Acrobat JavaScripts, it will tell you what you need
to know.

JavaScript Objects

Before we can look at the examples, we need to talk briefly about a concept that's central to JavaScript (as well as some other programming languages): the JavaScript Object. A JavaScript Object is a programming construct that represents some data or other thing of interest to the JavaScript language. JavaScript sees pretty much everything except the simplest data (such as numbers) as objects. There are objects that represent signatures, colors, sounds, and even the Acrobat application itself.

For example, the term "this" in a JavaScript refers to an object that represents the current document. The phrase `this.getField("toothDecayIncidence")` is a request to "this document" to get the field named `"toothDecayIncidence."`

Named references

In JavaScript, it is often convenient to name an object that we want to work with. The word "var" in a JavaScript line creates a reference to an object or other data, as in the following:

```
var fld = this.getField("toothDecayIncidence");
```

This line of JavaScript gets the field object named "toothDecayIncidence" and creates a reference to it named "fld." Later in this program, we can refer to the field object by this name:

```
fld.fillColor = color.white;
```

Script I: Changing Field Colors

This is an effect you see on Web sites sometimes: When the user clicks a field or tabs into it, the field changes color—the white background becoming some other color. It's a visual feedback trick that lets the user know for certain what field they're typing into.

Here, we will modify the Personal Profile questionnaire from Chapter 15 (Figure B.1). We shall change the text fields so that the backgrounds turn red and the text turns white when the user enters the field; when the user leaves the field, we shall make the background transparent again and set the text back to black.

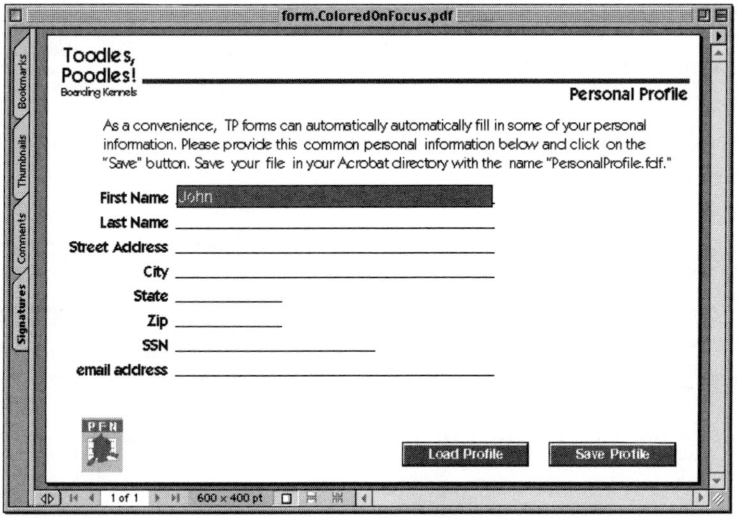

Figure B.1 Our first JavaScript example makes the text fields in this form turn red when the user tabs or clicks into them. The field turns transparent again, with black text, when the user leaves the field.

To do this, we must add two JavaScripts to each text field, one each for the On Focus and On Blur events (Figure B.2). Remember that On Focus occurs when the user clicks or tabs into a form field; On Blur occurs when the user tabs or clicks out of the form field again. These events were added in Acrobat 5, so I'm afraid our JavaScripts won't work in Acrobat 4. (Our form will still work in Acrobat 4; these JavaScripts will just never be triggered.)

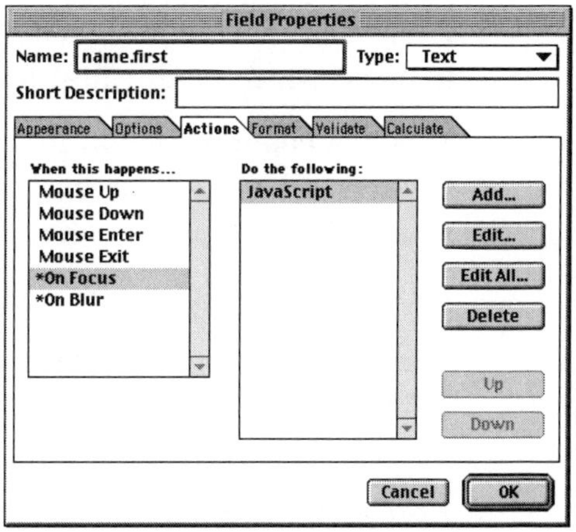

Figure B.2 We will attach JavaScripts to each text field's On Focus and On Blur events.

On Focus JavaScript

When the form field becomes the target of the user's input, the JavaScript action needs to change the field's colors. Here's how we do this (Figure B.3):

```
var txt = this.getField("name.first");
txt.fillColor = color.red;
txt.borderColor = color.black;
txt.textColor = color.white;
```

Let's look at this program line by line.

```
var txt = this.getField("name.first");
```

Figure B.3 This is the JavaScript for the On Focus event. We get a reference to the text field and then turn its background red, its border black, and the color of its text white.

Here the JavaScript asks the current document ("this") for the form field whose name is "name.first." We will refer to this field within the JavaScript by the name "txt" (which I chose, by the way; there's nothing special about it). The phrase "var txt" creates a reference name that may be assigned to a piece of data in a JavaScript— in our case, the name.first text field.

This is a common action in JavaScript: Get a reference to a form field and then do something with it. Here, we got a reference to name.first and now we shall change its colors.

```
txt.fillColor = color.red;
```

This line changes the color of txt's background color (written "txt.fillColor" in JavaScript) to a color named color.red.

JavaScript defines a whole set of standard colors that may be referred to by name; these colors are listed in Table B.1.

Table B.1 Standard Acrobat Colors

color.black	color.ltGray	color.cyan
color.white	color.red	color.magenta
color.gray	color.green	color.yellow
color.dkGray	color.blue	color.transparent

```
txt.borderColor = color.black;
txt.textColor = color.white;
```

In similar fashion, we set the color of the field's border to black and the color of its text to white.

On Blur JavaScript

Acrobat will execute the On Blur JavaScript when the user tabs out of our form field or clicks somewhere else in the Acrobat page. We want this JavaScript to undo the color changes that we made with our On Focus JavaScript. We shall make the field transparent again and return the text color to black.

Here it is:

```
var txt = this.getField("name.first");
txt.fillColor = color.transparent;
txt.borderColor = color.transparent;
txt.textColor = color.black;
```

This is very similar to the previous JavaScript. It differs only in that we are making the background color (txt.fillColor) and border color transparent and setting our text's color to black.

Script 2: Rollover Help

In Chapter 13, we created rollover help for our timesheet form in the form of a hidden text field that contained our help text. We made this field visible when the mouse moved over a button with a Show/Hide Field action (Figure B.4), and then hid it again when the mouse left the button.

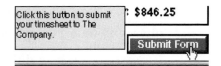

Figure B.4 In Chapter 13, we added rollover help to our Submit button with Show/Hide Field actions attached to the button's Mouse Enter and Mouse Exit events.

This works perfectly well for one or two controls that require help text, but there is a hidden flaw in this approach. The way we implemented rollover help in Chapter 13 requires a separate,

hidden text field for *each button.* This becomes unbelievably messy if
you have help associated with every field in your form (Figure B.5).

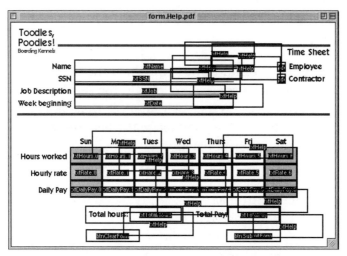

Figure B.5 Chapter 13's rollover help technique becomes very
untidy if *all* your form fields need rollover help. A separate text field
would be required for each control that has associated help text.

There is a better way.

The Chapter 13 technique associates two Show/Hide Field actions
with each control for which you provide help: one for the Mouse
Enter event and another for Mouse Exit. Each control's actions
show and hide the text field containing that field's help.

Here, we will take a different
approach. We shall have only a
single, hidden help text field for
the entire page (Figure B.6). Each
button's Mouse Enter action will
be a JavaScript (Figure B.7) that
does two things: It will set the text
field's text to the help information
for that button, and then make the

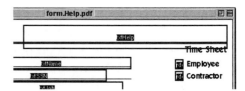

Figure B.6 Here we have created a text field
(txtHelp) that we shall use for all form fields'
help text. The Mouse Enter JavaScript for each
form field will insert text into this text field
and then make it visible.

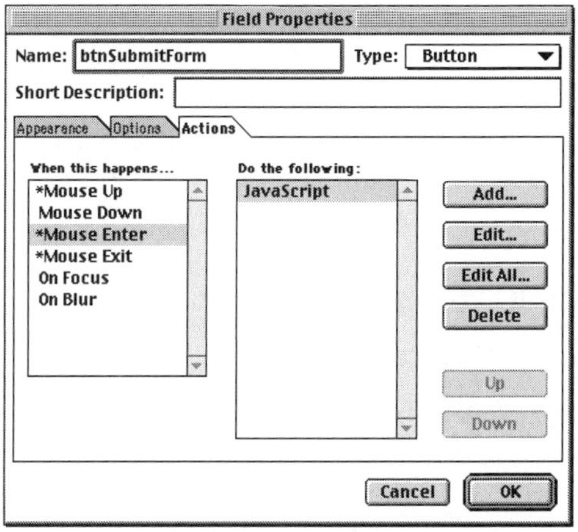

Figure B.7 We will attach a JavaScript to each form field's Mouse Enter event that will place text into the txtHelp field and then make that field visible. The Mouse Exit action will be Show/Hide field.

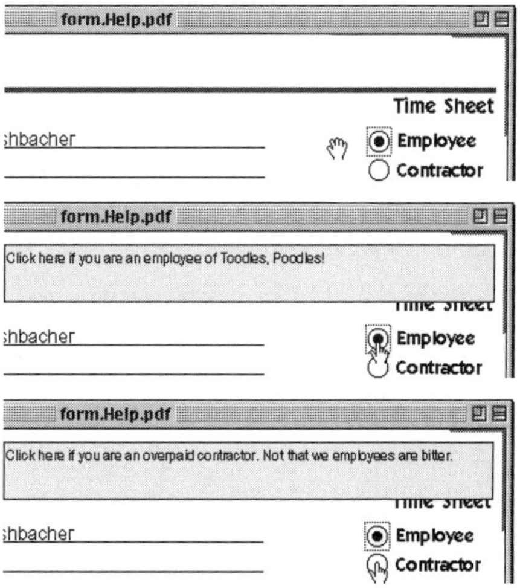

Figure B.8 The shared help text field is initially invisible (top). Each control's Mouse Enter JavaScript puts that control's particular help text into the text field (middle and bottom).

help text field visible. Rather than having a help field for each button, we shall have a single, shared help field into which each button places its particular help information (Figure B.8).

The Mouse Exit action for each control will remain a Show/Hide Field action, just as before; this action will hide the single help text field.

Mouse Enter Action

The Mouse Enter JavaScripts will be nearly identical for all the controls that have rollover help; the scripts will differ only in the text that is assigned to the various help text fields. The JavaScript below is for the Employee radio button.

```
var help = this.getField("txtHelp");
help.value =
  "Click here if you are an employee of T.P.";
help.hidden = false;
```

Let's look at the details:

```
var help = this.getField("txtHelp");
```

We start by getting a reference to the help text field, giving it the internal name "help."

```
help.value =
  "Click here if you are an employee of T.P.";
```

Our JavaScript sets the help text field's value (that is, the text that it displays) to whatever text is appropriate to that control.

```
help.hidden = false;
```

Finally, we set the hidden attribute of our text field to false, making the help text appear on the page.

Script 3: Field Visibility

In Chapter 9, we had a Job Application form with a combo box that was initially invisible; it became visible if the user clicked on a particular check box (Figure B.9). We did this using a Show/Hide Field action attached to the Boss' Child check box; the Mouse Up event caused us to show the Son/ Daughter combo box.

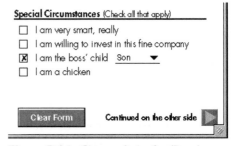

A weakness of this implementation was that once the combo box was made visible, it stayed visible: If we deselected the Boss's Child check box, the combo box didn't become hidden again. We will fix that here.

Figure B.9 In Chapter 9, the Son/Daughter combo box was invisible until the user clicked on the Boss' Child check box. Unfortunately, unchecking the check box did *not* make the combo box invisible again.

Mouse Up Action

The JavaScript in this section will be a replacement for the Show/Hide Field action we earlier assigned to the check box's Mouse Up action. When the user click the check box, our JavaScript will examine its value; if that value is Yes (the export value for the check box), then we shall make the combo box field visible; otherwise, we shall hide the combo box (Figure B.10).

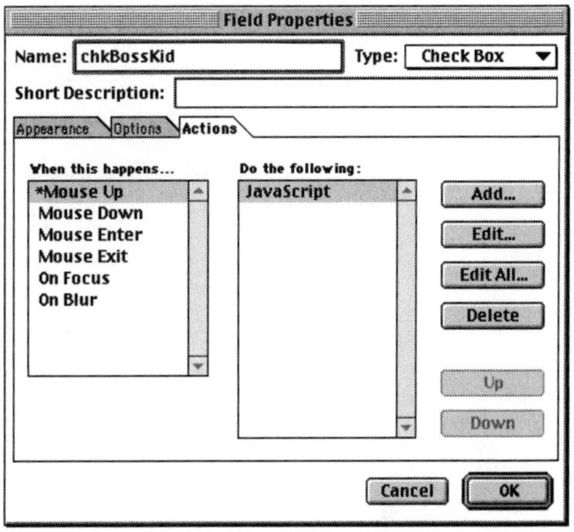

Here's the script for the Boss' Child check box:

Figure B.10 We shall attach a JavaScript to the check box field's Mouse Up action: It will make the combo box visible if the check box is checked, and hidden if the check box is unchecked.

```
var cbo= this.getField("cboSonDtr");
var chk = event.target;
if (chk.value == "Yes")
{
     cbo.hidden = false;
}
else
{
     cbo.hidden = true;
}
```

Let's examine this in detail:

```
var cbo= this.getField("cboSonDtr");
```

We get the field object for the combo box and assign it the internal name "cbo."

```
var chk = event.target;
```

We then get a second field object, this one representing the form field that generated the Mouse Up event. In Acrobat, the event object contains all the data associated with the event that caused the JavaScript to execute. The event.target property is the form field that caused the event—in our case, the Boss' Child check box.

```
if (chk.value == "Yes")
{
    cbo.hidden = false;
}
else
{
    cbo.hidden = true;
}
```

Here we see one of the more puzzling constructions in JavaScript. This is how you tell JavaScript to do one thing if something is true, and to do something else otherwise.

Translated into English, this block of JavaScript says: If the value of our check box is Yes then set the combo box's hidden attribute to false; otherwise set the combo box's hidden attribute to true.

The phrase in parentheses after "if" must be a comparison of some sort. In our case, we are looking to see if the value of our check box object is "Yes." (Yes is the export value for our check box field.) The two equal signs mean "is equal to."

If the phrase in the parentheses is true (in our case, if the value of our check box is Yes), then JavaScript will carry out the commands between the curly braces ({ }), setting the combo box field's hidden attribute to false and therefore making it visible.

If the phrase in the parentheses is false (meaning the check box's value is not Yes), then JavaScript carries out whatever is between the curly braces following the word "else."

Now, when users click the Boss' Child check box field, the Son/Daughter combo box will become visible or invisible, depending on whether the check box is checked or unchecked.

Sample 4: "Graying Out" a Field

In the Macintosh and Windows environments, controls that are unchangeable or inactive are typically "grayed out," meaning that they appear dimmer than other, active controls. In our final example, we shall see how to do this with an Acrobat form field. We shall do this with our Oath form from Chapter 11 (Figure B.11); when the user signs the form, the name field, initially in black text, will become a light gray (which also indicates that it's locked).

Figure B.11 In this example, we shall "gray out" the user's name when the form is signed.

You should enter this JavaScript into the Signature field's Signed panel (Figure B.12). Simply click the Edit button and type the script into the resulting JavaScript Edit dialog box.

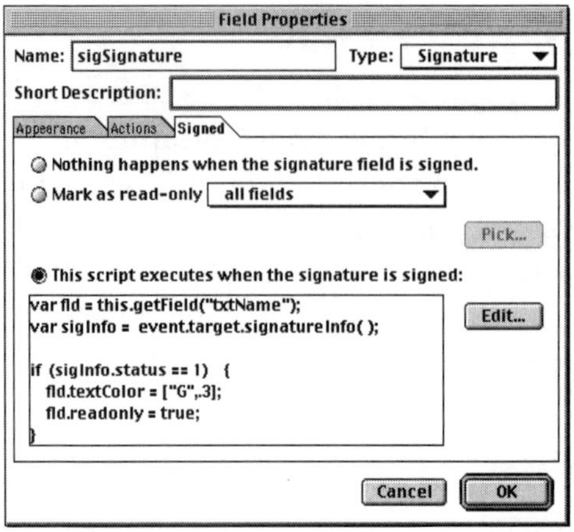

Figure B.12 We shall assign a JavaScript to the Signature field's Signed panel.

Here's the script:

```
var txt = this.getField("txtName");
var sig = event.target.signatureInfo( );
if (sig.status == 1)
{
        txt.textColor = color.ltGray;
        txt.readonly = true;
}
else
{
        txt.textColor = color.black;
        txt.readonly = false;
}
```

The details:

```
var txt = this.getField("txtName");
var sig = event.target.signatureInfo( );
```

Our JavaScript needs to fetch two objects for this task: first, the text field for the signer's name, which we give the internal name "txt." We obtain this with the getField command, as usual. Second, our JavaScript must acquire an object that represents our signature in the Signature field. We get this with the signatureInfo command and give the resulting object the name "sig."

```
if (sig.status == 1)
{
     txt.textColor = color.ltGray;
     txt.readonly = true;
}
```

Our sig object has an attribute called "status" that indicates whether the Signature field has been signed. This status is a numeric code that has a value of 1 if the field has been signed.

In our script, if the signature's status has a value of 1 (remember the double equal signs mean "is equal to"), we shall set our text field's textColor to a light gray and make its read-only attribute true. The text on the Acrobat page becomes light gray and unchangeable.

```
else
{
     txt.textColor = color.black;
     txt.readonly = false;
}
```

If the signature's status is not 1, then we shall set the text field's textColor to black and turn off the read-only attribute; the signer's name then becomes editable again.

Index

Binding control, 210
bit depth, 200
bits per pixel, 200
Bookmarks panel, 167, 168
books, Acrobat, 203–204
Boolean values, 42, 104
Border Color check box, 46, 83
Border controls, 46–47
Border Style options, 74
Browse button, 92
browsers. *See* Web browsers
Button Face Attribute controls, 75
Button Face When controls, 75
buttons, 70–86. *See also* radio buttons
    contrasted with links, 22
    copying and pasting, 78
    creating, 72–73
    labeling, 42, 74–75, 80–82
    purpose of, 42, 70

C

C/C++, 55, 178, 187
Calculate panel, 89, 96–98
calculated fields, 101–102, 150–152
CD-ROMs, distributing forms on, 191
Center command, 152, 153
certificates. *See* user certificates
CGI, 6, 19–20, 178
CGI Resource Index, 178, 189
Change Password panel, 135
Change Permissions password, 173
check boxes, 104–107
    creating, 106–107
    hiding/showing, 118–119
    labeling, 42
    properties for, 105–106
    purpose of, 42, 104
Check by Default property, 106
Check Style menu, 105
checkmarks, 104, 107
Citizenship combo box, 112–113
Clear Form button, 59, 75–78, 157–160
CMYK color, 16
code examples. *See* JavaScript
Color control, Link Properties, 30
color management, 214, 216
Color panel, 213–214
Color Picker, Macintosh, 30

Color Well controls, 46
colors
    background, 46, 83
    border, 46, 83
    changing field, 218–221
    CMYK *vs.* RGB, 16–17
    standard Acrobat, 220
    Web-safe, 17
combo boxes, 108–114
    contrasted with list boxes, 43, 108–109
    creating, 110–114
    properties for, 111
    purpose of, 42, 108
    showing/hiding, 224–227
    spell checking contents of, 111
    system considerations, 110
comments, form data, 65
Common Gateway Interface. *See* CGI
Common Properties controls, 48
Compare feature, 141
Compatibility menu, 209
compression
    Distiller options for, 210–212
    JPEG *vs.* ZIP, 199
    lossless, 211, 212
Content Layer, 23
controls. *See also* specific controls
    contrasted with form fields, 9
    examples of, 9
    inadvertently changing names of, 40
Controls Layer, 23
conventions, field naming, 37–39
Conversion Options dialog box, 199
Convert Gradients to Smooth Shades
    option, 214–215
Copy command, 78, 146
Create New User dialog box, 134
crosshair pointer, 24
Ctrl-drag technique, 146, 148
Cyber-SIGN, 127

D

data. *See* form data
data-processing programs, 186
date field, 103
date formats, 64–65, 103
Daughter/Son combo box, 113–114,
    117–120, 224–227
Default is Checked option, 124

H

Hand tool, 25
handles
    form field, 37
    link, 26
help, rollover. *See* rollover help
Help Guide, Distiller, 208
Helper Applications preferences, 193
Highlight menu
    Field Properties, 74, 83
    Link Properties, 29
HTML
    and data-submission process, 186–189
    as design tool, 2, 3
    and form data, 177–179
    limitations of, 3–4
    and signature data, 131
HTML files, 63, 177–179
HTML forms, 3–4
http://, 67
hyperlinks. *See* links

I

Icon Placement dialog box, 83
Illustrator, 4, 5, 13, 214, 216
images
    color/grayscale, 211–212
    compressing, 18, 210–212
    downsampling, 210–211, 212
    monochrome, 212
    resolution for, 211, 212
    scaling, 83
    using as button labels, 80–82
Import Form Data action, 54–55, 195
Import from File button, 139
Incremental Changes check box, 65
Inherit Zoom option, 34
initial view controls, 167
interactivity, 22
Internet Explorer, 192. *See also* Web
    browsers
Invisible Rectangle option, 28

J

Java, 186, 187
JavaScript, 55–59
    entering/editing, 56–58

and Event object, 94
examples
    calculating text field values, 96–98
    changing field colors, 218–221
    checking version number, 56
    converting text to uppercase, 94
    creating rollover help, 221–224
    emailing form data, 181–182
    "graying out" fields, 227–229
    moving document view, 56
    showing/hiding fields, 224–227
    spawning template, 164–165
    and forms validation, 96
learning, 58–59, 217
purpose of, 55
recommended books on, 58, 217
and rollover help, 160
and Selection Change panel, 115
JavaScript action, 55–59, 92
JavaScript for the World Wide Web: Visual
    QuickStart Guide, 58
JavaScript Object, 218
Job Application form
    adding radio buttons to, 124
    creating buttons for, 75–79, 84–86
    creating check boxes for, 104–107
    creating combo boxes for, 112–114
    creating jobs list for, 115–117
    creating text fields for, 98–103
    files for, 71, 88
    labeling buttons for, 80–82
Job Options, Distiller, 17–18, 208–216
JPEG compression, 199

L

labeling
    buttons, 42, 74–75, 80–82
    check boxes, 42
layers, placing links in, 23
Layout menu, Field Properties, 74, 81
legal documents, PDF files as, 125
Lexign, 127
Link Properties dialog box, 24–25, 26, 27–31
Link tool, 24
links, 22–34
    contrasted with buttons, 22
    and Controls Layer, 23
    creating, 22–25, 26
    editing, 26–27
    and Go to View action, 31–34
    properties for, 27–31

text editors, 57–58
text fields, 87–103
  aligning text in, 90
  calculating values for, 96–98
  creating, 89, 98–103
  formatting text in, 93–95
  limiting number of characters in, 90
  multi-line, 90, 91–92
  plain text, 98–100
  properties for, 89–98
  purpose of, 43–44, 87
  spell checking, 91
  validating user input, 95–96
TextPad, 58
thumbnails, 167, 210
TIFF files, 199
timesheet form, 144–145, 156, 161–165,
    221–224
tool tips, 72, 157
Tools menu, 40
Total Income field, 101–102
training. See tutorials/training
true/false values, 42, 104
TrueType fonts, 210
Trusted Certificates, 135, 137–138
tutorials/training
  Acrobat, 9, 52
  JavaScript, 59
  PDF, 204, 205
TWAIN driver, 197, 198
Type menu
  Field Properties, 36, 50
  Link Properties, 28

U

UltraEdit, 58
Underlined style, 47
URLs
  and Edit URL button, 67
  and Select URL button, 64–65
user certificates
  creating, 134–137
  defined, 127
  fingerprint numbers for, 136, 139
  installing, 137–139
  purpose of, 128
  sending to email addresses, 135, 137
  storing, 139
  and submission of form data, 131
User Information panel, 135

user interface design, 117
user profiles, 127–128, 132–134
User Settings dialog box, 129, 135

V

Validate panel, 89, 95–96
verification, signature, 140–141
view controls, Document Properties, 167
View Signed Version command, 141
views, Acrobat, 32, 167
visibility, field, 224–227. See also
    Show/Hide Field action
Visibility menu, 48
Visible Rectangle option, 28
Visual Basic, 178

W

WAV files, 61–62
Web browsers
  color considerations, 17
  and data-submission process, 186–187
  preferences settings for, 193
  viewing forms in, 192–193
Web Capture Preferences dialog box, 66
Web commerce, 3
Web page, linking to, 66
Web-safe color, 17
Web server, making forms available on,
    191–192
Web sites
  Acumen Journal, 52, 59, 204
  Acumen Training, 9, 52, 204
  Adobe Systems, 205
  CGI Resource Index, 178, 189
  Planet PDF, 58, 204
Width menu, Link Properties, 29
Width window, Field Properties, 47
window option controls, 167–168
Windows systems
  color palette, 30
  and combo boxes, 110
  and data files/folders, 195
  and Edit Menu Item action, 53
  and JavaScript editors, 57–58
  and Paper Capture plug-in, 202
World Wide Web Link action, 66–69

X

XML files, 63, 65, 177

Y

yes-or-no questions, 42, 104

Z

Zapf Dingbats fonts, 104, 213
ZIP compression, 199
Zoom tool, 33–34